CONTEMPORARY FICTION
AND CHRISTIANITY

CONTINUUM LITERARY STUDIES SERIES

CONTEMPORARY FICTION AND CHRISTIANITY

ANDREW TATE

continuum

Continuum International Publishing Group
The Tower Building, 11 York Road, London SE1 7NX
80 Maiden Lane, Suite 704, New York NY 10038
www.continuumbooks.com

First published 2008
This paperback edition published 2010

British Library Cataloguing-in-Publication Data
A catalogue record for this book is available from the British Library.

ISBN: 978-0-8264-8907-4 (hardback)
      978-1-4411-6175-8 (paperback)

Library of Congress Cataloguing-in-Publication Data
A catalog record for this book is available from the Library of Congress.

Typeset by Aarontype Limited, Easton, Bristol

Contents

Acknowledgements

My first debt is to the staff at Continuum. Thanks to all my colleagues and students in the Department of English and Creative Writing at Lancaster University, particularly to members of my classes on American and British Fiction for the MA in Contemporary Literary Studies. I am particularly grateful to Arthur Bradley, Jo Carruthers and Michael Greaney. I have benefited from many conversations over the last few years, but would like to mention the following friends and colleagues for their valuable input: David Ashbridge, John Batchelor, Andrew Dix, Alison Easton, Alison Findlay, Lee Horsley, Hutch, Simon Jones, Mark Knight, Emma Mason, Jon Roberts, John Schad, Patrick Sherry, Catherine Spooner, Steve Tomkins, Jonathan Taylor, Lindsey Walker, Chris Walsh, Thomas Woodman, Michael Wheeler, Terry Wright. I would also like to acknowledge precious feedback from conference participants in Lancaster, Oxford, Reading, Roehampton and Syracuse. The book could not have been completed without the encouragement of my parents, Chris, AM, Marie and Peter and, finally, Michaela, to whom it is dedicated. The mistakes are all mine.

Material from chapters 2, 3 and 6 appeared in earlier incarnations in book chapters and articles for *Figures of Heresy: Radical Theology in English and American Literature*, edited by Andrew Dix and Jonathan Taylor (Brighton: Sussex Academic Press, 2006); *The Glass* (number 16, Spring 2004), edited by Roger Kojeck; and *Biblical Religion and the Novel*, edited by Mark Knight and Thomas Woodman (Aldershot: Ashgate, 2006) respectively. I gratefully acknowledge the publishers for permission to reuse the material for this book.

Introduction: Re-enchanted Fictions

Now – here is my secret ... My secret is that I need God ...
(Douglas Coupland, *Life After God*, 1994)[1]

Then the elderly man said, 'I have a story that will make you believe in God'
(Yann Martel, *Life of Pi*, 2002)[2]

But how do we distinguish our truth from another's falsity ... except by the story we cherish? Our story of God. But, my friends, I ask you: Is God a story? Can we, each of us examining our faith ... can we believe anymore in the heart of our faith that God is our story of Him?
(E. L. Doctorow, *City of God*, 2000)[3]

This book focuses on the surprising and sometimes prophetic friction generated by the antagonistic but animated relationship between the contemporary novel and Christian theology. It also explores the complex religious impulses at play in the fictions of our postmodern moment. Major and emerging Anglophone novelists such as John Updike, Don DeLillo, Salman Rushdie, John Irving, Douglas Coupland, Yann Martel, Jeanette Winterson, Jim Crace, Michèle Roberts, Nick Hornby, David Maine and Jon McGregor persistently return, both explicitly and in less overt ways, to theological questions. Why does a 'secret' desire for faith in the transcendent appear to fixate the postmodern literary imagination? How can the novel accommodate transcendent experiences or encounters with the divine? Is it possible, in a rational era, that a piece of narrative might make a compelling case for theism? How might a writer address the idea of grace in a world apparently beyond belief? Can twenty-first-century fiction, a product of the so-called disenchanted, secular imagination, tell 'stor[ies] of God'? This introductory chapter examines the implications of 'post-secular' culture for the novel and identifies a number of distinct, if over-lapping, thematic approaches to Christianity that are crucial to the spiritual sensibilities of contemporary fiction; these include the question of religious reading; the return of the miraculous; the heretical impulse and the significance of apocalyptic visions.

After Secularization: The Post-Secular Imagination

There are, to say the least, a whole series of unexpected and rather peculiar affinities between contemporary literary fiction and this once dominant religion. Just as critics frequently predict the death of the novel, Christianity is a faith tradition that is judged, by some observers, to be in a state of terminal decline. The history of the post-Enlightenment 'civilized' world has been, according to this view, a story of gradual but undeniable secularization, which has necessarily involved the diminishing influence of the Church and a loss of belief in the supernatural.[4] 'Secularisation', states Callum Brown, is 'a salute to reason, the intellect and to progress'. Yet Brown, who is certain that such progress is unassailable, also describes this liberating theory as a 'narrative in crisis'.[5] More starkly, William E. Connolly argues that the 'historical modus vivendi called secularism is coming apart at the seams' and demands refashioning because it 'ignores or devalues some dimensions of being that need to be engaged more actively'.[6]

In recent years, the confident modernity vital to secularism has itself been subject to sceptical enquiry. 'The world today, with some exceptions . . . is as furiously religious as it ever was, and in some places more so than ever', claims Peter Berger, whose work in the 1960s advocated the so-called 'secularization thesis'.[7] The 'myth of secularization is dead', asserts another commentator who is convinced that religion remains 'an invaluable window into the whole edifice' of human activity despite inevitable change in spiritual practice and habits of mind.[8] 'Religion', in the words of Graham Ward, a leading British theologian, haunts 'once more . . . the imagination of the West'.[9] A sceptical response, however, might be to observe, dryly, that the spectral motif on which this claim depends is surely a sign that the era of belief has passed away only to be reawakened as an unhappy revenant. For many critics, including those who define themselves as religious as well as avowed secularists, this revival is a cause for alarm. The rise of fundamentalism, in a variety of theistic guises, has necessarily galvanized liberal opponents fearful that well-intentioned respect for religion inadvertently perpetuates the legitimacy of authoritarian belief. Others are concerned that public concessions to religion collude with theocratic regimes that censor rational debate and challenges to their power. Although this book is written from a Christian perspective, I believe that it is crucial for people of faith to take these criticisms seriously and to avoid retreating into defensive, backward-looking positions. Sarah Coakley, a leading Anglican theologian, argues that 'to be fruitful' theology must 'endlessly renegotiate its porous boundaries' with other disciplines 'whilst carefully maintaining its distinctive voice in speaking of *God*'. She also insists that theology 'is not just "high" academic discourse in constant interaction with philosophy' but is 'lived' out in popular culture, politics 'and in the bodily negotiations of everyday life'.[10] This book, in an exploration of diverse narratives of belief and unbelief, seeks to pursue a similar approach in its reading of contemporary fiction.

The study in this volume also recognizes that religious thinking is not the sole preserve of reactionary fanatics. This is not a point easily conceded by all commentators on religion and popular culture. 'The allure of fundamentalism', argues Zygmunt Bauman, 'stems from its promise to emancipate the converted from the agonies of choice'.[11] It is sometimes strategically easier to simplify matters of faith rather than to acknowledge ambivalences, differences and uncertainties. However, critical voices, on either side of the faith and scepticism debate, are keen both to give witness to their world view and to hear stories from radically different perspectives. Such ideologically inflected debates about the fate of faith (and particularly the future of organized belief) in the modern world inform a now widely recognized re-evaluation of religion or a 'sacred turn' in contemporary culture. As John D. Caputo observes, the re-emergence of religion is visible 'even among avant-garde intellectuals who have given it a new legitimacy by discrediting its discreditors, suspecting its suspectors, doubting its doubters, unmasking its unmaskers'.[12]

'The implosion of the secular', argues Graham Ward, 'has ... facilitated a new return to the theological and a new emphasis upon reenchantment: a return not signalled by theologians but by filmmakers, novelists, poets, philosophers, political theorists, and cultural analysts'.[13] However, Ward's assessment of what he names a 'postmodern sensibility' is ambivalent: the return of Christian motifs in a faithless context, according to Ward, announces 'an enjoyment of the absence of God by the commercialization of God's presence – through angels and miracles, through stigmatas and sacramentalisms'.[14] Ward hits on the generative paradox of postmodern culture: it both perpetuates modernity's disdain for providence and produces a longing for the divine. This surprising movement has been particularly significant in the traditionally sceptical-materialist fields of continental philosophy, popular culture and literary studies. Titles such as *The Trespass of the Sign: Deconstruction, Theology and Philosophy* (1989), *Theology and Contemporary Critical Theory* (1996, 2000), *Philosophy and the Turn to Religion* (1999), *God in the Details: American Religion in Popular Culture* (2001), *Towards a Christian Literary Theory* (2003) and *Negative Theology and Modern French Philosophy* (2004) share a cross-disciplinary infatuation.[15] As recently as the mid-1980s such flirtations and odd, triangular alliances between theology, cultural studies and continental philosophy might have seemed like an alarming and quixotic fatal attraction. Twenty-first-century thought, by contrast, has acquired a distinct taste for the hybrid and the impossible.[16] If religion has become a spectral force, stalking the disciplines that attempted to vanquish it, it is astonishing to note how often this ghost is now welcomed at the table of contemporary critical and cultural debate. Hent de Vries, a vital figure in mediating these novel associations, argues that 'religion' – however it might be defined – thrives on challenges and antipathies:

> The endless, if also inevitably limited, refutations of religion's truth-claims are so many reaffirmations of its ever-provisional survival, ad infinitum. In religion's perpetual agony lies its philosophical and theoretical relevance. As it dies an ever more secure and serial death, it is increasingly certain to come back to life, in its present guise or in another.[17]

Where does the novel fit into this apparent revival (or resurrection) of religion? Fiction, according to mainstream literary opinion, is the one narrative form that cannot bear the stigmata of active religious thought. Georg Lukács' frequently quoted description of the novel as 'the epic of a world abandoned by God' has become the paradigm for interpreting fiction in post-Christian terms.[18] 'Post-medieval literature records, among other things, the gradual withdrawal of God from the world,' argued J. Hillis Miller in 1963.[19] This interpretation of cultural history does not pursue a Nietzschean insistence on the death of the divine but accentuates an escalating (and for some writers, equally devastating) sense that God is silent:

> The lines of connection between us and God have broken down, or God himself has slipped away from the places where he used to be. He no longer inheres in the world as the force binding together all men and all things. As a result the nineteenth and twentieth centuries seem to many writers a time when God is no more present and not yet again present, and can only be experienced negatively, as a terrifying absence.[20]

The rich, if not always benign, influence of various expressions of the Christian faith on Western cultural heritage is rarely in dispute. Conservative critics, many of whom do not speak from a position of religious faith, frequently lament the death of a dominant, national religion to which the vast members of society assent primarily because of the negative effect that secularization has had on the arts and cultural production. The late Peter Fuller, who described himself as 'an incorrigible atheist', for example, expressed doubts as to whether art could 'ever thrive outside that sort of living, symbolic order, with deep tendrils in communal life, which, it seems, a flourishing religion alone can provide.'[21] Fuller's polemic is given particular strength in his audacious conclusion regarding the 'Christian' involvement in the built landscape: 'Unbelievers, of course, can enjoy the cathedrals; but we could never have made them'.[22]

The Problem of Religious Reading

One serious objection to a Christian interpretation of the novel (indeed of any text) is that the reader's prior creedal commitment will necessarily reduce the complexity of personal experience and public narration on which fiction depends – including the representation of trauma and joy – to fit the contours of another, privileged story. This sacred plot, the Christian (and originally Jewish) grand narrative of humanity's fallen state and need for redemption in the figure of an incarnate God, must determine the reception of all other fictions. As Paul S. Fiddes has argued, where 'literature tends to openness', doctrine, the authorized body of belief, is predisposed towards 'closure'.[23] A sceptic's view of religious habits of reading, then, might suspect that difference is quietly (but violently) erased by belief. James Wood, a critic and novelist with strong, if sceptical, theological interests, argues that religious faith and the belief required by literature (what he calls a kind of 'discretionary magic'), though analogous, are contradictory:

This is surely the true secularism of fiction – why, despite its being a kind of magic, it is actually the enemy of superstition, the slayer of religions, the scrutineer of falsity. Fiction moves *in the shadow of doubt*, knows itself to be a true lie, knows that at any moment it might fail to make its case. Belief in fiction is always belief 'as if'. Our belief is itself metaphorical – it only *resembles* actual belief, and is therefore never wholly belief.[24]

For Wood, fiction itself is secular because of the kind of relationship that it has with its reader. In traditional religious experience, the worshiper needs an unwavering faith in the object of worship, whereas in the act of reading, the reader – analogous, in Wood's analysis, with the position of the believer – is not only free to exercise disbelief, but the encounter between text and reader is positively charged with the possibility that s/he might, at any time, reject what s/he is reading; apostasy, as it were, is a vital escape clause for the disillusioned reader.

'Is Nothing Sacred?' (1990), a frequently quoted and prescient essay by Salman Rushdie, explores the premise that literature, even in an ostensibly secular age, might be holy or sanctified. The notoriously hostile context in which Rushdie was writing – shortly after he had become the target of a *fatwa* imposed by the Ayatollah Khomeini for the alleged blasphemy of *The Satanic Verses* (1988) – makes the brave clarity of the essay all the more impressive. Although it is a response to his most fierce censors, the article attempts something far more daringly ambivalent than a self-congratulatory salute to the autonomy of the writer. Rushdie also emphatically refuses the quasi-mystical vocation of the novelist as pseudo-priest. Literature, unlike religion, he suggests, must be afforded the freedom of uncertainty: 'The only privilege literature deserves ... is the privilege of being the arena of discourse, the place where the struggle of languages can be acted out'.[25]

If one literary tendency is for writers to be canonized rather than read, there is a simultaneous risk, as one critic has stated, that a liberal theological reading of culture seeks to 'baptize all moral heroism and tragic wisdom as anonymously Christian'.[26] Yet alternative, less muscular, models of Christian reading have emerged as part of a conversation between literature, theology and critical theory. If the visible church, the community of Christian readers, has historically practised a controlling, aggressive mode of reading, the gospels themselves feature images of a more generous, provisional form of interpretation. In the account of the woman taken in adultery in John 8, Jesus delays the judgement of the crowd when he stoops and writes in the dust. 'Religious reading', argues Stephen R. Haynes, 'does not necessitate reading uncritically. It does, however, require a faithful pursuit of textual clues until they yield a coherent religious theme, or until it becomes clear that one is lacking.'[27] Tracing the correlation between human suffering, incomprehensibility and acts of interpretation, Robert Detweiler claims that it 'is a task of the religiously-reading community to locate, disseminate and thus complete ... narratives' of hidden and unspeakable pain. 'A religious reading', he argues, 'will seek to identify and celebrate such fiction that provides these private, sanctified texts a public voice' rendering such stories 'bearable' without simultaneously making them 'profane'.[28]

Another concern expressed by spiritually inclined critics is that the novel actively marginalizes religious experience. Sara Maitland, perhaps the most combatively theological British prose writer of the last 25 years, suggests that the lack of 'echoes of eternity' in twentieth-century fiction is unsurprising since the novel 'is *the* genre of the post-Enlightenment'.[29] There is, she argues, a visible fissure between the continuing reality of spiritual belief, in its dizzyingly plural forms, and the novel, her chosen genre, which appears to be 'so singularly bad at recording, exploring and testing religious experiences, theological ideologies or faith-based motivations':

> Religious experience (as opposed to the social experiences of people who happen to be religious) is markedly absent from the modern novel. Religious characters are usually comic, villainous or mad, and their religious peculiarities consume their whole presence in the novel.[30]

Other writers, like Blake Morrison, the contemporary poet and novelist, regard the absence of God as cause for good cheer ('If God's gone at last, that's a relief') rather than despair. However, this liberation is rarely as serene as the word might suggest: Morrison's allegedly 'mild' form of disbelief, for example, which he identifies with George Orwell's image of the 'Anglican Atheist', is coloured by an anger that he politely attempts to evade. He is happy to wander 'about the ruins of the C of E', enjoying the occasional nostalgic foray into a public worship, but insists that 'belief in deities or an afterlife [is] childish nonsense'. Finally, he claims that he does not yearn for the absent God to 'turn up' and would, in fact, 'want him imprisoned or executed if He did'.[31] Morrison's view, expressed in one of a series of short, personal essays on the subject 'God and Me' in a special issue of *Granta* on religion, *God's Own Countries* (2006), is part of a literary lineage of diffident disbelief. James Wood states that the 'velocity' of his 'flight from belief has not been constant: there have been hesitations, interruptions, acute nostalgias'.[32] Morrison and Wood's shared, quiet antipathy for transcendent, theistic religion coupled with a mild nostalgia for aspects of its form resonates with the nineteenth-century rationalist fiction of George Eliot. Later in that century, this cool rationalism mutated into a form of anger with the divine: Thomas Hardy, for example, limned the 'ache of modernism' explicitly in relation to the decline of traditional Christian faith. In novels such as *Tess of the D'Urbervilles* (1891) and *Jude the Obscure* (1895), the 'terrifying absence' of God is tempered only by the fear that the world may be subject to the laws of a capricious and malign deity.[33] Hardy's near contemporary, Henry James, explores the legacies of the traditional Puritan hostility towards the very form of the novel in his seminal essay 'The Art of Fiction' (1884). 'The old superstition about fiction being "wicked" has doubtless died out in England,' he argues, but also claims that the spirit of it lingered in a certain oblique regard directed toward any story that does not more or less admit that it is only a joke ... It is still expected, though perhaps people are ashamed to say it, that a production which is after all only a "make-believe" (for what else is a "story"?) shall be in some degree apologetic – shall renounce the pretension of attempting really to represent life. This, of course, any sensible, wide-awake story declines to do ... The old evangelical hostility, which was explicit as it was narrow, and which regarded it as little less favourable to our immortal part than a stage-play, was in reality far less insulting.[34]

If, as James suggests, the secular distrust of any narrative aspiring to a persuasive realism bears the trace of an earlier 'evangelical hostility' to fiction, it is ironic that religion itself is the sphere of human activity about which the novel is most circumspect. Terry Eagleton, one of the most theologically literate critics working in the language, has suggested that the everyday, routine concerns of the realist novel mean that while it 'may still retain some religious beliefs ... it is as nervous of religious debate as a pub landlord'.[35] Yet contemporary fiction, despite this legacy of theological reticence, is noisy with God-talk: to extend Eagleton's (very English) bibulous metaphor, the twenty-first-century novel appears to have become garrulous under the influence of the spirit. Conversion narratives, moments of epiphany, sacred motifs, religious idioms, glossolalia, unexplained healing, miraculous visions, prophetic voices and resurrected Christ figures crowd the pages of the late twentieth- and early twenty-first-century novel. Indeed, Lukács' emphasis on the absence of God from fiction now seems charmingly obsolete. In fact, postmodern fiction, notorious for its epistemological scepticism and corrosive irony, repeatedly records the cultural return of divinity, a homecoming that many devout rationalists might find alarming. John Updike, perhaps the most spiritually acute of twentieth-century American novelists and whose brand of holy heresy is the subject of Chapter 3 of this book, claims that literature must always be analogous to visionary experience, even when it is produced by an unbelieving mind:

... it remains curiously true that the literary artist, to achieve full effectiveness, must assume a religious state of mind – a state that looks beyond worldly standards of success and failure. A mood of exaltation should possess the language, a vatic tension and rapture.[36]

The idea that literature can achieve a form of mystical truth is forcefully denied by certain materialist critics. In *The Visionary Moment* (2002), for example, Paul Maltby presents a self-styled 'postmodern critique' of literary epiphany:

An old theory of truth still enchants us. According to this theory, truth, in the sense of 'higher' spiritual knowledge, can be apprehended in an illuminating instant. The theory has a long history and today remains deeply inscribed in religious, literary, and colloquial discourse . . . this theory of truth has survived in spite of wave after wave of antimetaphysical thinking.[37]

However, the ecstatic mode of epiphany is not necessarily a product of orthodox faith, and what Updike names literature's 'vatic tension' points to the erosion of a clear line between the sacred and the secular. As Caputo argues, 'the distinction between theism and atheism is a little more unstable than people think, including most popes and bishops'.[38] To that list, we might add sceptical novelists who are hostile to the absolutes of religious authority – sometimes following unhappy personal experiences of faith, sometimes out of intellectual hostility – yet who also express a longing for the transcendent in their fiction. The contextual argument for a great divorce between faith and fiction is both straightforward and problematic. Dominic Head, for example, claims that 'the fact of a predominantly secular society is really a 'given' for [British] novelists in the entire post-war period'.[39] If this is the case, can the novel continue to be an active broker of religious ideas? Head's historicist position certainly implies that the passing of the Church's moral and social influence will inevitably lead to a parallel decline of an explicitly Christian mode of writing, if there ever was such a form. Although Head is writing about British culture, his view is echoed by Donna Tartt, the American author of *The Secret History* (1992) and *The Little Friend* (2002), who has written that there is a 'constant tension' between her committed Christian faith, also rooted in the Roman Catholic tradition, and her 'vocation as a novelist . . . since the novel in its history and genesis is an emphatically secular form'.[40]

Callum Brown concludes his contentious secularization thesis, *The Death of Christian Britain* (2001), with the claim that the 'Christian-centred culture' that previous generations might have regarded, even unconsciously, as a template for their attitudes, morality and expectations, has expired. 'If a core reality survives for Britons,' he notes, 'it is certainly no longer Christian'.[41] However, this is a radically different account of secularization from the now standard view that religious belief met its ruin in the mid-nineteenth century as a consequence of the new scientific scepticism. Indeed, Brown argues that the 'salvation economy' or 'machinery and ideas' of Evangelical culture shaped the Victorian popular consciousness in a way that it is hard to imagine today.[42] Secular Britain, he suggests, is really a product of shifts that took place in the 1960s, a decade in which 'a suspicion of creeds arose that quickly took the form of a rejection of Christian tradition and all formulaic constructions of the individual'.[43]

James Robertson's uncanny, sensitive and intensely theological novel *The Testament of Gideon Mack* (2006) reads like a fictional response to Brown's account of secularization. The narrator recalls the impact on his father's ministry of the 1960s, the 'American decade' that 'demolished privacy' and encouraged 'people to explore their inner selves'. The social revolution of those years meant that by 1970 the recently full church pews 'were more than half-empty . . . those for whom organised religion meant nothing any more went out with the tide and did not return'.[44] Robertson uses religious practice as a way of exploring the politics of an era: devolution, the impact of laissez-faire economics, cultural isolation are all read through the prism of a clergyman's private crisis. In one interview, the novelist suggested that a key theme of his work was to consider whether 'the absence of a spiritual or moral structure such as the Kirk once provided' implies 'a greater absence in our lives, or has that been filled by the products of rampant consumerism?'[45] The novel bears a close family resemblance to James Hogg's *The Private Memoirs and Confessions of a Justified Sinner* (1824): like Hogg's Gothic tale, *The Testament of Gideon Mack* deploys the device of a discovered manuscript, is similarly stalked by demonic doubles and also explores Scottish national identity and its Calvinist inheritance. 'What is the history of Christianity in this dark wee country,' reflects Gideon, 'but a history of doubts and fears, grasping at metaphysics from hard stone and wet bog?'[46] This 'grasping at metaphysics' remains a vital part of the contemporary novel, despite the decline of the institutions that encode belief.

'Waiting for a Miracle': The Return of the Miraculous

In an influential introduction to the 'study of literature and religion' published in 1989, David Jasper observes that these two cultural phenomena 'are never far apart'.[47] Is this still the case? Has the so-called 'postmodern condition' (to use Jean-François Lyotard's famous term) of late-twentieth- and early twenty-first-century culture, in which trust in an overarching story of history has largely failed, undermined the close and creative association between religious practice and literature? If previous generations of spiritually literate writers, including Graham Greene and William Golding, offered, with exceptions, comparatively rationalist fictions, postmodern writers increasingly test the limits of realistic narrative strategies. In the early twenty-first century, novelists are fascinated by the implications of miraculous occurrences. Indeed, rationalist hostility to miracles is subverted by the extraordinary 'sacred turn' followed by many questing artists and critical theorists during the last decade. This post-secular movement towards the miraculous in fiction includes improbable stories of faith healing, fulfilled prophecy and experiences of epiphany; as I have noted, many writers, both sceptical and devout, have re-imagined the life of Christ; ghosts, angels and mystics are now common figures in serious literary fiction. Is this eclectic spirituality indicative of a postmodern 'Great Awakening' or simply the death-throes of a sentimental, decadent late capitalism? If modernity banished mystery from the world, should we regard its return with hostility or cautious optimism? Chapter 4 focuses on the representation of miracles and the sceptical legacy of the eighteenth-century philosopher David Hume's challenge to the miraculous. A miracle is most easily defined, observes Richard Swinburne, as 'an event of extraordinary kind brought about by a god and of religious significance'.[48] These ideas are explored in relation to novels by, among others, Don DeLillo, Nick Hornby, David Guterson and Jodi Picoult.

Chapter 5 develops the focus on the representation of miracles with a specific focus on John Irving's *A Prayer for Owen Meany* (1989). Can fiction that takes the supernatural seriously be considered as serious fiction? In his path-finding study, *Theology and Literature* (1988), T. R. Wright notes that the 'liberal humanist ideology' that came to dominate realism – with George Eliot's *Middlemarch* (1870–1) the greatest achievement of this world view – was challenged in the twentieth century primarily by Catholic novelists such as Evelyn Waugh, Graham Greene and Flannery O'Connor: 'all of whom can be seen to challenge the unexamined assumptions of the "modern" secular world, the "rational" view that miracles never happen and that religious experience is an illusion'.[49] Realist ideas are certainly no longer taken for granted in Anglophone fiction. Daniel Underwood, the narrator of Douglas Coupland's *Microserfs* (1995), believes that new technology reflects a deep-rooted and desperate craving for an encounter with the transcendent. Technology and the miraculous blur even if the one is merely a simulated version of the other:

> Flight Simulation games are actually out-of-body experience emulators. There must be all of these people everywhere on earth right now, waiting for a miracle, waiting to be pulled out of themselves, eager for just the smallest sign that there is something finer or larger or miraculous about our existence than we had supposed .[50]

'All fiction contains two primary impulses: the impulse to imitate daily life and the impulse to transcend it,' claims Gillian Beer.[51] These twin impulses only partially explain the turn to the supernatural in contemporary fiction. Twenty-first-century accounts of the miraculous are not exclusively confined to genre fiction or to worlds whose imaginary laws of gravity of necessity feature supernatural phenomena. Indeed, encounters with the uncanny, the unexplained and, occasionally, the divine have slipped their generic boundaries and quietly crossed the threshold into the predictable world of everyday, mimetic realism. A defining aspect of the detraditionalized, post-religious imagination is, as Graham Ward has suggested, an inclination to 'employ a magic realism of various kinds . . . The supernatural comes from the other side of C. S. Lewis's wardrobe and enters the house, garden and urban landscape itself.'[52] 'Magic realism', as practised in Anglophone literature by novelists such as Angela Carter, tends to be explicitly materialist, in spite of its debt to folklore and Gothic fiction.[53] However, a rather different strand of fiction, more open to the supernatural, has emerged alongside its sceptical sibling. This incursion of the miraculous appears in many different forms, some of which thrive on the occult or angelic while other narratives explore a more muted, if no less spiritually significant, version of 'signs and wonders'. At one extreme, it is visible in Gothic stories of the spectral, including Hilary Mantel's *Fludd* (1989) and *Beyond Black* (2005), for example. Can such supernatural tales, despite their explicit use of religious allusion, be read as part of a postmodern turn to theology? 'The haunted is a degenerate form of the sacred,' John Updike claims, in response to Nathaniel Hawthorne's guilt-driven characters.[54] Whether or not the ghosts that stalk so many twenty-first-century fictions belong to Freud, Marx or to an altogether less rational worldview, they certainly expand the imaginative possibilities of narrative. For some novelists, narratives of the numinous are necessarily theological. John L'Heureux – a former Jesuit priest – examines the fragile division between faith and unbelief in *The Miracle* (2002). The novel's protagonist, Father Paul LeBlanc, is an angst-ridden young priest – a man caught between a worldly-wise pragmatism and the desire to 'obliterate the self' – whose faith is transformed by an apparent miracle.[55] This event is not even a comparatively mundane encounter with a piece of weeping marble statuary or a momentary epiphany but a full-scale bodily resurrection, the very form of miracle that Hume defined as the ultimate impossible wonder. L'Heureux's miraculous narrative is by no means unique and its tropes and implications – literary and theological – are discussed in relation to the significant body of contemporary novels that include similar, reason-defying phenomena in Chapter 4.

One subplot in Jonathan Coe's *The Rotters' Club* (2000), continued in its sequel *The Closed Circle* (2004), offers a playful and painful account of a collision between the miraculous and the mundane. Coe's sixth novel narrates the intersecting lives of a group of teenagers and their families in the 'brown times' of Britain in the 1970s, with a plot that both exploits comic nostalgia for innocence lost and examines more disturbing memories of the political changes that marked the era.[56] Terrorist violence, trade union corruption, offhand racism, ugly far-right politics and the rise of Margaret Thatcher do not merely provide a milieu for the rites of passage stories of Ben Trotter and his friends, but represent the core experiences that coalesce to define their adult lives. Against the grain of this realist narrative, Coe includes an apparent eruption of the miraculous: on Thursday 7 March 1974, faced with the appalling prospect of swimming in the nude (the sadistic sportsmaster's standard punishment for the heinous sin of forgotten trunks), Ben apparently finds God. This encounter with the divine follows a desperate (and first ever) prayer: what begins as casual blasphemy 'somehow evolved' into an act of supplication (*TRC*, p. 71). A pair of shorts – dripping wet and outsized – suddenly appears in a locker and Ben is delivered from one of the many routine humiliations of adolescence. In some comic fiction, this kind of reprieve would serve only as catharsis for a traumatic, if amusing, episode. However, in *The Rotters' Club*, the event sparks a long-lasting and sincere conversion. Immediately after this moment of allegedly miraculous rescue, Ben's sense of the divine is deepened as he listens to Francis Piper, an elderly poet associated with the Bloomsbury group, read from his work. Coe deploys the language of epiphany as Ben's 'newly devotional ears' hear 'echoes of some psalm or hymnal' and 'Divine Grace' appears to be 'everywhere' (*TRC*, p. 73).

The tone of this conversion narrative is played somewhere between the genres of chaotic farce and the raptures of spiritual autobiography. Ben's miracle is ordinary, secular, comic and even banal but it also changes his world view and leads him to faith. Recalling this 'strange moment of revelation' three years later, he concludes 'that religious belief, at its most sincere, was an essentially private thing, a wordless conspiracy between oneself and God' (*TRC*, p. 273). Ben's eventual discovery of its origins, twenty years later, in the novel's sequel, *The Closed Circle* (2004), is devastating. His belief that the salvific trunks had been provided by 'the breath of God' is debunked when he discovers, via one of the novel's many coincidences, that the trunks had been stolen and abandoned by Piper, who proves to have been as much a voyeur as he was a sublime poet. This revelation points towards the contingency of religious belief but the final epiphany of *The Rotters' Club*, constructed around a vast, chapter-length meandering sentence, an echo of the end of James Joyce's *Ulysses* (1922), is a celebration of comic grace: 'it seemed to me then that not only does God exist, but he must be a genius, a comic genius, to have made everything in the world so funny, everything form Sam and his crazy predictions right down to the dark beery circle my glass has just left on this green coaster' (*TRC*, p. 399). In a sense Ben's discovery of the origins of his 'miracle' in the sequel is less revealing (and certainly less compelling) than this moment of joy. Coe suggests that the sacred is found in the midst of the profane, rather than as some utterly separate sphere of existence.

In fact, this exuberant blurring of supernatural phenomena and realist narrative has an ancient precedent. Hans W. Frei notes that in 'biblical stories . . . nonmiraculous and miraculous accounts and explanations are constantly intermingled'. Frei's path-finding study *The Eclipse of Biblical Narrative* (1974) contrasts the 'jaundiced eye' of modern historical narrative which necessarily rejects miracles with the scriptures in which 'even . . . miraculous accounts are history-like or realistic if the depicted action is indispensable to the rendering of a particular character, divine or human, or a particular story'.[57] More recently, Mark Knight and Thomas Woodman have argued that

> the biblical sacred is not so much the miraculous in the sense of extraordinary wonders as the natural seen in its ultimate depth. From this perspective realism may even prove the preferred option for the expression of biblical categories of the sacred in fiction, provided it is a realism conceived in sufficient depth and openness.[58]

David Maine's *The Flood* (2004), published in the US as *The Preservationist*, and the first of his series of biblically themed novels, embodies the realist aesthetic described by Knight and Woodman. Maine's novel rewrites the deluge described in Genesis 6–8 and imagines the response of the key human figures who appear in the narrative. Maine's narrative collapses the normal distinctions between realism and myth: in *The Flood*, Noah, or 'Noe', routinely hears the voice of God and miracles take place. However, the characters are still subject to the same laws as any figure in a realist novel would be. The ark remains a symbol of earthly rescue and spiritual salvation, but it also reeks of human and animal waste and is similarly full of danger, doubt and despair. The novel's timely sense of hesitant wonder is best expressed by Japheth, cast as Noe's youngest, mischievous son.

> I know when I'm in the presence of something mightier than myself. It happens during thunderstorms and earth tremors and clear nights with no moon, and here it's happening again right in front of me. I'd be stupid to say otherwise.[59]

The Flood is not merely an iconoclastic recasting of a foundational piece of religious mythology: it displays a vivid impression of awe for creation and takes its source material seriously. However, as a rewriting of scripture it does dare to challenge the hegemony of authorized accounts of sacred history. In this sense, it testifies both to contemporary fiction's fascination with the miraculous and a more subversive impulse for heresy.

Fiction and Heresy

A primary aim of this book is to determine that the sensitive literary exploration of religious questions is emphatically not the exclusive terrain of confessional, 'religious' writers: sceptical and sometimes openly atheistic novelists, including Jim Crace, whose novel *Quarantine* (1997) follows Jesus into the Judean desert, have produced narratives that prioritize engagement with belief in all its complexity. Few of the novelists discussed in detail in this study, with the exception of John Updike and Rhidian Brook (discussed in more detail in Chapters 3 and 4 respectively), are likely to assent to the Apostles' Creed. Yet all of them illuminate, problematize and enrich ideas that are fundamental to Christian tradition. 'The story of Christianity', argues Valentine Cunningham, 'is a story of heresy'.[60] Heresy, he notes, is derived from the Greek *haeresis*, meaning 'literally choice, taking a position' and a term that 'soon came in the Christian era to mean mistaken choice, taking up a bad theological position'. Cunningham develops a defence of 'the necessity of heresy' as a vital principle for a thriving literary culture: 'To put it plainly and extremely, literature in English thrives on heresy, wishes to be heretical and is so. Heresy has been and is a grand creative principle with us'.[61] In the tradition of 'canonical' literary heretics cited by Cunningham, including Emily Dickinson, James Joyce, Matthew Arnold and Samuel Taylor Coleridge, we might add a provisional, and ever expanding new list of contemporary writers. A variety of heretical usurping of the gospels is discussed in Chapter 2, for example, and Updike's consciously theological brand of heresy is the focus of Chapter 3.

Oranges Are Not the Only Fruit (1985), Jeanette Winterson's first novel, a *künstlerroman* and semi-autobiographical fiction of unconversion, prophecy and self-discovery, is part of this vibrant heretical tradition. The novel ends with its narrator returning to her home town, climbing its neighbouring hill and reflecting on her severed relationship with God. In some senses it re-enacts the exemplary modernist endings of James Joyce's *Portrait of the Artist as a Young Man* (1916) and Virginia Woolf's *To the Lighthouse* (1927). Just as Stephen Daedalus finds a new vocation in art, which allows him to wrest himself from the faith of his fathers and, similarly, Lily Briscoe attains liberation in her moment of quasi-religious aesthetic vision, so does Jeanette finally move from child-evangelist to author of her own past, present and future. This evidently faithless ending to a 1980s novel is perhaps a peculiar, disorientating narrative with which to begin a study of contemporary fiction and theology. Jeanette's journey is not, after all, a solitary leap into the sea of faith, but an ascent to a space of subjective, humanist freedom.

Jo Carruthers, responding to Harold Fisch's claim that the engagement of the novel with scripture 'has been profoundly antithetical', explores the ways in which Winterson's debut 'rails against the evangelical Protestantism in its form as well as its content. By naming the chapters after the books of the Bible, Winterson overwrites the Genesis narrative with her protagonist's beginnings and in her chapter "Ruth", evokes Ruth and Naomi's relationship with reference to her protagonist's lesbian relationship'.[62] Yet there is a tension in Winterson's narration of new-found autonomy between the ecstasy of independence and the melancholy of spiritual homelessness.[63] The narrator's confession that she grieves for the absence of God is, to an extent, surprising since her story has been one of Promethean rebellion against a tyrannical, irrational and patriarchal system of religious belief. In another sense, however, her wrestling with the divine and the integral yearning for some spiritual absolute is inscribed by her zealous religious heritage: the Puritan/Evangelical tradition in which she has been raised is characterized by its emphasis on personal regeneration, the death of the old, corrupted self and its rebirth as a new creation. This frame would suggest that Jeanette's paradoxical search for a kind of wholeness both in independence and interrelatedness is a displacement of religious narratives engraved in the consciousness and which, as many lapsed believers will testify, are singularly difficult to escape. We might read the kicking against/desire for God in Romantic, Christian or psychoanalytic terms but ultimately it embodies crucial aspects of the 'post-secular' condition of contemporary culture in the late twentieth and early twenty-first centuries. The motif of ascent coupled with a panoramic vision that affords witness through time as well as space is distinctively spiritual, echoing the solitary figures of Romanticism, seeking consolation from the turmoil and sorrows of urban life in the gloom and glory of the created landscape. Jeanette King notes that the mixture of 'adult registers' in the novel's early sections, when the young schoolchild is unable to understand fully the 'connotations and appropriacy' of these different voices, 'articulates her experience of religion as an integral part of everyday reality, rather than a distinct realm of experience for Sundays and holy days'.[64]

James Wood's first novel, *The Book Against God* (2003), similarly explores the heretical impulse via a struggle between a believing parent and their sceptical offspring. Its narrator, Thomas Bunting, like Gideon Mack, is a disbelieving son of the manse. As his name suggests he is defined by doubt, a devout secularist for whom 'life is always a struggle for freedom'.[65] The titular 'Book Against God' is Thomas's diversion from completing a doctorate in philosophy and is considerably less grand than it sounds: 'I copy out apposite religious and anti-religious quotations, and develop arguments of my own about theological and philosophical matters . . . the day would disappear into theology and anti-theology' (*TBAG*, p. 3). In this palimpsest of scepticism, Thomas displays contradictory instincts and tastes: he is an aesthete who enthuses about 'beautiful objects, rich foods, rare atmospheres' but who is also drawn to the astringency of the Psalms. The interplay between Thomas and his father, Peter – both named for disciples who betrayed Christ – embodies a much more complex religious dimension to the story than its narrator would allow. As Peter notes, 'belief and unbelief are not absolutes, and not absolute opposites. What if they are rather close to each other, I mean belief shadowed by unbelief and vice versa?' (*TBAG*, p. 46). This blurring of the boundaries between belief and scepticism is troubling for both believers and sceptics.

The late Flannery O'Connor, celebrated novelist of the grotesque and a practising Roman Catholic who wrote in and of the belligerently Protestant south of the United States, argued that a committed faith should allow readers to engage with literature that disturbs rather than consoles. O'Connor, whose religious views were far from liberal, rejected the view that reading serious, adult literature is not the business of the committed Christian:

> It is when the individual's faith is weak, not when it is strong, that he will be afraid of an honest fictional representation of life; and when there is a tendency to compartmentalize the spiritual and make it resident in a certain type of life only, the supernatural is apt generally to be lost. Fiction, made according to its own laws, is an antidote to such a tendency, for it renews our knowledge that we live in the mystery from which we draw our abstractions.[66]

Philip Pullman's controversial trilogy of children's fantasy novels, *His Dark Materials* (1995–2000), is very different from the kind of literature that O'Connor wrote, both in theological and aesthetic terms. However, the novels do test the limits of O'Connor's call for a courageous approach to fiction by believers. Pullman's series, comprising *Northern Lights*, *The Subtle Knife* and *The Amber Spyglass*, represents the most sophisticated antagonistic critique of Judaeo-Christian theology to be articulated in recent popular culture. In many ways, it is representative of the religious complexities of the modern imagination. Just as C. S. Lewis's Narnia series may have indicated British society's continuing rootedness in Christianity during the 1950s, Pullman's 'other-world-and-ours' allegories signify a more widely accepted hostility to the same religion at the dawn of the twenty-first century. Yet it too has its origins in the very tradition which it critiques, since it is an explicit rewriting of one of the epics of Christian literature, John Milton's *Paradise Lost* (1667); *His Dark Materials* is an allusion to Book II of the poem. Milton's epic, the high point of the Puritan imagination, was itself a creative (and not unambiguous) response to the

Genesis narrative of humanity's fall from grace. Despite Pullman's real hostility to Christianity – in particular its emphasis on a God who is both omniscient and personal – his fiction is, ironically, rooted in the text against which he is rebelling: the 'book of Books', the Judaeo-Christian scriptures. Michael Edwards has argued that 'if the biblical reading of life is in any way true, litera-ture will be drawn strongly towards it. Eden, Fall, Transformation, in whatever guise, will emerge in literature as everywhere else.'[67] The emphatic return of these ideas, even in antagonistic, consciously heretical forms, is part of a re-enchantment of popular culture.

Spirituality, Re-enchantment and the Apocalyptic

In Douglas Coupland's apocalyptic novel, *Girlfriend in a Coma* (1998), Richard Doorland reflects that in the absence of traditional forms of faith, he and his friends have instead been 'exposed . . . day in, day out, to a constant assembly line of paranoia, extreme beliefs, and spiritual simplifications'.[68] Coupland's fiction, the focus of Chapter 6, embodies the yearning for faith in the post-modern era. His work is marked by an escalating interest in apocalypse, both in the sense of end-time narratives and as sudden, visionary experience. One of the defining theological anxieties of the era relates to the loss of traditional pictures of heaven. Is it still possible to imagine an afterlife and bodily resurrection? In the closing chapter of David Lodge's *Paradise News* (1991), Bernard Walsh, erst-while priest and sceptical theologian, delivers a lecture on the deterioration of traditional Christian visions of the afterlife. 'The question facing the theologian today is . . . what can be salvaged from the eschatological wreckage?'[69] Walsh laments the loss of Christianity's traditional emphasis on a 'teleological and apocalyptic' narrative that 'presented both individual and collective human life as a linear plot moving towards an End, followed by timelessness: death, judgement, hell and heaven'.[70] Lodge's novel contrasts the idea of an earthly paradise, of heaven today, with the theological idea of a future Kingdom of grace and love and suggests that the former will always be disappoint-ing and the latter has become nearly impossible to believe. A yearning for the hope of a transformative future life animates much fiction of the last fifty years. Robert Detweiler, for example, identifies novels by Kurt Vonnegut, Italo Calvino, John Barth and Walker Percy, among others, as part of a theological trend that embodies 'an eschatological impulse, a longing for a different and better world, for a new creation that at last looks much like the old, for an ideal version of the original creation'.[71] Coupland continues this tradition but recuperates the hope of bodily resurrection as a challenge to disenchanted modern culture.

Coupland's audacious recasting of theology for a culture supposedly beyond religious belief is part of a wider paradigm shift. 'All in all,' argues Zygmunt Bauman, a less obviously theological interpreter of global culture, 'postmoder-nity can be seen as restoring to the world what modernity presumptuously, had taken away; as a *re-enchantment* of the world that modernity tried hard to *dis*-enchant'.[72] Bauman claims that the modern era's emphasis on reason as autonomous, free from prejudice and utterly objective, 'has been dismantled' by a new re-enchanted sensibility: 'It is that artifice and that reason, the reason of the artifice, that stands accused in the court of postmodernity'.[73] This influential claim should not be understood as a call for the return of superstition and authoritarian religion: ironically, Bauman reminds modern readers that modernity itself, for all its 'meaning-legislating reason', is not without its superstitions and shibboleths. For Terry Eagleton, modernity was always religious, despite its loud protestations: the Enlightenment did not really kill God but merely give him a 'series of majestic new names, like Nature, Man, Reason, History, Power, Desire, and so on. Rather than dismantling the whole outdated apparatus of metaphysics and theology, we have simply given it a new content'.[74] Postmodern culture is highly suspicious of these artificial names for divinity.

Although Bauman's account of 're-enchantment' is primarily sociological, the idea has given shape to many theological explorations of culture. In a 1995 article, John A. McClure argues that late twentieth-century American culture and the literature of postmodernity should be read as a post-secular phenomenon in which 'many postmodern texts are shot through with and even shaped by spiritual concerns'. McClure cites Bauman's description of the collapse of modern disenchantment in an essay that focuses on Thomas Pynchon and Don DeLillo. He also emphasizes the idea of the return of religion to an apparently secular sphere such as the novel:

> In order to understand what is going on in American postmodern culture, then, we need to think in terms of something like a religious revival: a resurgence . . . of spiritual energies, discourses, and commitments. And in order to understand postmodern fiction, we need to attend to the ways in which it maintains and revises a modernist tradition of spiritually inflected resistance to conventionally secular constructions of reality.[75]

McClure was one of the first literary critics to identify the new religious sensibility of postmodern fiction. His use of the term 'spiritual', however, is particularly significant. Spirituality, like postmodernism, has become a notoriously elastic term that is applied to so many rival phenomena, activities and beliefs that it has forfeited any clear meaning. 'Quite simply, the term "spiritual" has suddenly become rather spongy,' notes Martyn Percy, 'it seems to lack definition, and yet soak up virtually everything'.[76] Indeed, in the provocative title of a journal article, one researcher asks: 'Is the Term 'Spirituality' a Word that Everyone Uses, But Nobody Knows What Anyone Means By it?'[77] The article reviews the results of a questionnaire regarding the term which were inclusive of most forms of twenty-first-century human engagement including sport, art, humanitarian action and state funerals: 'Overall, membership of, or belief in, a particular religion was not thought to be prerequisite for the experience of the spiritual'.[78] Similarly, Alister McGrath has observed that the 'cherished deities of reason and logic' have apparently been 'dethroned, to be replaced with angels, spirits, forces – not to mention Jesus'. The emergence of so-called 'New Age' spirituality is, for McGrath, a sign that the culture of postmodernity is 'fed up with the rather boring platitudes of scientific progress, and longs for something rather more interesting and exciting.'[79] However, as Philip Sheldrake argues, the concept of spirituality becomes more evocative when traced to its roots in the Hebrew and Christian traditions. For Christianity, Sheldrake notes, 'spirituality refers to the way our fundamental values, life-styles, and spiritual practices reflect particular understandings of God, human identity, and the material world as the context for human transformation'.[80] Although these concepts have evolved (and in some cases been diluted) in secular and post-secular culture, the core concepts remain vital and provide a useful framework for a religious critique of the contemporary novel.

Conclusion: Writing God

In an article entitled 'Is the Postmodern Post-Secular?' Brian D. Ingraffia explicitly responds to and argues against McClure's view from an orthodox Christian position. The postmodern strategies of Pynchon and DeLillo, he suggests, in no way affirm a genuine recovery of the sacred.[81] Indeed, in a longer study that explores the trajectory of modern disbelief from Friedrich Nietzsche and Martin Heidegger through to Jacques Derrida, Ingraffia argues against a 'synthesis' of postmodern theory and theology and instead proposes 'an either/or'.[82] 'Theology continues to be that against which postmodernism defines its freedom,' reasons Ingraffia, and this 'autonomy' is not simply the evasion of 'a transcendent God' but also a freedom that allows 'the free play of interpretation against belief in any final, authoritative meaning'.[83] Although Ingraffia's critique displays an admirable alertness to the continuities between postmodernity and the modernity that it supposedly displaces, I cannot accept the logical conclusion of his argument that contemporary culture has to recover the scandal of biblical revelation to be of any religious value. If fiction is, by definition, a human construct, it will always constitute a jumble of sacred longing and ordinary failure. However, Ingraffia's argument vividly illustrates the difficulty that postmodern culture, including literary fiction, is faced with in speaking of God.

'Theology has lost its object,' argues Philip Blond. 'It can no longer point to anything with ostensive certainty and say the word "God" '.[84] Similarly, in an exploration of theology and film, Roy M. Anker has observed that the word 'God' is no longer either 'evocative' or 'precise', 'having long since become the great cosmic catchall for anything slightly strange, repressive, or, for that matter, unjust – either in politics or personal life'.[85] Rhidian Brook's *The Testimony of Taliesin Jones* (1996), a relatively rare novel of religious conversion rather than loss of faith that is discussed in more detail in Chapter 4, explores the difficulties of imagining the divine. The novel's eleven-year-old protagonist, Taliesin, is confused by the lack of clarity in descriptions of God:

For some, it seems, God is made up, He can't be located, no one seems to have seen Him, He hasn't featured in the news. For others He is as real as an apple; He can be found in everything, even inside of us. Is there a right or wrong answer, or does it just depend? Is there a completely utterly categorical yes, or an absolutely totally definite no?'[86]

Brook's novel wrestles with the possibility that God might be encountered in the everyday and, in a quiet way, offers a bold narrative of emerging faith. In many other instances, however, when God is invoked in the contemporary novel, it is frequently to deride or refute the validity of the term. For example, in Salman Rushdie's millennial, pop culture-saturated rewriting of the Orpheus and Eurydice myth, *The Ground Beneath Her Feet* (1999), the term 'God' becomes fraught with power struggles. Rai, the novel's rationalist narrator, who describes himself as 'the least supernaturally inclined of men', reacts angrily to a casual benediction uttered by a friend: 'Thank god? No, no, *no*. Let's not invent anything as cruel, vicious, vengeful, intolerant, unloving, immoral and arrogant as god just to explain a stroke of dumb, undeserved luck'.[87] In fact, the imaginary 'god' who is the target of Rai's indignation is close to the figure N. T. Wright suggests that 'most people' invoke in the contemporary west, 'the god of Enlightenment Deism': a 'far-off, detached being' who 'is basically remote, inaccessible, and certainly not involved with the day-to-day life, let alone the day-to-day pain, of the world as it now is'.[88] Despite Rai's assertive atheism, Rushdie's novel suggests that the 'ground beneath' all manner of philosophies and religious persuasions, including aggressive secularism, is uncertain. In its exploration of the continued search for transcendent experience in a supposedly godless era, *The Ground Beneath Her Feet* is an emphatically post-secular novel.

Martin Amis offers a similarly sour account of the human need for God in 'The Janitor on Mars' (1997), a troubling short story of first contact with extraterrestrial life. Drawing on the defamiliarizing tactics of the so-called 'Martian poets' – exemplified in Craig Raine's *A Martian Sends a Postcard Home* (1979) – the narrative offers an illuminating, skewed vision of human endeavour in art, politics, science and religion. Amis's Martian 'janitor' is a kind of cybernetic angel, but one who offers a message of judgement without grace. The pitiless machine finds 'terrestrial religion and its scarcely credible tenacity' both ludicrous and intriguing. His godlike perspective allows him to compare the life-forms of other planets where 'they just kick around a few creation myths for a while and then snap out of it when science gets going' with humanity that seems to need religion in spite of science. During the millennia of waiting to deliver his message, the robot appears to have become familiar with the theology of Søren Kierkegaard and John Updike's fiction as well as human anthropology: 'One of your writers put it succinctly when he said that there was no evidence for the existence of God other than the human longing that it should be so . . . What *is* this longing?'[89] This science-fiction incarnation of the avenging angel, who casually informs humanity that its cosmically inconsequential world will be destroyed imminently, presents a distinctly Graeco-Roman understanding of the relationship between God and creation:

> Everyone else wants 'God' too – but from a different angle. For us, 'God' isn't top-down. He's bottom-up. Why yearn for a power greater than your own? Why not seek to become it? Even the most affable and conciliatory Martian would have found your Promethean urge despicably weak ... This entity, through his surrogate the Third Observer, created life on Mars. And what am I supposed to do about Him? *Worship* Him? ... That's *your* thing. When all is said and done, you *are* very talented adorers.[90]

Despite the tone of contempt for theistic religion deployed in Amis's short story, the janitor is unable to rationalize the persistence of worship and wonder as fundamental to human identity. Indeed, the fact that the writer's dystopian vision of future earth looks beyond itself for meaning resonates with the tradition of transcendent theology: Amis represents humanity as fallen, flawed, floundering and in need of a redemption that lies outside its own powers.

Yann Martel's Booker Prize-winning novel, *Life of Pi* (2001), takes a more positive approach to the ways in which God is addressed and imagined. Indeed, it is framed by a claim in the preface that the novel tells a story '*that will make you believe in God*'.[91] This, as the narrator notes, is something of 'a tall order' and there is little evidence that the streets were filled with newly converted believers, leaving behind their atheism, after the novel's publication. However, *Life of Pi* is an extraordinary novel of the power of narrative and religious belief to transfigure catastrophe and loss. Piscine Molitor Patel ('Pi') is raised in a secular household in Bombay (like Rai in *The Ground Beneath Her Feet* his father is not religious) but undergoes a series of conversions. He cherishes a sequence of transformative adolescent encounters with Hinduism (to which he owes 'the original landscape of [his] religious imagination'), Christianity and Islam and maintains the practices of each religion.[92] The novel becomes a kind of syncretistic version of John Bunyan's *Pilgrim's Progress* (1678–84) and the strange story of Pi's shipwreck, the devastating loss of his family and his own unlikely survival is a powerful elegy for the miraculous possibility of storytelling. Rather than capitulate to despair, Pi draws on the strength of combined spiritual traditions to refigure his traumatic experience. 'Reality', claims T. R. Wright, 'is at least in part a matter of faith, of what we choose to be the case'.[93] The anxiety of choice between world views or alternative accounts of reality is one of this novel-parable's fundamental themes. This echoes the clash of interpretations described in *The Ground Beneath Her Feet*, between those who believe that the 'true miracle of reason ... is reason's victory over the miraculous' and others 'for whom the miraculous had long ago supplanted the quotidian as the norm, and who would have been utterly lost, without ... angels and devils, in the tragic jungle of the everyday'.[94] Significantly, in his adult life, Martel's Pi seems to bridge the gap identified by Rushdie as he becomes both a man of science and a person of faith: at university he studies

Zoology and Theology and expresses kinship with atheists as 'brothers and sisters of a different faith'. In fact, he has more respect for those who consciously reject religious belief than for agnostics: 'We must all pass through the garden of Gethsemane ... To choose doubt as a philosophy of life is akin to choosing immobility as a means of transportation'.[95] Doubt, as James Wood might argue, seems to be the accepted mood of the novel in all its 'true secularism'.[96] However, *Life of Pi*, alongside other twenty-first-century narratives, challenges the notion that the journey of faith, rather than one of burgeoning disbelief, is necessarily detrimental to morally complex, demanding fiction.

'Postmodernity has opened up breathing space once again to consider what is "other" to our theories', claims Kevin Vanhoozer. This 'breathing space' has included a new engagement with the 'repressed' other of theology.[97] Sadly, this return has been accompanied by the spectacle of violence on a global scale, sometimes perpetrated in the names of a variety of gods, not all of which are supernatural. Yet this is not the end of the story or, indeed, the only story. The remaining chapters in this volume will explore the dynamic variety of ways in which Christianity, in its plural forms, interacts with fiction. Keith Ward notes that the 'Christian faith has many interpretations, and many different forms of interpretation' but that beyond these disparities 'the gospel itself ... rests on the revelation, the self-disclosure ... of God in the life and death of Jesus, and on the experience of his risen presence in the fellowship of his disciples'.[98] Chapter 2 pursues this foundational idea and analyses the Christological implications of a variety of fictional interpretations of the figure of Jesus, with detailed reference to Jim Crace's extraordinary novel *Quarantine*. Chapter 3 explores John Updike's representation of Christian belief and his fascination with the interlinking phenomena of sin, heresy and unwarranted grace. Chapters 4 and 5 both examine the return of the miraculous in contemporary literature, moving from a wide overview of fictional miracles in Anglophone fiction to a more specific examination of John Irving's *A Prayer for Owen Meany* (1989). The apocalyptic – and occasionally miraculous – fiction of Douglas Coupland is the focus of Chapter 6. The conclusion identifies some of the major theological trends in contemporary fiction and argues that the novel, even in its most determinedly secular forms, now articulates religious questions more forcefully than has been widely recognized.

2

This Other Christ: Jesus in Contemporary Fiction

'The problems of greatest concern to me are not the modern world's famous inability to believe in God,' states William C. Placher, 'but the world's characteristically trivial images of God'.[1] Do these 'trivial images' of divinity include the multiple representations of Jesus in contemporary literature and culture? Is it possible to create any such interpretation, visual or literary, that does not diminish the object of worship? Contemporary spectators, alienated from the traditions of biblical narrative, might be rather uninspired by what N. T. Wright has described as 'the stained-glass Christ-figure of much Christian imagination . . . in the Catholic, Protestant, Orthodox or evangelical traditions'.[2] Yet, in spite of the sentimental images that dominate popular representations of Jesus, post-Christian, postmodern cultures continue to be fascinated by this strange and elusive figure, the man who claimed to be God. The focus of Pat Barker's *Double Vision* (2003), a novel that explores a variety of twenty-first-century traumas, is the construction of a vast sculpture of Jesus. More specifically, this statue is a fifteen-feet tall representation of the risen Christ. Its creator, Kate Frobisher, is not a confessional religious sculptor (indeed, she makes 'no secret of her lack of belief') but has been commissioned by an Anglican cathedral to produce what she calls '[m]y Christ'.[3] The agnostic artist, struggling to find an appropriate vision and idiom for her work, dislikes 'all representations of Christ':

> If they were good, they underlined the folly of her thinking that she had anything new to contribute to a tradition that had lasted 2,000 years. If they were bad – like the painting in the Lady Chapel of Christ in a chiffon nightie, its diaphanous folds failing to hide the fact that there was nothing to hide – they seemed to invite her mockingly to add to their number. (*DV*, pp. 28–9)

This aesthetic antipathy for the traditions of Christian art parallels Placher's more explicitly theological disdain. Both philosopher and sceptical artist, from different perspectives, recognize that inadequate images of divinity have come to dominate the contemporary religious imagination. Kate's gradually evolving Christ, slowly carved and shaped by an artist who is in both physical and emotional pain, serves an interesting purpose in a novel that is not ostensibly about religious belief. Barker's narrative deals with the impact of violence and its mediation in the modern world; central to this theme is an exploration of the ethical implications for narratives of human suffering in an age in which spectacle shapes the prevalent perceptions of violence. Shortly before the action of the novel, Kate's husband, Ben, a war-zone photojournalist, was killed in Afghanistan; their friend, Stephen Sharkey, a correspondent who collaborated with Ben in reporting global conflict, is writing a book on the relationship between war and its popular representation. Kate's sculpture of Jesus, bearing the wounds of torture, becomes a motif that both makes human suffering visible and, more radically for a disbelieving artist, represents the possibility of resurrection. While the crucifixion, an image of intense personal pain, has unmistakable resonance for an age of war, it is harder to accommodate the resurrected Christ to such an era. Can a traditional and irreducibly theological image of redemption be of any secular use?

In fact, Barker's icon of a mute but expressive risen Christ reiterates a long-term debate about the depiction of the sacred and, in particular, the idea of incarnation. Rowan Williams, for example, has identified a fundamental question for theologically oriented art and literature: 'In a cultural environment where Christian images are not very accessible, how do you express the differentness of Christ?'[4] In *Double Vision*, Kate Frobisher's Christ is a startling, defamiliarizing and unique presence; his is an uncanny, transfigured body whose meaning is open to interpretation but one that unlocks an alternative view of the novel's psychological and political themes. The punning title suggests both a dazed encounter with the twenty-first-century landscape and the necessity of multiple perspectives on reality. Even Kate's process of sculpture – slow, meticulous and self-critical – is at odds with the visual zeitgeist of an 'accelerated' culture. Instead of countless disposable images, ready to be consumed and discarded, Kate works in a medium that demands attention and focus on a single material reality from both creator and reader-spectator. *Double Vision* is also a reminder that it is impossible to represent the figure of Christ – even incidentally, as statue rather than flesh and blood character – without enmeshing narrative in Christological debate.

This chapter will focus on another contemporary novel that displays a form of 'double vision' regarding the figure of Jesus. *Quarantine* (1997), Jim Crace's disquieting rewriting of Jesus Christ's forty-day fast in the Judean wilderness, risks both the rage of conservative Christians and the contempt of secular critics. A devout reader might believe Crace to be guilty of heresy; alternatively, a dedicated materialist might also have condemned the writer for perpetuating what Mieke Bal has named 'deplorably fashionable . . . sentimental returns to a God generated by millennial anxiety'.[5]

Quarantine is a novel of mission: its author has a pious conviction of what he names the 'powerful persuasion' of his faith; similarly, his fiction is informed by sensitivity towards the miraculous qualities of existence. Yet Crace is not a Christian; indeed, he describes himself as an atheist who is 'impatient with the simple-mindedness of orthodox religion, its lack of imagination, its bafflegarb'. He defines his atheism, however, as 'something richer than just the bleak and heartless absence of belief'.[6] For Crace, the rejection of God is not merely nihilistic; instead, it is a creative act of denial, one which engenders the birth of a new creed.

Crace, the unbeliever, illustrates what John Updike describes as a necessary 'vatic tension' in his literary encounter with Jesus.[7] In an article he wrote to introduce *Quarantine* to American readers, he clarified the irreverent objective of his narrative:

> It would be a simple matter. Take a venerated Bible story . . . add a pinch of hard-nosed fact . . . and watch the scripture take a beating. *Quarantine* with Science as its sword would kill Christ after only thirty days in the wilderness. There'd be no Ministry or Crucifixion. The novel would erase two thousand years of Christianity. This would be my party-pooper for the Millennium.[8]

Crace's reading of the gospel narrative is intransigently materialist. The story of Jesus' successful forty-day abstention from food and water – his *quarantine* – contradicts all the evidence of modern medicine; without supernatural intervention, it would not be possible for a man to survive such an ordeal, and, since such beliefs are fictions associated with a pre-scientific world, the rational reader must necessarily interpret the episode only as a myth. *Quarantine*, however, is a distinctively late modern piece of myth-making, one that arbitrates between the phenomena of the everyday and the impossible. Indeed, from one perspective the narrative resonates with the style of the many interpolated tales recorded in the gospels. '[A]s with Biblical parable the focus is . . . the immediacy of the quotidian and mundane, a world bound by familiarities,' argues Philip Tew.[9] However, the novel that emerges from Crace's confirmed scepticism emphasizes an utterly rational reading of the Christ story. It suggests that Jesus was delusional, convinced of his role in a providential scheme and desperate to meet with his God in the most godforsaken of landscapes, a desert space in which 'Creation was unfinished' and 'where the world was not complete'.[10] Crace's Jesus is frail, mortal and misguided to the point of possible psychosis. In fact, in an interview with Tew, the writer has revealed that, alongside a visit to the Judean desert, the novel, with its cast of idiosyncratic outsiders, was partly inspired by his observations of a local group of people receiving psychiatric 'care in the community' in the 1980s.[11] It is no surprise then that Jesus, this eccentric 'Gally', suffers from a very modern form of anomie, a social isolation associated with outcasts who cannot find a place in the conventional patterns of life.

The fact that *Quarantine*'s friendless Jesus dies alone in a cave, the victim of his own mania, rather than as a subversive nailed to a cross, a man unable even to begin his ministry, still less to cure the sick or to rise from the dead, appears to locate the narrative in an aggressively anti-theological tradition. Superficially, the novel certainly resembles what Patrick Sherry names a possible 'non-redemptive or anti-redemptive art', since it appears to purge Jesus of his divinity and, in the language of Christian soteriology, deny the possibility of atonement and salvation.[12] Paradoxically, however, this fictional exploration of a formative Christian narrative also resonates with orthodox theologies of the Incarnation, particularly with the notion of kenosis, the self-emptying, vulnerable nature of God incarnate. *Quarantine* is caught between a modernist need to illuminate superstition – to 'slay' false creeds – and what Lane calls 'a sliver of redemption' which 'is still there, constantly undermining rationalism'. 'Any hint of nihilism in Crace', he suggests, 'appears to undergo transformation; nihilism becomes affirmation.'[13] Indeed, instead of outraged censure from Christian readers, Crace discovered that the novel 'had been received by many British readers as a spiritual and scriptural text, an enrichment rather than a challenge to their faith':

> Correspondents ... claim that *Quarantine* could not have been written by an atheist. 'The Grace of God', they say, 'was standing at your shoulder as you wrote.' They're wrong, of course ... Novels and their writers are not mere mirror images. It's the imp of story-telling at our shoulders, not the Grace of God.[14]

Paradoxically, Quarantine foreshadows Rowan Williams's claim that 'the most effective depictions of God and grace and Christ these days are going to be sideways on and a bit different'.[15] This chapter examines the theological implications of Crace's sceptical-materialist account of the wilderness experience of Christ in comparison with other contemporary fictional Christs and their own 'temptations'. My account emphasizes the Christological possibilities of the novel and engages with a number of theological perspectives on Christ's body, including work by Jürgen Moltmann, Charles Gore, John McQuarrie and Richard Kearney. I give particular prominence to the theoretically inflected theology of Graham Ward, with its emphasis on the suffering Christ. Ward negotiates between the ostensibly incongruent but complexly interrelated fields of the Christian tradition and sceptical postmodern theory: the result is a properly incarnational account of Christ's suffering – and its indivisible relationship with all human pain. As he observes, '[s]uffering is a mode of embodied experience: a theological account ... must concern itself with what it means to be a soul enfleshed'.[16] My reading of *Quarantine* draws, therefore, on a series of essays by Ward that emphasize the kenotic nature of Christ.[17] It is also attentive to Ward's reminder in *Christ and Culture* (2005) that '[t]o do Christology is to inscribe Christ into the times and cultures we inhabit'.[18]

The encounter between Crace's Jesus, 'not much more than an adolescent', represented as a wilfully self-denying but potentially divine mystic, and the quasi-Satanic Musa, an abusive and manipulative merchant, provides the novel's central drama. I will argue that in the attempt to demythologize an ostensibly miraculous event, Crace confronts the limits of his own atheism and causes the Christian reader to confront the wholly/holy strange nature of Christ, the incarnation that Karl Barth has described as 'this infinitely surprising thing, that never existed before and cannot be repeated'.[19] The complex endeavour of *Quarantine* echoes wider shifts in contemporary consciousness regarding the problematic distinction between sacred and secular activity. The so-called 'sacred turn' at work in popular culture and critical theory is widely – if ambivalently – regarded as an intellectual softening towards the spiritual and the sublime. The 'postmodern mind', suggests Zygmunt Bauman, 'agrees to issue [religion and other concepts difficult to define], maltreated or sentenced to deportation by the modern scientific reason, with a permanent residence permit'.[20] Bauman's highly influential model of postmodernism's potential 're-enchantment' of a world robbed of spiritual possibility by high modernity has been explored by a number of contemporary theologians and literary theorists. John McClure, for example, argues that postmodernism is coterminous with the advent of a new 'sacralized', post-secular worldview reflected, in particular, in the holy yearnings of contemporary American fiction.[21] Graham Ward offers a more cautious and critical assessment of the postmodern theological land-scape: he argues that a 'deepening sense of godlessness is the apotheosis both of the secular worldview and, simultaneously, the generator of theological ques-tions, motifs, images, and mythemes articulated by a variety of secular sources in contemporary culture'.[22] Brian D. Ingraffia's critique of postmodern culture is considerably less forgiving and, in fact, repudiates the entire 'post-secular' thesis; he suggests that a Christian appropriation of postmodern theory is mis-guided. Ingraffia asserts that the 'central scandal of the Christian faith' – the defeat of death by Christ's death and resurrection – 'is in no way recovered in postmodern thought'.[23]

Yet *Quarantine*, despite its atheist conception, might be differentiated from much 're-enchanted' or post-secular culture since it focuses not on an obscure, unspecific sense of spiritual yearning but on a single person. There is an unex-pected echo of Barth in the specificity of Crace's focus: 'When we pronounce the name of Jesus Christ, we are not speaking of an idea. The name Jesus Christ is not the transparent shell, through which we glimpse something higher – no room for Platonism here!'.[24] There is certainly 'no room for Platonism' in Cra-ce's unkempt and awkward Galilean. This figure, who at first appears like an effect of light in the haze of the desert heat, becomes too rudely personified, too corporeal to be an 'idea', though the author would not refer to him, or any other man, as the Christ. As Kevin Vanhoozer has also argued, the Incarnation, in all of its violent particularity, resonates in the postmodern repudiation of 'disem-bodied' knowledge: 'On this point, postmodernity and incarnational Christian faith are agreed.'[25] The burden of representing this body – miraculously, both human and divine according to the traditions of incarnational theology – is one challenge of the sacred turn.

The Word made flesh made words

'Christian language begins with the disappearance of its "author"', asserts Michel de Certeau, the polymathic Jesuit cultural theorist. His essay, 'How is Christianity Thinkable Today?' (1971), emphasizes the paradox of Christian belief: its originator must be absent for the body of believers to exist. To be a Christian, according to this view, is to be in a constant state of lack: 'That is to say that Jesus *effaces himself* to give faithful witness to the Father who authorizes him, and to "give rise" to different but faithful communities, which he makes possible'. De Certeau evokes the competing, individual voices generated by the absent founder who 'is incorporated and takes on meaning in a plurality of "Christian" experiences, operations, discoveries, and inventions'.[26] This 'plurality' of 'inventions' includes stories unauthorized by the visible Church, those heterodox or heretical images proliferated by writers such as Jim Crace.

In a collection of highly theorized responses to the figure of Jesus and his followers that bears the distinctly Pauline title, *Writing the Bodies of Christ* (2001), John Schad, via Thomas Carlyle and Jacques Derrida, has noted that, from the mid-nineteenth century, 'the sheltered life of the church is exposed to the strange, dangerous and multidimensional space of writing'.[27] 'Every month or two some publisher comes up with a blockbuster saying that [Jesus] was a New Age guru, an Egyptian freemason, or a hippie revolutionary', notes N. T. Wright.[28] Jesus is especially conspicuous in contemporary literature, film and critical theory: he is, for example, the figure who connects a devout Roman Catholic actor-director with a Marxist-Lacanian cultural theorist. Mel Gibson's contentious film *The Passion of the Christ* (2004) screened the violent final hours of Jesus' life from a creedal perspective and generated an unprecedented public debate on the meaning of the crucifixion. Slavoj Žižek, the Slovenian cultural theorist and self-professed 'fighting materialist', is a strange companion for Gibson; yet he, too, from a very different perspective, has celebrated the redemptive act of the cross.[29] Gibson's presentation of the crucifixion as violent spectacle was preceded by Russell T. Davies's similarly audacious play for television, *The Second Coming* (2003); in this contemporary drama, Jesus is incarnated as an awkward, self-deprecating, thirty-something Mancunian who discovers his divinity after a drunken kiss with an old school friend.

Quarantine, then, is a significant postmodern addition to the tradition of what Theodore Ziolkowski calls 'fictional transfigurations of Jesus'.[30] In a piece of odd publishing synchronicity, the novel was published not just in the same year but in the same week as Norman Mailer's less well-received, curiously reverent *The Gospel According to the Son*. Mailer's rival 'transfiguration' of New Testament source material is in the tradition of 'fifth gospel' narratives, fiction that plays on the conceit of suppressed scriptures whose very discovery (or invention) questions the trustworthiness of the canonical gospels. 'While I would not say that Mark's gospel is false, it has much exaggeration. And I would offer less for Matthew, and for Luke and John, who gave me words I never uttered,' reflects 'the one who came down from Nazareth to be baptized by John.'[31] This apparent challenge to orthodoxy is less subversive than this early warning suggests: Mailer's narrative does little to undermine the idea that Jesus performed miracles, for example, or, indeed, that he was the son of God. In allowing 'the son' to speak for himself, Mailer echoes the device used by Michèle Roberts in *The Wild Girl* (1984), an explicitly feminist gospel according to Mary Magdalene. Roberts's vision is both radical and in keeping with elements of Christian tradition. Although the narrative departs from scripture by eroticizing the relationship between Mary and Jesus, it also locates itself in a specifically theological aesthetic tradition. In following a convention of 'Medieval and later . . . art, hagiography, legends, poems and plays', Roberts merges the 'figure of Mary Magdalene' with Mary, sister of Martha and Lazarus and 'the sinful woman who anoints Christ'.[32] Roberts's novel is prompted not just by debates in twentieth-century feminist theology but also, as she acknowledges in the prefatory note, on the Nag Hammadi gospels. These alternative gospels, discovered in Egypt in 1945, including the famous 'Gospel of Thomas', presented a challenge to the authority and uniqueness of the accounts included in the New Testament. Although many biblical scholars have questioned the credibility and importance of these lost scriptures, their discovery has prompted imaginative possibilities for writers of theologically inflected fiction such as Roberts.[33]

The Wild Girl's interpretation of Mary presents her as a sensual mystic, raised in a Jewish household, but fascinated by the competing spiritualities of her world: she is prone to ecstatic visions and spontaneous bursts of song that her mother believes 'belong to the rites of the pagans' (*TWG*, p. 13). Mary's meeting with Jesus is the catalyst for her spiritual development and prophetic critique of accepted religious traditions, and particularly those that marginalize women and punish female sexuality. 'Like other prophets before her, however,' notes Jeanette King, 'Roberts's Mary Magdalene claims to be leading her listeners back to the truth'.[34] Should these rewritings of the New Testament trouble Christian readers? Francis Watson has expressed the anxiety that the 'constant manufacture of images' of Jesus indicates that the Son of Man has become 'little more than a blank screen onto which individuals and cultures may project their own aspirations and fantasies'.[35] How does Crace's frail Jesus contribute to the traditions, both literary and theological, of understanding the mystery of Incarnation?

The Word in the desert

Crace's scriptural source, Jesus' temptation by Satan in the desert, is narrated in each of the synoptic gospels: Matthew 4.1–11, Mark 1.13 and Luke 4.1–13; the Gospel of John does not describe the encounter. Each of the synoptic gospels follows a sequence that begins with Jesus' baptism by John and continues with his journey into the desert, prompted by the Spirit. This order of events and the wilderness location are the only elements common to all three versions: the fast is described only in Matthew and Luke, who also give alternative accounts of the mode of Satan's temptation. Mark gives the briefest, most elliptical narration, but, unlike Matthew and Luke, includes a reference to other presences in the wilderness:

And immediately the spirit driveth him into the wilderness.
And he was there in the wilderness forty days, tempted of Satan; and was with the wild beasts; and the angels ministered unto him. (Mark 1.12–13)

Ulrich Mauser notes that this 'cryptic' account is read, following Jewish 'adaptations of biblical themes', in two ways. The first of these interpretations views Jesus as the second Adam, who, by resisting temptation, 'restores Paradise' (this is the reading explored by Milton in *Paradise Regained* (1671)). An alternative tradition, however, reads Jesus as 'the protagonist in God's struggle against Satan'.[36]

Crace's fiction is characterized by his engagement with the particulars of landscape and the inexorable push and pull of the environment; indeed, he has been described by one critic as 'the poet of detail, the laureate of the mineral, the bacterial and the gaseous'.[37] Similarly, Tew has argued that the 'rhythmic insistence' of the novelist's 'style often prioritizes the strong presence of landscape as a characterized presence, rather than a sense of internal subjectivity'.[38] In *Quarantine* this environmental stimulus emerges, in that the novel is interested less in making a distinction between the Jesus of history and the Christ of faith than it is in evoking a pilgrim of ancient Galilee. Crace, *pace* the evolving 'quest' of Albert Schweitzer, N. T. Wright and others for the 'historical Jesus', appears to have begun a mischievous parallel search for the geographical Jesus. The wilderness common to the temptation narratives and to Crace's postmodern rewriting of an event that, as a rationalist, he cannot accept, is an infertile space paradoxically rich with spiritual associations. Indeed, the imaginative horizons generated by real and fictive barren ground form the basis of a significant recent study: David Jasper's *The Sacred Desert* (2004), a theological exploration of wilderness, ranges between Elijah and the films of Wim Wenders, drawing on autobiography, the holy wanderings of de Certeau, Michael Ondaatje and the Desert Fathers (as well as on Crace's work itself). '[T]here are always miracles in the desert', asserts Jasper, 'as it suspends normal categories of human experience.'[39]

Hugh Pyper reminds us that the desert is 'a liminal space where the constraints of social life are stripped away and both destruction and transformation are possible', and that it is '[l]ife-threatening yet liberating in its unbounded spaces and solitudes, for [in] the biblical tradition it stands in contrast to the orderliness of the city, which may represent security but can also be claustrophobic, violent and decadent'.[40] Douglas Coupland, in *Life After God* (1994), a collection of interrelated, post-secular narratives, has developed the tradition of theologically seasoned wilderness temptation stories. The anonymous narrator of 'In the Desert', for example, recounts a formative encounter with the 'Nothingness' of the scorched American landscape which led to a spiritual crisis and a rethinking of his beliefs. Lost in the Mojave desert during an aborted drug run, the narrator, cocooned in his car, listens to the 'enthusiastic and committed' but also 'whacked out and extreme' voices of the many Christian radio stations specific to America. The narrative echoes Watson's suggestion that, in the postmodern moment, Jesus has become a blank screen on to which people might simply project their 'aspirations and fantasies':

> The radio stations all seemed to be talking about Jesus non-stop, and it seemed to be this crazy orgy of projection, with everyone projecting onto Jesus the antidotes to the things that had gone wrong in their own lives. He is Love. He is Forgiveness. He is Compassion. He is a Wise Career Decision. He is a Child Who Loves Me.[41]

Despite his scepticism and inability to connect with the alleged reality of Jesus described by these born-again callers, the narrator locates this fortuitous encounter with rather facile religious broadcasting, when surrounded by a biblically parched and barren landscape, as the beginning of his own erring pursuit of holiness. Although 'cut off' from the fervent, estranging belief of these disembodied voices, he recognizes that previously 'lost' souls appear, at least, to have found purpose and meaning. The plot follows a pattern of painful conversion when the abstractedly penitent narrator abandons his cache of stolen drugs and then, his car refusing to start, seeks a way out of the wilderness. Facing death in the desert, the narrator serendipitously meets a fellow drifter, a taciturn traveller 'with skin like beef jerky' who gives him food and shows him the right path to civilization (p. 200). In a short story that reflects on the encounter of the lost with 'the face of Jesus' it is tempting to read this mysterious stranger as a displaced Christ, ready to redeem lost souls in the desert (*LAG*, p. 184). Although Coupland evades any supernatural solution – the drifter is 'simply a very far-gone desert rat', long since alienated from the quotidian, urban world – the story is nevertheless charged with theological implications (*LAG*, p. 207). The encounter is not supernatural, and the drifter is neither god nor devil, but it resonates with Jasper's claim that 'there are always miracles in the desert'. In this instance, the miracle is simply one of rescue 'by a stranger', a miracle of 'the possibility of forgiveness and kindness' (*LAG*, p. 212). 'In the Desert' suggests that wilderness spaces continue to represent a metaphorical mediation between temptation (the abandoned drug run) and salvation (the rescue by a stranger).

Just as Pyper and Coupland figure the desert as a liminal space, we might argue that the gospel temptation narratives themselves represent a transitional stage between Jesus' baptism and the acknowledgment of his sonship and the beginning of his ministry of miraculous healing and teaching. Pyper asserts that though '[h]uman violence may be evaded by fleeing into its solitudes', the desert sojourner becomes prey to 'the assaults of the demonic'.[42] As a materialist, Crace reverses the latter assertion but his desert space still echoes the very Biblical tradition that he rejects. Images of emptiness dominate the novel, and the Judean wilderness of *Quarantine* takes on a quasi-theological shape. Crace's Jesus, a misguided mystic, encounters the desert as a place of absence and negation; it is a 'wilderness that [is] large and inexplicable':

Look at the lack of trees, he'd told himself, the thinness of plants and grasses. God would be at work still. This was the edge of god's unfinished universe . . . Where were his fingerprints? . . . Every Galilean knew that vegetation was the fruit of god's union with the earth. There was no vegetation on these slopes. Perhaps there was no god either. Perhaps this was the devil's realm. (*Q*, pp. 75, 77)

This godless landscape, bereft of life and signs of creation, frames a narrative which is drawn, in spite of its scepticism, to the notion of Jesus' own act of self-emptying, the divesting of divine authority for human form. Although *Quarantine* is a sceptical retelling of a specific group of Biblical stories, it also represents an act of wrestling with the larger story of Jesus' claims to divinity and, in particular, the mythology of his death and resurrection. Against this landscape of lack, Crace's human Jesus enters the desert without comfort or esteem, stripped of dignity, and, as he reflects, scorned by his family:

Their god-struck, visionary boy . . . who'd hid himself in gabbling scriptures, had gone off in a temper to the hills. Their Gally was absurd. Look at his bleeding feet. Look at his flaking lips. Observe that holy, love-lorn look across his face. See how he hardly manages that little climb up to the ridge. (*Q*, p. 76)

Miyahara Kazunari argues, with some justification, that 'Crace's Jesus is too meek, too vain, too inappropriate, too human' to be 'entitled the Saviour'.[43] Yet what this reading omits is Crace's recuperation of the shocking, scandalous nature of the Incarnation and also his strange, alienating protagonist. This atheist writer, in his attempt to disparage Christian tradition, paradoxically strips away a patina of propriety and produces an image of Christ (a term that Crace only uses in his later essay: in the novel he is always Jesus or 'Gally') that echoes N. T. Wright's notion of the 'crazy, subversive wisdom in which ordinary human wisdom, and conventional Jewish wisdom, would be stood on its head'.[44] *Double Vision* explores a similar idea in Kate Frobisher's search for a credible vernacular through which to sculpt her Christ. She is burdened by what she views as the somewhat timid, polite traditions of Christian art:

All her instincts had been for a nude figure – there's no logical reason why the Risen Christ should go on wearing the dress of a first-century Palestinian Jew for the rest of eternity, and even less reason for him to have got stuck in the robes of a medieval English king, and yet she knew that a naked Christ would cause uproar. A lively faith in the Incarnation often goes with a marked disinclination to have the anatomical consequences staring one in the face. (*DV*, p. 66)

The offence that Kate speculates a nude Christ would cause might be less a product of middle-class manners than a legacy of theological difficulty in facing the consequences of a 'lively faith in the Incarnation'. These two fictional iterations of Jesus – the one a starving desert dweller, the other a work-in-progress by a struggling artist sponsored by the church – both disturb refined, aloof modes of Christology that somehow erase the vividness of the figure of God incarnate.

The wounded body: Grace and kenosis

'For those who believe in the transcendence and total otherness of God, [the Incarnation] radically diminishes him', argues Frederick Buechner. The notion of a transcendent creator-God becoming human, subject to pain and suffering, animates the paradoxical centre of Christian belief: 'For those who do not believe in God, it is the ultimate absurdity. For those who stand somewhere between belief and unbelief, it challenges credulity in a new way.'[45] Yann Martel's *Life of Pi* (2001) offers a re-energized perspective on the scandal of the incarnation when, as a fourteen-year-old 'contented Hindu', Piscine Molitor Patel has an encounter with the Christian gospel. Initially, Pi is shocked and appalled by the idea that God allows himself to be mocked, beaten and murdered by his own creation. The idea of a vulnerable deity made flesh inverts all that this young spiritual seeker believes about the divine order of the universe:

> The Son . . . who goes hungry, who suffers from thirst, who gets tired, who is sad, who is anxious, who is heckled and harassed, who has to put up with followers who don't get it and opponents who don't respect Him – what kind of god is that? It's a god on too human a scale, that's what.[46]

This defenceless being appears to confound ideas of supernatural power and to diminish religion. Pi's queries about Jesus of Nazareth echo theological doubts that have been articulated for two thousand years: 'Why would God wish that upon Himself? Why not leave death to the mortals? Why make dirty what is beautiful, spoil what is perfect?'[47] The plain answer that Pi is consistently given by a patient priest (but which is perhaps less often given in theology) is that 'love' alone explains this irrational action. Fascinated by the self-denying love of this strange, messy Christ 'who is alive', Pi embraces Christianity while remaining a faithful Hindu.[48]

The strange holiness imaged in Martel's novel and in the figure of Grace's desert sojourner echo a tradition of *kenotic* theology that emerged in the nineteenth century. It was greeted by both traditionalists and radicals as a dangerous, untenable doctrine, yet it continues to inform many of the most dynamic contemporary Christologies. John Macquarrie notes that kenosis, or self-emptying, is a theory of Incarnation which proposes that the *Logos* or eternal word of God 'was able to manifest itself in the finite life of a human being' by radically self-limiting its divine attributes.[49] Macquarrie shows that the theory was, in part, a response to new challenges to the truth of Jesus as the unique son of God, and also a critique of the dualistic Chalcedonian Christology inherited by orthodox believers. According to kenotic theology, developed in Germany by Gottfried Thomasius (1802–73) and in England by Charles Gore (1853–1932), the nature of God was found in the modest, self-emptying nature of Jesus in his life of poverty, and, ultimately, in his separation from eternity in his death on the cross.[50] The key biblical passage for this theology is found not in the gospels but in Paul's Epistle to the Philippians, 2.5–8:

> Let this mind be in you, which was also in Christ Jesus: Who, being in the form of God, thought it not robbery to be equal with God: But made himself of no reputation, and took upon him the form of a servant, and was made in the likeness of men: And being found in fashion as a man, he humbled himself, and became obedient unto death, even the death of the cross. Wherefore God also hath highly exalted him, and given him a name which is above all things.[51]

Crace's interpretation of Jesus cannot, in a literal sense, be described as Christology; as an atheist, such taxonomy is not available to him. Furthermore, his Jesus dies in the desert before a ministry can begin; the cross, symbol of shame and sacrifice, plays no part in the novel. Yet Crace's wild, naked Jesus, who starves in a cave, echoes the kenotic image offered by the apostle:

> He'd ... be ... glad ... to defile himself on those kept out of temples – lepers ... prostitutes, the blind, even the uncircumcized – if they would listen to him, if it would cause discomfort to the priest. These were the ones, he thought, that god had created weak and blemished and imperfect by design ... These people were his family. (*Q*, pp. 150–1)

Crace's 'Gally' is an outcast who identifies with the dispossessed; for much of the narrative, he is defined by his absence, hidden from his fellow desert dwellers, refusing to participate in the miracles they desire. The atheist writer does not interpret this as a sign of holiness but recognizes it as an inversion of egotistical religion, in which a Nietzschean will-to-power is ironically manifested. For Charles Gore, the 'real incarnation involves a real self-impoverishment, a real self-emptying, a real self-limitation on the part of the eternal Word of God'.[52] Colin Gunton has offered a doctrine of Incarnation indebted to the nineteenth-century tradition of Gore and, in particular, Edward Irving: 'the self-emptying or kenosis of the Son of God in the incarnation and crucifixion is not the depotentiaton of his deity, but its expression', he argues.[53]

The Jesus who enters the desert in *Quarantine* is part of a mortal world, destined to die if he carries out his task. Negation, death and lack are the dominant tropes of the novel and each of these signifiers of absence finds resonance in the etiolated figure of the Galilean: the desert landscape is dotted with the hollow spaces of caves; Marta, also pursuing quarantine, is anxious about her empty womb; faces are imaged as 'empty water-bag[s]' (*Q*, p. 140); the demonic

Musa dreams of the purses he will empty as he learns the tricks of the 'Gally'. Ultimately, Jesus' body becomes 'an empty bag' (*Q*, p. 129). As he reads the scriptures, this modest, unscholarly figure determines that God is found not in the words but 'in the spaces, he was sure. God went to the very edges of the page' (*Q*, p. 135). The 'Gally' views his task as an act of negation rather than affirmation, following in the tradition of 'what Achim the psalmist called the Task of Not', the discipline of wanting nothing from the world. 'Seek wakefulness instead of sleep, the psalmist said and pain instead of comfort . . . look only for the peace that's found in wretchedness and not the peace that's found in love' (*Q*, p. 130). A Christian reader might argue that Crace fails to perceive the connection between the 'wretchedness' of Christ's embrace of human form and the divine love that it signifies. Crace's openly 'godless' frame suggests that signs themselves are always devoid of meaning and that Jesus' act of self-abnegation is an empty gesture before an absent God. Yet a Christian kenoticism, as offered by Keith Ward, for example, would argue that the divine act of self-emptying 'is also pleroma (fullness) involving self-realization as well as self-giving'.[54]

In *Double Vision* Kate Frobisher's Jesus, commissioned by and for a believing community, might be located in a secular version of this tradition. The artist's interpretation of – 'her way of seeing' – the sculpture evolves during its construction; this is partly because Kate discovers that her assistant, Peter Wingrave, is a psychologically disturbed individual, obsessed with both the artist and her work. Late at night, Kate secretly watches her enigmatic colleague don her clothing and imitate the process of sculpture with what, at first, appears to be an act of vandalism against the statue. On closer inspection, it becomes clear that this vandalism is merely performative, a strange ritual of mimicry. Peter's betrayal of Kate's risen Jesus in an echo of his namesake's biblical denial of Christ (Matthew 26.70; Mark 14.68; Luke 22.57; John 18.17, 25–7). Yet Kate's alarming discovery appears to deepen her sensitivity towards the physicality of her Christ and, in particular, the reality of his wounds:

> Chest and neck gouged . . . Pockmarks everywhere . . . Beaten up. Somebody with a talent for such things had given him a right going over. This was the Jesus of history. And we know what happens in history: the strong take what they can, the weak endure what they must, and the dead emphatically do not rise. (*DV*, pp. 180–1)

Although Kate is unable to believe in the literal resurrection of the body of Christ, the process of creating the sculpture, together with her uncanny encounter with Peter, have rendered the wounds of Jesus all the more visceral. Barker, like Crace, is not consciously invoking the traditions of Christian kenoticism, yet they both represent Jesus as wounded, self-sacrificing figures.

Graham Ward has traced the recent re-emergence of kenotic readings of Jesus in two very distinctive theological traditions. The first instance appeals to the a/theologies of the death-of-God school, exemplified by the work of Thomas J. J. Altizer and Mark C. Taylor. In this 'postmodern, nihilistic' framing, Jesus' obedience to death is construed as a 'metaphor for the absence of God in the contemporary world'.[55] Yet Ward also identifies kenotic theology as a key strand in the conservative theology of such writers as Jean Luc Marion. Ward notes that this theology views kenosis as 'linked to the Word becoming flesh, the gift of God's presence, in Jesus Christ and in the eucharist. The kenotic economy is inseparable from a Trinitarian "philanthropy" as it operates for the salvation of the world and is evidenced in the incarnation, cross and resurrection'.[56] Elsewhere, Ward identifies a postmodern, consumerist conflation of 'suffering and bliss', which he reads as 'a sign of decadence announcing a sado-masochistic culture'. In the face of this decadent culture, he offers Christ's mode of 'sacrificial suffering (as *kenosis* and passion), which undoes the economics of sin'.[57] For Crace, of course, a salvific economy is a logical impossibility and so one might assume that his version of Jesus' suffering has a clearer connection with postmodern a/theologies.[58] Where Ward asserts that 'a certain suffering is endemic to incarnate living, a suffering that always made possible the sacrifice on the cross', *Quarantine* cannot envisage a hoped-for grace.[59] Yet neither does the novel simply capitulate to the notion of God as void.

Crace's interrogation of the temptation, superficially at least, transforms supernatural influence into psychopathology; the Spirit does not drive this Jesus to the desert. Rather, he argues with his family, who fear for his sanity, and enters the desert with the desire to 'encounter god or die' (*Q*, p. 22). The 'wild animals' and 'angels' of Mark's account become four other travellers, similarly in pursuit of divine knowledge or healing, who have embarked on their own 'quarantine'. The figure of Satan is represented not by a supernatural presence but by a corpulent and fraudulent trader, named Musa, who is abandoned for dead at the beginning of the narrative by his cousins and his wife, Miri, who happily digs a grave for him. The first encounter between Jesus and Musa is only obliquely one of temptation: the Galilean enters the ailing trader's tent to ask for a little water before he begins his fast, which he steals as his host lies unconscious. Blithely, Jesus pronounces a blessing over Musa: 'So, here, be well again', a litanic refrain in the novel (*Q*, p. 26). This moment parallels the serendipitous meeting between the lost narrator and the desert drifter in Coupland's 'In the Desert': in this instance, the 'Gally' performs a simple act of kindness that appears to be salvific. Crace parodies the image of Jesus the divine healer: Jesus, a reluctant thief, accidentally causes the Satan figure to be resurrected, following a casual benediction. This, in itself, might seem blasphemous to a conservative Christian reader, as would Jesus' apparent lack of knowledge that he is the son of God; indeed, Crace's Jesus is simple in his faith – he has a 'village view of god, that was not scholarly. He believed he was the nephew of his god' (*Q*, p. 109).

Norman Mailer's account of Jesus' desert temptation is, superficially at least, more respectful of the biblical material. *The Gospel According to the Son* has none of the ironic distance of *Quarantine* from its aspiring messiah. Unlike Crace's Jesus, Mailer's Galilean coolly narrates his experience of the barren landscape, a space marked with signs of mortality and in which 'in every direction was emptiness' (*TGATTS*, p. 37). Obedience to the voice of the spirit is not represented as a symptom of mental instability but as a mark of spiritual courage. Jesus encounters a devil quite unlike the repulsive Musa: instead he is visited by a man as 'handsome as a prince' who is well versed in the scriptures; the range of temptations echo those narrated in some of the New Testament accounts (*TGATTS*, p. 45). Mailer extends the succinct accounts of the temptation offered in the canonical gospels with some rather Gnostic ideas propounded by the urbane Satan figure: 'Your Father is but one god among many . . . You would do better to consider the breadth of His rages; they are unseemly for a great god' (*TGATTS*, pp. 48–9). Yet Mailer's gospel, defended by its holy narrator as a corrective to the inadequacies of the second-hand, authorized accounts of his life, never questions the divinity or resilience of Jesus. Unlike Crace's vulnerable nomad, Mailer's Jesus leaves the wilderness strengthened by his trial. Where Mailer remythologizes the biblical narrative, with the supplement of novelistic detail, Crace's confrontational approach to the source material locates him in a tradition of demythologizing scripture that has its roots in the nineteenth-century quest for the authentic Jesus of history.

In 1906 Albert Schweitzer, writing of the failure of the pursuit for Jesus among the ruins of history, notoriously claimed that '[a] "life of Jesus" can be written out of hate – and the greatest of their kind were written with hate'. Schweitzer was describing the epochal biographies of the human Jesus by Reimarus and David Friedrich Strauss, both of which challenged the prevailing doctrines of the incarnation: 'It was not so much hate directed against the person of Jesus as against the supernatural nimbus with which he had come to be surrounded'.[60]

This recovery of the human face of Jesus, the attempt to separate myth from objective history, apparently so shocking to the orthodoxies of nineteenth-century European Christianity, has since been at least partially accommodated by even the most traditional of believers. The 'supernatural nimbus' identified by Schweitzer represents the accretion of superstition perpetuated by the powerful institution of the visible Church – both Roman Catholic and Protestant – which many post-Enlightenment scholars viewed as wholly untenable. Passionate believers, whose view of the incarnation was untroubled by a critical attitude to scripture, wanted to recuperate the image of Christ as a man of sorrows. Evangelicals and Dissenters might have responded with vitriol to the apparently blasphemous images of Jesus that emerged in both Strauss's *Das Leben Jesus, kritisch bearbeitet* (1835–6) and Ernest Renan's *La Vie de Jesus* (1862), yet their late-twentieth-century inheritors would understand that Christianity must emphasize the suffering, physical Jesus as well as the transcendent, eternal world of God.

Crace's militant atheism is, of course, rather more radical than the gentle post-critical challenges of Strauss and the heirs of the higher criticism. We should not, however, mistake his non-belief for a wholly objective lens through which to read the Christ-event. Renan once argued that only a former believer was qualified to write religious history; without the experience of faith, the writer could not expect to comprehend the world view that he described. Equally, this religious historian must no longer be a believer since it would be impossible to attain a neutral perspective.[61] Our own historical moment is more hostile to the claims of objectivity. Crace, by his own admission, is not seeking to judge the gospels with dispassionate detachment. A sentimental story of easy redemption that one might expect to find in a pre-critical Christian construal of the narrative is replaced by a sceptical fiction, though one which reveals the internal conflicts of committed unbelief.

In *The Crucified God* (1974), Jürgen Moltmann argues that both 'Christians and non-Christians' often create 'an image of Jesus which suits their own desires':

> They have idolized Jesus ... He has become the archetype of the divine authority and glory which men have longed for. He has become the teacher of a new morality to mankind. He has become the resistance fighter from Galilee. An analysis of the changing ideas of Christ and portraits of Jesus in history shows that they correspond so much to the needs of their age, place of origin and intended purpose that one cannot avoid the suspicion that they are illusory and artificial.[62]

Gunton makes a key distinction between past and present Christologies, both of which he views as problematic:

> whereas ancient thought tended to abstract Jesus Christ from history by eternalizing him – by making him, as human, a timeless theophany – modern thought tends to abstract him from eternity by making his temporality absolute.[63]

Crace's novel thereby joins a culture of debate that has focused on the person of Jesus. Orthodox models of the incarnation have been critiqued since the mid-nineteenth century, but in the last twenty years the post-critical tradition has become something of an industry. In 1985, for example, Robert Funk, together with other radical theologians, founded the 'Jesus Seminar' in New York. The figure that emerged was described by one journalist as a 'non-Christian Jesus' and a 'Jesus for the America of the third millennium'.[64] Richard Kearney has argued that the so-called 'cult' of 'the historical Jesus is a form of idolatry' as it traduces both flesh and spirit. Crace's Jesus is a more complex figure who, in his death, exceeds what Kearney calls 'an idol of presence': in the novel he becomes 'a voyager, at last, between the heavens and the earth' (*Q*, p. 193).[65]

Narrative resurrection

In *Double Vision*, Barker's sceptical sculptor looks at her near complete statue and recognizes that it, oddly, has been transformed: 'Didn't look human ... Strong, though. She felt its strength. Christ in a nightie it was not' (*DV*,

p. 289). Peter, the biblically named betrayer, briefly returns to the studio and is invited to inspect the risen Christ. His casual blasphemy ('My God') contains the trace of reverence: it is an unconscious act of worship when confronted with a sign of grace (*DV*, p. 291). In a novel crowded with evidence of humanity's capacity for violence, an image of the risen Jesus suggests the possibility of rebirth. Similarly, Crace confesses that although '*Quarantine* did slay Christ ... novels have a way of breaking loose from their creators': 'Science does not triumph unambiguously in the book ... Jesus does not let me kill him off entirely'.[66] Indeed, in the final pages of the novel, two characters witness a risen Jesus, his ruined body departed from the grave and leaving the desert. 'The empty tomb is the condition of possibility for a spiritual knowledge', observes Michel de Certeau: the Christian community is precipitated by a gap where a body should lie.[67] According to the troubling gospel accounts, this corpse, God made flesh, arose from the grave and *Quarantine* ends with an uncanny encounter, a Biblical echo, as two of the desert 'trespassers' see a risen Jesus (*Q*, p. 226). Is this final, most outrageous miracle – the resurrected body – merely a simulation of the sacred? In 'The Precession of Simulacra', Jean Baudrillard argues that with the evaporation of the real, and the dissolution of God into a 'plethora' of signs, it becomes impossible to distinguish 'the false from the true, the real from its artificial resurrection'.[68]

The first of these witnesses in *Quarantine* is Musa, the inverse of Jesus, greedy, violent and ultimately a rapist. He calls out to the figure who will not speak: 'he had never seen a man appear so weightless and invincible as Gally seemed to be' (*Q*, p. 205). Musa is hardly a reliable spectator, but a second witness, the godly Marta, a Jewish woman who was raped by Musa on the night of Jesus' death, also encounters this strange resurrected figure. She tells her surrogate sister, Miri, of her experience: 'I saw *him*. I knew it had to be the Gally ... Just skin and bones. He was as near to me as you are now. I could have touched him. But he touched me. He touched my cuts and bruises. And then he kissed my feet' (*Q*, p. 225). This moment echoes both John 13.5 (Jesus washes the feet of his disciples) and Mark 14.3 (a woman anoints Jesus with expensive perfume). Marta's experience resonates with Kearney's recent work on transfiguration and *persona* – a sense of spirit beyond traditional categories of spirituality – which represents an 'eschatological aura of possibility ... It is another word for the otherness of the other'. The figure of Jesus comes to Marta as a body but as more than a body; as Kearney notes, contrary to some 'spiritualist illusions', 'the *persona* is not some disembodied soul. It gives itself in and through the incarnate body'.[69] Marta believes that her empty womb has been filled by the healing, kenotic touch of this abject but resurrected Galilean. Her encounter may even be in a dream but it is no less real. In this way, Crace unconsciously echoes the eschatological hopes of Christianity: Jesus heals Marta and disappears. The episode embodies the 'now' and 'not yet' of Ward's kenotic theology. Christian kenosis, he argues, is not a 'bad infinite' – in which desire can never be fulfilled – but a hopeful one that represents both 'longing for God' and/or 'God's longing for us'.[70]

A final image of Jesus is witnessed by Musa, who intends to capitalize on his encounter with the man he believes healed him:

> His Gally was no longer thin and watery, diluted by the mirage heat, distorted by the ripples in the air . . . as he came closer to the valley floor his outline hardened and his body put on flesh. (*Q*, p. 243)

'Is this just a mirage upon mirage – a double miracle of desert seeing?', asks Jasper.[71] The risen Jesus is revealed to sinner and saint, Jew and Gentile, even in a novel that rejects the miraculous. As the fleshy, indulgent Musa leaves the desert, he readies himself with new, immaterial merchandise: he intends to 'trade the word' (*Q*, p. 242). The story of this 'man who had defeated death' is not a revolutionary experience for Musa but a means of securing power (*Q*, p. 242). From the figure of Jesus, Musa is intent on creating an idol: the Gally will become a conjurer, a mystic with access to the secrets of life and death. Crace appears here to parody what Rowan Williams has called 'the almost infinite corruptibility of religious discourse'.[72] Musa becomes a disciple of an idol in his own image: within the economy of the novel he is a corrupt church, the founder of an ersatz faith who will 'preach the good news' (*Q*, p. 242). Similarly, in Mailer's pseudo-gospel, Jesus reflects that, though he did rise on the third day, '[m]any of those who had been near me were given to exaggeration' (*TGATTS*, p. 236). His transfigured Jesus speaks with a new omniscience in the novel's most polemical passage of the 'rich and pious' who dare to call themselves Christian, but who 'are often greater in their hypocrisy than those who condemned me then' (*TGATTS*, p. 239). For Mailer's Jesus, the promise of redemption is 'hidden in the faces of the poor' who inspire 'an immutable compassion, and . . . the will to live again and rejoice' (*TGATTS*, p. 242).

Neither the Jesus of history nor the Christ of faith will be tamed. As de Certeau notes, 'he is impossible to grasp and "hold" ': 'there is the disappearance of an "idol" which would freeze our view and give us the truth in a singularity'.[73] Crace's Jesus is no idol, nor is he a rival to the 'man of sorrows' and God-made-flesh of the gospels. Yet the novel recuperates some of what Buechner names the 'raw, preposterous, holy' quality of incarnation misplaced in the multitude of sacred but sanitized re-imaginings of the Christ. 'When the culturally dominant pictures of God have come to be simplistic,' claims Placher, 'it becomes hard to arouse much excitement about the news of divine incarnation – or much sense of its meaning'.[74] Crace's novel, committed to a radically materialist view of Jesus, performs a paradoxical act in generating debate about the 'news of divine incarnation' and 'its meaning'. In *Quarantine* the strange, etiolated body of the Gally, this *other* Jesus, is transfigured, and so, too, are the limits of Crace's secular vision.[75]

3

John Updike's Holy Heresy:
Between Grace and 'the Devil's motley'

[T]he Christian faith has given me comfort in my life and, I would like to think, courage in my work. For it tells us that truth is holy, and truth-telling a noble and useful profession; that the reality around us is created and worth celebrating; that men and women are radically imperfect and radically valuable . . .[1]

John Updike, the creator of Harry 'Rabbit' Angstrom and Henry Bech, fictional chronicler of suburban-bourgeois American life since 1959, author of more than twenty novels and dozens more volumes of poetry, short stories and critical prose, is a theological writer with a peculiar penchant for sin. His narratives are replete with the chaotic consequences of minor indiscretions, comically juvenile bad behaviour and the tragedy of serious transgression. As Marshall Boswell has argued, a fundamental conviction of Updike's fiction is that 'the world is fallen, and there is no human way to correct that flaw in creation'.[2] Yet these sinful fictions are redeemed by an apparently inexhaustible creator's sympathy for the erring individuals who are as prolific in their repeated misdemeanours as Updike is in his compulsive literary production. The writer's many adulterous anti-heroes are extravagantly multiple in their betrayals and his liars create untruths which beget yet more falsehoods. The 'radically imperfect' lives of these fragile and sometimes unrepentantly corrupt characters illuminate daring and richly problematic fictions of guilt, unwarranted grace and the cruel economies of human relations. In *Seek My Face* (2002), an elegiac novel of the post-war American art world, Updike returns to the concept of sin. Hope Chafetz, an elderly painter, gives an account of her gloriously messy past – including two failed marriages to near mythical figures of the post-war New York art scene – that is troubled by a sense of 'creaturely' guilt. In her conversation with the serene, aloof art critic, she identifies a lingering guilt from her childhood roots in the Quaker tradition:

'My Quaker blood distrusted anything of the creature –'
'Creature?'
'Our bodily self. The *world's* bodily self. Color, sex, ostentation. You know, the sins. You've heard of sins?'[3]

Updike is fascinated by the implications of sin as both a theological idea and a worldly activity. This New England novelist's turn towards the transgressive is not, in itself, unique but a kind of repetition or echo. Good fiction and the Christian metanarrative are, after all, both dependent on their protagonists making disastrously bad choices. Indeed, Michael Edwards maintains that

> Literature occurs because we inhabit a fallen world. Explicitly or obscurely, it is part of our dispute with that world, and of our search for its and our own regeneration. It begins in alienation, and stands over against a reality which it perceives as exilic and mortal.[4]

As a genre, the novel, which of all literary forms best represents the movement of the individual conscience and consciousness through the disarray of history, seems most to need original sin.[5] Without a fall, in orthodox terms the deliberate rejection of truth and responsibility, narrative has no beginning. If Dickens's Pip had renounced pride, stayed in the forge and emulated Joe Gargery's Christian humility, there could be no *Great Expectations*. Should James Gatz have recognized the futility of pursuing a chimerical American dream, Nick Carraway would not have narrated *The Great Gatsby*. Pip and Gatsby misread the world and, in so doing, they simultaneously fall into sin and create the occasion of story, with all its disorderliness and hope.

Updike's fiction, though freighted with a specifically Christian theology, rarely offers up conventional pilgrim journeys of fall, painful conversion and glorious redemption. Indeed, in these novels wickedness often seems to prevail, the immoral go unpunished and the morally pure are ruined. Although we can rarely take unambiguous spiritual succour from novels like those in the *Rabbit* tetralogy (1960–90) – novels, as David Lyle Jeffrey suggests, 'whose protagonists bear the consistent character of the fallen Adam' – Updike limns a world stripped of consoling illusions rather than one without redeeming grace.[6] Indeed, his work might embody Patrick Sherry's argument that a writer's 'seeming preoccupation with evil' is often 'linked closely with a desire to suggest the action of grace'.[7] The unpredictable 'motions of Grace', in a phrase of Blaise Pascal's used by Updike as the epigraph to *Rabbit, Run* (1960), lead the writer to some desolate places, both figurative and literal, often far without the consecrated and secure ground of orthodox faith.

Judgement of this spiritually complex American novelist seems to fix around the polarities of enthused devotion and disappointed contempt. Is he a heroic narrator of the troubled Christian life or merely a fractious, if refined, stylist who is guilty, as one early critic pronounced, of having 'nothing to say'?[8] This chapter will address the conflicting constructions of Updike and the ambivalent conclusions that have been drawn regarding the spiritual value, or otherwise, of his fiction. It concentrates on modes of heresy and the representation of sin across a range of Updike's writing. The structure and consequences of heretical thinking and behaviour in Updike's 1986 novel *Roger's Version* (1986), with its disorderly blurring of sex and spirit, orthodoxy and dissent and acute configuration of the heretic as a force even in late, rationalist modernity, is its focus. However, the chapter will also consider ideas of apostasy, dissent and the search for God in Updike's more recent novels, *Seek My Face* and his ambitious re-reading of twentieth-century US history, *In the Beauty of the Lilies* (1996).

Truth in Heresy

On 11 September 1997, Updike, in his sixty-sixth year, was awarded the Campion Medal by the Catholic Book Club as a 'distinguished Christian person of letters'. In his acceptance speech, the novelist indicated that for a middle-class Protestant American the receipt of such an award, named for St Edmund Campion, the 'brilliant Jesuit' who was tortured and martyred in 1581, was somewhat 'disconcerting':

> It is all too easy a thing to be a Christian in America, where God's name is on our coinage, pious pronouncements are routinely expected from elected officials, and churchgoing, though far from unanimous, enjoys a popularity astounding to Europeans.[9]

G. R. Evans echoes Updike's discomfort with a nation in which religious belief is an easy element of a citizen's cultural capital and, in fact, argues that '[t]he "American Way of Life"' might itself be regarded as a more or less conscious performance of the Pelagian heresy, 'for it teaches that people can both be good and "get on in life" simply by trying hard'.[10] Against the conventional image of nominal middle-American piety – which is the religious world that Updike knows best – the novelist further insists that to be authentically Christian 'in this day and age, as in the time of imperial Rome, is to be unorthodox'. Even in accepting a Roman Catholic sponsored honour, Updike insists that the authentic Christian heritage originates in heretical challenges to authority. He also admonishes religiously minded readers who seek easy consolation or 'glimpses of mollifying holiness' in literary fiction created by authors who also happen to be Christians. Such a hope, he notes, is likely to be dashed in the frequently desolate literary fiction of such twentieth-century believers as Muriel Spark and Flannery O'Connor. Elsewhere Updike has argued that the 'bleak world they display, often comic in its desolation and inconsequence' is most certainly

> – not the world of arrived faith and its consolations but the fallen world whose emptiness, perhaps, led them to make the leap of faith. And given the limits of hagiography [biography of saints] and the ineffability of God, isn't that all a novelist can be expected to deliver – *this* world, in its pain and mangled glory?[11]

Yet, for all his emphasis on the realities of struggle and failure, this recipient of an award named for a Christian martyr has since been described as 'of all theological writers, one of the most complacent'. While Updike confesses that ambiguity and 'hollowness' are integral to an authentic Christian experience, James Wood, in his provocative 1998 study *The Broken Estate*, claims that this novelist's supposedly spiritually driven fiction only 'stages theological arguments which are foreclosed. Doubt, or its opposite, fervency is not taken seriously in [his] work'.[12] Harold Bloom, the great proponent of literature's Oedipal wrestling bouts, is similarly caustic about Updike, who he claims 'evades every agonistic encounter with the force of the literary past'. Like Wood, Bloom sees in Updike's fiction a certain serene indifference that means the novelist 'rarely fails, but nothing is got for nothing, and the American Sublime will never touch his pages'.[13] For Bloom, the powerful (but rather nebulous) term 'American Sublime' is a surrogate form of religious experience, one that might displace the formal strictures of the Christian doctrines that inform so much of Updike's writing. In fact, Bloom's argument sounds more like a criticism of one of Updike's more passive heroes, men determined to avoid failure and the burden of disappointment by refusing to participate in life wholeheartedly, refusing to take a Kierkegaardian leap of faith. A moment in *Seek My Face*, for example, in which one painter is dismissed by his passionate aesthetic peers as 'too glib for sublimity, lacking in the proper American passion', reads like a sly acknowledgment of Bloom's criticism (*SMF*, p. 11).

Similarly, David Lyle Jeffrey hears in the biblical cadences of Updike's fiction not a genuinely Christian voice but the fading echo of dying tradition; he believes the novels seek 'to demonstrate their moral seriousness by pillory of any available living traces' of the 'tarnished' 'legacy of decadent New England Puritanism'.[14] Updike's most robust defender as a significant theological artist has been James Yerkes, who argues that '*the religious consciousness in Updike may best be characterized as our sense of an unavoidable, unbearable, and unbelievable Sacred Presence*'.[15] This trinity of negation (the God or, more vaguely, the 'Sacred Presence' who is '*unavoidable, unbearable, and unbelievable*') is indicative of Updike's ambivalent negotiations with theology and its crucial, if frequently painful role in his fiction. *In the Beauty of the Lilies*, Updike's most vividly historical novel and an account of the twentieth century via four generations of an American family, begins in 1910 on the day that the Reverend Clarence Wilmot loses his faith. This unconversion is rendered in distinctive, bodily and scientific terms: Wilmot feels 'the last particles of faith leave him' as both a 'visceral surrender' and a 'ruinous pang'.[16] This quiet moment of apostasy typifies modernist rationalism and in the work of a determinedly atheist writer might be figured as a trope of ecstatic liberation. Yet, far from experiencing a benign sense of new found agency or wonder, the doubting minister's crisis of faith is coterminous with a loss of appetite for the material world . The passage describing the unconversion deploys a dialectic of corporeal delight and displeasure on which Updike's fiction frequently depends:

> Without Biblical blessing the physical universe became sheerly horrible and disgusting. All fleshly acts became vile ... The reality of men slaying lambs

and cattle, fish and foul to sustain their own bodies took on an aspect of grisly comedy – the blood-soaked selfishness of a cosmic mayhem. (*ITBOTL*, p. 7)

A. O. Scott argues that Clarence's apostasy 'is the obverse of the strain of faith, derived from Kierkegaard, Chesterton and Barth, that Updike has, in novel after novel, defended against glib voices of pragmatic and liberal Christianity'. The austere conclusion of this view is that '[i]f you can't have the objectively existing God, however unknowable, then you have nothing'.[17] The novel also has a ruthlessly punitive narrative logic: Clarence's reluctant decision to abandon his faith and, for integrity's sake, his vocation, has disastrous consequences for every principal character in the novel. Indeed, the violent conclusion of the novel, in which Clarence's great grandson becomes part of a separatist cult, is connected with the original loss of faith. In the absence of a religious tradition, Clark, who has grown up with every material comfort but no sense of spiritual belonging, is seduced by the violent absolutes of a millennialist cult. Updike's plot implies that abandoned religion does not always simply evolve into cool rationalism but might mutate into sadistic fundamentalism. Clark, like Clarence, longs for a God who appears to be absent.

Seek My Face, Updike's twenty-first novel and a kind of thematic companion piece to *In the Beauty of the Lilies*, returns to the theme of a God who seems to be defined by his absence. Its protagonist Hope Chafetz, a septuagenarian painter and shrewd witness of the evolving culture of the American century, was raised in the ascetic and muted traditions of Quaker belief. The solitary painter reluctantly shares her experience with Kathryn, a young and mildly pompous arts commentator from New York, who confronts her with a statement made in the catalogue for her last exhibition of the 1990s:

> For a long time I have lived as a recluse, fearing the many evidences of God's non-existence with which the world abounds. The world, it has come to me slowly, is the Devil's motley, colorful instead of pure. I restrict my present canvases to shades of gray ever closer together, as if in the pre-dawn before light begins to lift edges into being. I am trying, it may be, to paint holiness. (*SMF*, p. 5)

Updike's fiction, like Hope's catalogue and subsequent confession to Kathryn, abounds, simultaneously, with a fear of '*the many evidences of God's non-existence*' and a figurative desire to 'paint holiness'. For Martin Corner, the spiritual desertion that is especially resonant in Updike's most recent novels comes close to suggesting that 'the only acceptable God is one defined by his absence, the only viable spirituality one that looks, hopefully but almost without expectation, to the place where God might once have been'.[18] Corner is right to identify the ambivalence with which Updike's characters greet epiphanies (including anti-epiphanies, moments of spiritual sightlessness) but he also underestimates the specifically theological framing of these experiences. We might locate Updike in the tradition of Christian literary dissent explored by Valentine Cunningham's essay on 'the necessity of heresy', in which he argues that heterodox, dissenting readings often represent the search for a purer mode of understanding. For Cunningham there is an inevitable, creative play between orthodoxy and heresy that generates engaged spirituality and dynamic literature. In this line of argument, not only is the narrative of Christianity 'a story of heresy' but the interplay between '[h]eresies and orthodoxies are often – and in classic deconstructionist style – utterly parasitical the one upon the other'.[19] Similarly, in the relatively conservative *Brief History of Heresy*, Evans uses the example of the church reformer Jan Hus (c.1369–1415), whose criticism of Rome led to his excommunication and death at the stake: he sought purity and was damned as a heretic. In *On Reading the Books of Heretics*, Hus cited St Paul's counterintuitive defence of dissent even in the search for unity in the body of believers : 'For there must be also heresies among you, that they which are approved may be made manifest among you.' (1 Corinthians 11.19). According to Hus's perspective '[t]he books of the heretics . . . have the capacity to stir up spirituality, to clarify the truth, and, paradoxically, to encourage the reader to seek the truth so as to avoid falling into the same errors': 'The books of the heretics are to be read, not burned, so long as there is truth in what they say'.[20]

Theological Architecture

Roger's Version is one of Updike's three, non-sequential contemporary retellings of Nathaniel Hawthorne's *The Scarlet Letter* (1850), the first truly great American work of prose fiction. This thematic trilogy, including *A Month of Sundays* (1975) and *S* (1988), tests its nineteenth-century progenitor and, just as Hawthorne was wrestling with the ghosts of Puritan New England, including those of his own apparently tyrannical ancestors, so does Updike enter into a contest with Hawthorne's representation of Christian identity. Donald J. Greiner has traced Updike's engagement with *The Scarlet Letter* and argues that the trilogy 'bows to Hawthorne even as it challenges Hawthorne's "war" between flesh and spirit'.[21] In an essay on the tormented New England writer's 'creed', Updike describes *The Scarlet Letter* as '[America's] classic novel of religious conscience and religious suffering'; it is the text with which all narrators of the American sacred experience, in its exalted and despairing forms, must come to terms. For Updike, the elliptical, tortured Puritan world evoked by Hawthorne's prose is a curious, threatening phantom:

> A very vivid ghost of Christianity stares out at us from his prose, alarming and odd in not being evenly dead, but alive in some limbs and amputate in others, blurred in some aspects and otherwise basilisk-keen.[22]

This spectral or 'undead' faith, so troubling to Hawthorne, is a restless spirit and one that continues to haunt the house of fiction. The claims of historic Christianity, as well as its expedient language, invigorate the contemporary British and American novel to ambivalent effect. The post-secular pilgrimage of Douglas Coupland, for example, is marked by his characters' urgent search for belief in an eternal, personal God; by contrast Jim Crace, committed to an atheist-materialist creed, has confronted the limits of his own non-belief in rewriting Jesus Christ's sojourn in the desert in *Quarantine* (1997). Philip Pullman's Romantic belief in a 'Republic of Heaven' as represented in his subversive re-interpretation of *Paradise Lost, His Dark Materials* (1995–2000) is nonetheless dependent on a challenging encounter with the Old Testament. For Updike, however, theology is more than an aesthetic or ethical digression; rather it is fundamental to the architecture of his fiction. His narratives absorb, contest and are shaped by conflicting traditions within Christian theology. No other major exponent of prose fiction, perhaps since Bunyan, has confronted the disciplines of Protestant divinity so explicitly. Few of Updike's more than twenty novels evade the burden of this continual Christian wrestling with writing about God, and a number carry epigraphs from his alternative theological forefathers. The tormented existential faith of Søren Kierkegaard, the liberalism of Paul Tillich and, most notably for this chapter, the neo-orthodoxy of Karl Barth pervade his work. In a recent article on the novel's theology, J. Todd Billings argues that, in common with Paul Tillich 'and other theologians of culture, Updike in *Roger's Version* is unsatisfied with a self-congratulatory secular narrative'.[23] It is less clear whether he views the body of the church as a viable alternative to the failing aspirations of the world. Where Billings traces the liberal echoes of Tillich, I want to focus on his use of Barth, another heretical figure. This father of neo-orthodoxy rejected the traditions of nineteenth-century liberal theology and proclaimed that God can never be fathomed, approached or defined by humanity but must remain *totaliter aliter*, wholly other. Updike uses Barth, and in particular, the 1956 lecture 'The Humanity of God', to reappraise Hawthorne's narrative of religious guilt. Updike believed that Hawthorne's Christianity was one of radical dualism: where 'orthodox doctrine bridges matter and spirit with a scandalous Incarnation, Jesus Christ' for Hawthorne 'matter verges upon being evil; virtue, upon being insubstantial.'[24] The Barthian elements of *Roger's Version* deconstruct the gnostic tendencies of its parent text.

Updike, like all heretics, is engaged in acts of textual appropriation: these might be viewed as violent or recuperative. His process of rewriting is a multiple transgression against Hawthorne: three times he denies and capitulates to his literary forefather. This 'sin', however, might be read as a kind of religious literary strategy. James Schiff, who has offered the most comprehensive exploration of the trilogy's intertextual relationship with Hawthorne's romance, crucially defines *The Scarlet Letter* as a mythic text of the American imagination. He argues that the novel reflects upon 'the formation of America as the New Eden'.[25] Hawthorne was able to see the disparity between the exalted visions of his Puritan forefathers and the destructive, inhumane severity of their colonial regime. Updike, writing almost a century and a half after Hawthorne, narrates a further falling away of John Winthrop's vision of New England as a 'city upon a hill'.

Terry Eagleton has famously argued that '[a]ll literary works . . . are "rewritten", if only unconsciously, by the societies which read them; indeed there is no reading of a work which is not also a "rewriting" '.[26] Such acts of revision, of course, are not a one-way process, in which an enlightened present can appropriate and renovate the imaginative worlds of a less sophisticated culture. 'The past was not dead', proclaims Hawthorne in his digressive memoir-preface to the novel. 'The Custom House' reflects on the forceful re-emergence of repressed histories and contests the confidence of the present-day, mercantile America to transcend the terrors of its Puritan past.

The Scarlet Letter haunts the secular-sacred world of *Roger's Version*. Updike uses the triangular relationship, adulterous plot and theological anxiety of its urtext and relocates this classic narrative sequence to the (1980s) present, into the context of Reaganomics, the rise of the religious right and, less explicitly, connects it with the annihilation anxieties of cold war science. Retrospectively we might read this authoritarian moment, when the American people turned towards an obdurately conservative administration, as a kind of reiteration of the decadent Puritan theocracy of the seventeenth century, with its fear of chaos and disruptive desire, as narrated by Hawthorne in *The Scarlet Letter*. The Puritan past, Updike implies, is not dead but restless and threatening to take its revenge on a superficially liberal, democratic United States nostalgic for a mythic, misplaced stability. 'The haunted is a degenerate form of the sacred', Updike reflects in the essay on 'Hawthorne's Creed', and *Roger's Version* narrates the reanimation of a spectral New England Puritanism, seeking a new host in the body of contemporary America.[27]

Natural Theology vs Karl Barth

In Roger Lambert, a licentious theology professor at a New England Divinity school, Updike creates an echo, at once faithful and ironic, of Hawthorne's quasi-demonic Roger Chillingworth. The cuckolded manipulator of *The Scarlet Letter*, so often associated with occult ritual and fleshly vengeance, is brought to both the (a)moral and narratological centre of the reimagined fiction. Where Chillingworth is a ghostly parasite who executes a secret punishment of his wife's anguished lover (the zealous, guilt-ravaged Puritan minister Arthur Dimmesdale), from the blurred margins of the narrative, Updike's Roger is a garrulous, eloquent and candid opponent. His antagonist is a young, awkward evangelical who believes the existence of God might be proved via rapidly evolving information technology. He confronts Updike's wildly unreliable narrator, whose area of research focuses on heresy in the early Christian church, with a thesis that, if proved correct, will render Roger and his fellow theologians, brokers of the ambiguous sphere of religious belief and interpretation, superfluous: 'What I'm coming to talk to you about', Dale Kohler announces, 'is God as a *fact*, a fact about to burst upon us, right up out of Nature'.[28] In Hawthorne's text, Roger Chillingworth destroys a man of faith who had usurped his sexual status. By contrast, Updike's Roger, who believes that the parvenu pietist Dale is also conducting an affair with his wife, Esther, faces intellectual, as well as erotic obsolescence by the endeavours of his rival.

Dale Kohler is the novelist's second re-vision of Arthur Dimmesdale subsequent to the Revd Thomas Marshfield, the earthy but rather pompous Barthian narrator of *A Month of Sundays*. This [Dimmes] Dale inherits a similar spiritual intensity to Marshfield (and, we are led to believe, a more than equal sexual athleticism) but his confidence that Christianity might be vindicated by a modernist recuperation of natural theology inverts his predecessor's insistence on a God who is necessarily wholly other.

Schiff observes that, while this sober postgraduate gains his Christian name from Hawthorne's tortured minister, his family name is 'apparently' derived from a Jewish scholar, 'Kaufman Kohler, one of the most influential theologians of Reform Judaism in America', whose 'quest for the reconciliation of traditional faith with modern knowledge is one shared by' Updike's character.[29] This delicate intertextual overlapping of borrowed Christian and Jewish identities typifies a novel that seems simultaneously to fear and celebrate the loss of clearly defined boundaries from contemporary America. In a reading of the novel more dependent on Updike's fondness for Roland Barthes than his engagement with Karl Barth, John Duvall views this unstable 'play of difference[s]' as a means of exploring the connection between the theological and the sexual.[30] However, the assured distinctions between such cultural binaries as science and religion, student and professor, orthodoxy and heresy are continuously pressurized in the narrative, suggesting a radical instability. For example, though Dale's search for divine proof of God's existence places him in the Enlightenment tradition, he is also a confessional Christian who uses Evangelical language and tells Roger that Christ is his 'saviour'. Lambert is another lapsed minister (in a sense the figure of Dimmesdale is split between Dale and Roger – Roger, like Hawthorne's minister, is guilty of adultery both within the novel and in the years before the narrative). Updike continually collapses the boundaries between the two men, both erotically and theologically.

Dale seeks Lambert's support for a research proposal that will '*demonstrate from existing physical and biological data, through the use of models and manipulations on the electronic digital computer, the existence of God, i.e. of a purposive and determining intelligence behind all phenomena*' (*RV*, pp. 75–6). Roger, by contrast, echoes Marshfield, in that he is a Barthian believer, who cherishes the notion of a God who is 'wholly other'. Appalled by Dale's project, he propounds Barth's theology of revelation and insists that the scientist's proof-hungry nature is heretical as it ignores the

> God Who acts, Who *comes to us*, in Revelation and Redemption, and not one Who set the universe going and then hid. The God we care about in this divinity school is the living God, Who moves toward us out of His will and love, and Who laughs at all the towers of Babel we build to Him. (*RV*, p. 22)

Karl Barth's crisis theology, the neo-orthodoxy that stresses the 'wholly other' nature of God, has long been recognized as a key animating influence in Updike's work with *Roger's Version*, in particular, read as a fictional apologia for the Barthian critique of natural theology and a fierce vindication of his opposition to the liberal tradition.[31] The novel is prefaced by four epigraphs, including a quotation from Barth's 1956 lecture, 'The Humanity of God'. Although critics rightly note the neo-orthodox flavour of Roger's religion, and its close proximity to Updike's Barthian tendencies, there is a too easy conflation of this theological rogue with his creator. As such, although Lambert's status as an unreliable and manipulative narrator is acknowledged, the consistency of his theological arguments has rarely been challenged. The rather radical misuse of Barth's ideas undertaken by Roger Lambert is rarely observed; he is an eloquent apologist for Barthian theology but, in practice, a very bad Barthian. I want to argue that the novel is in conversation with Barth's neo-orthodoxy as much as it is a rewriting of *The Scarlet Letter*.

The Novelist as Heretic

When read in isolation and in ignorance of the lecture/essay from which it was taken, Barth's epigraph merely amplifies the novel's sense of despair at what Roger calls 'the tower of Babel' of human effort to reach God: 'What if the result of the new hymn to the majesty of God should be a new confirmation of the hopelessness of all human activity?' The question, when torn loose from its context in epigraph form, as all epigraphs must be, appears to be both rhetorical and foreclosed. In the original text, it is neither and the answer that Barth supplies does not conform to expectations:

> What if it should issue in a new justification of the autonomy of man and thus of secularism in the sense of the Lutheran doctrine of the two kingdoms? . . . God forbid! We did not believe nor intend any such thing.[32]

The 'what if' of Barth's interrogative is a kind of starting point for *Roger's Version*. (Indeed, the 'what if' is a question with which all fiction must begin.)[33] In this instance it asks: if all human effort is 'hopeless', why commit to any activity beyond one's selfish lusts? Yet, Barth insists, the 'new hymn to the majesty of God' was intended to engender worship, new understanding and belief in the redemptive work of Christ, not despair. It is difficult to believe that Updike was not aware of the counterintuitive conclusion to Barth's spiritual query. In a sense, the novelist acts as a kind of heretic in transforming the implications of the original textual source; interpretation, with its necessary occlusions and omissions, becomes heresy.

Roger mocks Dale for his attempt to seek theological certainty. His desire to take 'the kingdom of heaven by force' as the narrator, quoting Barth, comments is, indeed, contrary to the Christian tradition on the virtues of sightless faith. Roger's meditation on Barth's claim in 'The Problem of Ethics' that '[t]he god who stood at the end of some human way . . . would not be God' resonates with a belief in grace but is used merely as a way of dismissing a rival interpreter; it becomes intellectual capital, rather than spiritual encouragement.

'The Humanity of God' represented a reappraisal of Barth's rather austere crisis theology. Although the essay maintains the majesty and mystery of God as '*deity* – a God absolutely unique in His relation to man and the world, over-poweringly lofty and distant, strange, yes even wholly other', it also marks a recuperation of incarnational Christology. Barth repents, in part, for the impli-cation of earlier theology that culture, all that is created by fallen humanity, is necessarily hopeless:

> All this, however well it may have been meant and however much it may have mattered, was nevertheless said somewhat severely and brutally, and moreover – at least according to the other side – in part heretically. How we cleared things away! And we did almost nothing but clear things away![34]

Roger's contempt for humanity, his repudiation of all effort to transcend the sinful nature as a 'tower of Babel', echoes Barth's analysis of the limits of his early work. He is a gleefully iconoclastic Protestant who is happy to 'clear things away' without the need to reconstruct belief. Lambert justifies a certain lofty contempt – for Dale, for his niece, and for the wider world – via his use of Barth. 'The Humanity of God', however, emphasizes that God's intended rela-tion to man is defined by communion and creativity: 'He does not despise men, but in an inconceivable manner esteems them highly just as they are, takes them into His heart and sets Himself in their place'.[35] Furthermore, he insists that participation in the body of believers, as compromised, dishonest and spiri-tually barren as it might be, is vital to a true Christian understanding of the 'humanity of God': 'The Lord's Prayer is a *we*-prayer and only in this way also an *I*-prayer. "We" are the Church.'[36] Dale, in his awkward missionary fervour, embodies a faint '*we*-prayer'. Roger, the lapsed minister, who rejects commu-nity and communion, evades this kind of incarnational Christianity. Although Dale's rather dubious natural theology marks him out as a likely villain in Updike's world, he might, to Roger's horror, unconsciously be the more authentic Barthian of the novel. Roger professes admiration for Barth, and is able to quote him, but uses the theology as an excuse to evade commitment and engagement with the world. Dale's wrestling with the big questions, those Tillichian questions of 'ultimate concern', that for the too-content Roger have merely become academic conundrums, marks him of the two men as the more theologically serious. Wood's argument that the novel sets up a theological debate with a predetermined conclusion would have more credibility if Dale were a less articulate exponent of his faith position. His project might verge on the heretical but he takes both good and evil far more seriously than Roger and, in his attempt to engender belief and integrity, he echoes Barth's vision in 'The Humanity of God':

... man is *not* good but rather a downright monster. But even if one were in this respect the most melancholy skeptic, one could not . . . say that culture speaks only of the evil in man.[37]

Creativity, ideas, and the pursuit of God, might be fatally compromised, but, in Barth's terms, this 'attempt of man to be man and thus to hold the good gift of his humanity in honor and put it to work' is inevitable.[38] Dale seeks to 'hold the good gift' where Roger holds it in contempt.

The sexual connections between these two 'heretics', as between Chillingworth and Dimmesdale in *The Scarlet Letter*, is the occasion for theological exploration. John Duvall has read the novel in terms of its metaphorical conflation of heresy with pornography, the twin illegitimate fixations of Lambert, and connects these non-official forms of discourse with a homoerotic subtext.[39] For Schiff, the novelist 'endeavours to transform the *Scarlet Letter* myth by affirming corporeal impulse and thus reconciling body and soul'.[40] *Roger's Version* certainly confronts the chaotically incarnate aspects of life, with unruly desire and adulterous couplings represented in such repugnant detail that some critics have decried the novelist's descent into a kind of exclusive, theologically literate pornography. Shortly after publication, Frederick Crews observed, of one of Roger's graphic reveries on Esther and Dale's frantic infidelity, that 'we scarcely know whether we are supposed to read the scene or rent it'.[41] In 2003, the mainstream Evangelical magazine, *Christianity Today*, reflected, in an otherwise appreciative piece on the author's achievement that 'some of his novels . . . seem only thinly disguised excuses to parade the gaudy excesses of America's sexual fetishes. Even when you know he's up to something else – that his sexual explicitness has a cultural critique, even a theological agenda, behind it – it's pretty hard to stomach'.[42]

Updike's fiction has long been informed, perhaps even over-determined, by a fascination with the relationship between sexuality and religious belief. Indeed, one critic has observed that in the novelist's interpretation of 'the American Protestant creed, erotic desire, religious belief and worldly ambition are three aspects of the sacred drive to connect the self with the world'.[43] Updike has written of his two great, opposing theological heroes' perceptions of sexuality, including Tillich's alleged multiple infidelity and predilection for pornography and Barth's surprisingly liberal views of infidelity.[44] In a sense, both of these emerge in the figure of Roger Chillingworth. Can Roger be said to pursue Barth's advice to 'undertake an active opposition to this disorder, and to secure bridgeheads within the confusion'?[45] He seems to recognize himself as a transgressor only in so far as his infidelity is a pleasingly illustrative echo of the heretical texts that dominate his professional life. Late in the narrative, after he has finally had sex with his niece, Verna, one of three Pearl figures in the narrative, Lambert confesses:

> ... in my sensation of peace *post-coitum*, of sweet theistic certainly beneath the remote vague ceiling, of living *proof* at Verna's side, I was guilty of the heresy of which the Cathars and Fraticelli were long ago accused amid the thunders

of anathema – that of committing deliberate abominations so as to widen and deepen the field in which God's forgiveness can magnificently play. *Mas, mas.* But *thou shall not tempt the Lord thy God.* (*RV*, p. 289)

There is no repentance on Roger's behalf, merely a playful reflection with a theological tradition of devout heretics that, consciously or not, signals moral and spiritual self-satisfaction. God might be 'wholly other' for Roger, but this is merely because a Barthian transcendence assures him that he might pursue hedonistic pleasure without the need to recognize the incarnational value of other people: Verna becomes a sexual target to conquer, Esther an erotic figure to please the idolatrous eye and Dale an enemy to vanquish.

The opening words of *Roger's Version* ('I have been happy at the Divinity School') introduce its religiously inflected spatial setting and adumbrate the rather smug theological complacency of the narrator. Both are crucial to Updike's exploration of heresy and its antagonistic but inextricable relationship with Christianity in its mutating historical self-definitions. Updike's temporal shifting of Hawthorne's original to the 1980s is balanced by his preservation of its Boston setting; though the name of city and university are never made explicit, it is clear that the Divinity School is inspired by the influential faculty at Harvard with its fertile theological history. Roger's reflection that his own fondness for Barthian neo-orthodoxy is contrary to the zeitgeist of 'this liberal seminary dominated by gracefully lapsed Unitarians and Quakers' (*RV*, p. 27) is a subtle intertextual joke which suggests that Hawthorne, the reluctant inheritor of Puritan guilt, is not the only New England heretic whose ghost stalks *Roger's Version*.

In 1838, Ralph Waldo Emerson, a vital voice in the so-called American Renaissance, himself a 'gracefully lapsed Unitarian', delivered his notoriously heterodox 'Divinity School Address' to the apprentice clergymen of Harvard, the mid-nineteenth-century predecessors of Roger Lambert's radical generation of students. The affinities and antagonisms between Roger and Emerson are typical of Updike's playfulness: both men, for example, repudiated their 'legislative' positions as Christian ministers in favour of less spiritually responsible and accountable careers as interpreters. Emerson left his Unitarian pastorate in 1832, following his disillusionment with the efficacy of Communion, and became a radical, questing, Romantic experimental essayist. Roger Lambert informs his reader on the novel's first page that he abandoned the 'active ministry' fourteen years ago for a more interpretative career. Emerson is a liberal dissenter in a conservative world; Lambert, a neo-orthodox heretic, with privately libertarian tastes, in a tolerant, consciously heterodox world.

The Relativity of Heresy

Emerson, the visionary Transcendentalist, is memorably named elsewhere by Updike as a sort of self-proclaimed 'post-Christian prophet' who, in Updike's view, crucially lacked the debilitating guilt of Hawthorne or Melville and emphasized the radical discontinuity between the message of Christ and the ossified teachings of the gathered Church.[46] Emerson's lecture echoes the devotional fervour of Jonathan Edwards, the eighteenth-century preacher most closely associated with the Christian revivals of the first 'Great Awakening' of the 1740s, and the address makes a similar call for the repudiation of ritual in favour of a new, American spirituality of individual experience. Edwards, like Emerson, was viewed as a threat to the church establishment and banished from his pastorate. In a further echo, Emerson argues, as did Edwards, that divine revelation must and will be uttered by individuals in the contemporary world: 'Men have come to speak of the revelation as somewhat long ago given and done, as if God were dead', laments Emerson.[47] Despite the compelling cadences of his revivalist rhetoric and their continuities with the Protestant tradition, Emerson's theology effectively rejected creedal Christianity and, like a number of his European Romantic contemporaries, he sought to deify humanity ('If a man is at heart just, then in so far is he God') and to challenge the Trinitarian creed of Christ's unique divinity and salvific sacrifice:

> Jesus Christ belonged to the true race of prophets. He saw with open eye the mystery of the soul ... But what a distortion did his doctrine and memory suffer in the same, in the next and in the following ages! (*DSA*, pp. 1149, 1151)

Emerson's lecture so incensed the institution and the conservative Christian establishment that the ex-Unitarian minister was publicly decried as a heretic and exiled from Harvard for 30 years. Abhorred by the orthodoxy of his own moment in history, by the end of the twentieth century his immanentist, mystical and syncretistic arguments have prevailed, suggesting the historical relativity of heresy. Indeed, Dale's attack on the disciplinary vagueness of the current curriculum implies that an Emersonian-style heterodoxy shapes the modern Divinity School:

> What you call religion around here is what other people would call sociology. That's how you teach it, right? Everything from the Gospels to *The Golden Bough*, Martin Luther to Martin Luther King, it all happened, it's historical fact, it's anthropology, it's ancient texts, it's humanly *interesting*, right? But that's so safe. How can you go wrong? Not even the worst atheist in the world denies that people have been religious ... So what? (*RV*, p. 19)

In an article commemorating the bicentenary of Emerson's birth, Harold Bloom asserts that the writer 'remains the central figure in American culture, as well as our unofficial religion, which I regard as more Emersonian than Christian, despite nearly all received opinion on this matter'.[48] Elsewhere, Bloom has described this 'unofficial religion', and particularly its New Age manifestations, as an 'endlessly entertaining saturnalia of ill-defined yearnings'.[49] Both Dale's hunger for absolute scientific assurance for his theism and

Roger's dislike of syncretism indicate that they are heretics against the eclectic 'postmodern mind' which, as Zygmunt Bauman notes, is 'altogether less excited than its modern adversary by the prospect (let alone moved by the urge) to enclose the world into a grid of neat categories and clear-cut divisions'. The fact that theology has become a form of sociology is indicative of what Bauman further notes is 'the nasty habit things have of spilling over their definitional boundaries, or even by the premonition that the drawing of such boundaries with any degree of lasting reliability defies human resources.'[50] The heterodox world envisioned by Emerson is inherited by new prophets without honour in the form of Roger and Dale, both seeking the assurance of alternative forms of orthodoxy.

The Divinity School might once have been a legislative arena but now, to appropriate Bauman's formulation, it has become an interpretative space.[51] Where formerly the school would have trained ministers to preach a comparatively unambiguous (Protestant) gospel, the liberal, secularizing forces of the nineteenth and twentieth centuries have transformed it into a discursive space where categories of orthodoxy, theological realism and ethical absolutes are anathema. As Roger laments:

> This generation, which by and large has lost all inculturated instinct for the Judaeo-Christian sacral, has displaced much of its religiosity onto anti-pollution, ranging from the demand for smoke-free zones in restaurants to violent demonstrations in front of nuclear-power plants. (*RV*, p. 6)

Debate, political radicalism and a celebration of multicultural America define the liberal project of the contemporary Divinity School. In Roger, however – a white, middle-class academic, approximately the same age as Updike – we have a figure who is lost amidst the relativism of the age, and who subconsciously grieves the loss of a world of verifiable absolutes and defined hierarchies. Despite Roger's enthusiasm for heresy in its various historical forms and his libertarian defence of pornography, he is a deeply conservative figure. When confronted with a contemporary heresy in the form of Dale's project, Roger is outraged. However, this indignation in some senses undoes complacency and the novel becomes a sequence of highly charged theological debates, owing something to Oscar Wilde's dialogic essays.

The narrative mediates the encounter between materialist and mystical 'versions' of the world, as modes of interpreting scripture and experience collide and create alternative and destabilizing hermeneutic possibilities. Dale Kohler's project, as unlikely and hubristic as it might seem, provokes examination of one's own religious convictions. Should the devout seek to prove God's existence and triumphantly controvert the atheistic assumptions of contemporary science? Can Christianity simultaneously persist as a public, ethical force and as a relational faith tradition in which the self is remade by interaction with God? Certainly his potentially 'blasphemous' project to demonstrate the miraculous force behind all existence contradicts the arguments of both Emerson and Barth, the two diametrically opposed heretical thinkers whose work, in various ways, informs the novel. In the heterodox Divinity School Address, Emerson, in words that seem to prophesy both Dale's project and the marketing of the miraculous by 1980s TV Evangelists refutes the pursuit of the remarkable: 'To aim to convert a man by miracles, is a profanation of the soul' (*DSA*, p. 1151). Barth, from his distinctly non-Emersonian vision of a Deity who is far beyond human sensation and reason, declared in 'The Humanity of God' that the God of the Bible, of revelation and redemption, was 'no universal deity capable of being reached conceptually'. This later argument shapes Roger's view and, in a sense the professor of heresy is vindicated. Dale's attempt to reach God 'conceptually' meets with failure: a fleeting image of a hand appears on a computer screen only to fade, a ghostly half-presence, or as Roger names God, 'that tender shadow on the underside of our minds' (*RV*, p. 249). Dale leaves New England, and, Roger suggests, abandons his faith, destroyed by the encounter with decadent Boston liberalism and its Puritan ghosts. Yet this troubled avatar of Arthur Dimmesdale is one of the most articulate defenders, in postmodern literature, of a theistic reading of the world:

> Materialism is a faith just like theism: only it asks a lot more in the way of miracles. Instead of asking we believe in God it asks we don't believe in ourselves; it asks we don't believe in our own awareness, our own emotions and moral sensations. (*RV*, p. 165)

If the reader can make one final leap of faith and trust Roger's undependable, heretical version of events, Dale leaves more than a legacy of anguished faith in New England. Esther, he implies, is pregnant with a child conceived of their supposed affair. Where Arthur Dimmesdale embraced death on the scaffold, Dale's exit from the narrative is coupled with the incarnational hope of new birth.[52]

Roger's Version, refracted through the self-serving consciousness of a single, morally dubious narrator, is no more prescriptive than any other literary novel of the late twentieth century. Nonetheless, for all Updike's modernist curbing of omniscient intervention, its narrative demands a theological or atheological response. In a rare moment of spiritual insight and generosity Roger, asks of Dale's project: 'What was this desolation in Dale's heart, I thought, but the longing for God – that longing which is, when all is said and done, our only evidence of His existence?' (*RV*, p. 67)

Updike, who might be regarded as either confoundingly orthodox or vertiginously antinomian depending on one's theological perspective, is fascinated by the abject, aberrant and erotic status of the heretic. Roger and Dale, for example, exist on the peripheries of their own intellectual communities, unable to participate fully in, respectively, the pluralist or atheist-materialist ideologies of liberal divinity or rationalist science.

The novel negotiates with the unofficial history of Christian belief. Believers or atheists, we are all, Updike implies, forced to choose not between eternally fixed orthodoxy and dissent but between a variety of heresies. Theology, he argues in a comparative essay on Barth and Tillich, 'is not a provable accumulation, like science, nor is it a succession of enduring monuments, like art. It must always unravel and be reknit.'[53]

Roger's Version acknowledges the attraction of Puritan absolutism and Transcendentalist optimism, but repudiates both. The legacy of the latter tradition is a key part of contemporary America. Updike, however, cannot share the sanguine Transcendentalist view that the realm of selfhood, so championed by Emerson and Whitman, is the only reliable space for transformative, authentic encounters with the divine. Our only view of interiority in the novel, after all, is that of an unpleasant casuist, who gorges himself on pornographic fantasy.

The evidence of *Roger's Version* is that a religion based purely on subjective criteria is also tragically bound up with a postlapsarian world; collective, authorized expressions of faith, the '*Cultus*' so abhorred by Emerson, might well engender flaccid and legalistic traditions but the pursuit of a unique spiritual identity is similarly destined to fail. The final set-piece of Roger's narrative sees this master manipulator challenged by his wife, who leaves the domestic space to attend church. 'Why would you do a ridiculous thing like that?' demands the flustered Roger. 'Oh ... To annoy you' (*RV*, p. 329). Esther's new choice is a kind of heresy, against her own scientific rationalism and Roger's egocentric isolationism, as she seeks out communion and connectedness and, in so doing, confronts the theological complacency of her heresy-obsessed husband. As Evans argues '[h]eresy has been a great shaker-up of complacency' and Roger, though no sudden convert to re-engagement with humanity, has been forced to recognize the costly dynamics of desire and responsibility: he and Esther are the new guardians for Verna's neglected child.[54]

Updike does not write in what one writer of Christian fiction has called the 'major key of faith' but, instead, belongs in the complex, living tradition of American literary heretics. Sherry's view that it 'is difficult to convey the workings of grace in any medium, but the simplest way to start is to imagine a world without grace' has resonance for Updike's often desolate literary landscape.[55] His characters might seek transcendence in all the wrong places but many of them, somehow, stumble into what Frederick Buechner calls that 'crazy, holy grace', authored by a God who is both wholly other and intimately caught up in the lives of his creatures.[56] Desperate and depraved as many of his characters are, Updike's fiction is a space in which grace and forgiveness might, indeed, 'magnificently play' (*RV*, p. 289).

4

Miracles and the Mundane:
Signs, Wonders and the Novel

What place can miracles, visions, faith healing and other supernatural phenomena have in serious literary fiction? Should the evocation of supernatural events
be exclusively confined to the genres of fantasy fiction and Gothic romance? For
Salman Rushdie, who is both one of the twentieth century's most famous literary heretics and a candidly theological writer, the era's materialist fictional
trends are not adequate to represent the complex dynamics of religious belief.
Reflex cynicism about the numinous, he suggests, undermines the possibility of
empathy with believers:

> If one is to attempt honestly to describe reality as it is experienced by religious
> people, for whom God is no symbol but an everyday fact, then the conven-
> tions of what is called realism are quite inadequate. The rationalism of that
> form comes to seem like a judgement upon, an invalidation of, the religious
> faith of the characters being described. A form must be created which allows
> the miraculous and the mundane to co-exist at the same level – as the same
> order of event. I found this to be essential even though I am not, myself, a
> religious man.[1]

In Rushdie's essay ('In God We Trust', 1985; 1990), reworked in response to
the fatwa imposed upon him after the publication of *The Satanic Verses* (1988),
the novelist offered a quixotically generous view of the connection between imagination and spiritual conviction. Curiously, he simultaneously stands outside
of theology – insisting that he is not religious – and asserts that the novel form
needs to review its own insistence on pure reason in order to be just to those who
hold a God-centred worldview. The realist 'conventions' to which Rushdie
alludes are a legacy of modern incredulity towards the miraculous that we
can trace back to David Hume's *Enquiry Concerning Human Understanding* (1748).
'A miracle is a violation of the laws of nature,' Hume famously observed, 'and as
a firm and unalterable experience has established these laws, the proof against a
miracle, from the very nature of the fact, is as entire as any argument from
experience can possibly be imagined'.[2] What one critic has named Hume's
'Enlightenment anti-theology' informs the now widely accepted rational scepticism regarding divine intervention in everyday life.[3] Although, as Robert
Bruce Mullin argues in *Miracles and the Modern Religious Imagination* (1996), it is

easy to overstate the immediate impact of Hume's ideas, all modern theological thought has had to address the philosopher's critique of miraculous phenomena and its foundational purpose in revealed religion.[4] Hume's intervention is now regarded as a turning point in the history of Western belief because, as William C. Placher notes, pre-modern 'theologians had generally made no sharp distinction between the "natural" and the "miraculous"'.[5] The 'miracle' stories of the Jewish and Christian scriptures were the primary influence on the pre-Enlightenment belief that God acts through revelation in history. However, as Howard Clark Kee observes, these narratives have 'no notion of natural law determining how the universe operates' and so, though a 'miracle is usually recounted as an extraordinary event it is never portrayed as a violation of the laws of nature'.[6]

The implications of the *Enquiry* for Christian belief are wide-ranging: Hume asserts that the testimony of those who claim to have witnessed mystic phenomena can never be regarded as genuinely reliable, as on the balance of probabilities they are deluded or mistaken; consequently belief in the alleged authenticity of supernatural interventions should not be regarded as a sound basis for religious conviction: 'we may establish it as a maxim, that no human testimony can have such force as to prove a miracle, and make it a just foundation for any such system of religion.' Most devastating of all is the suggestion that Christianity is not only dependent on its early accounts of miracle, but 'even at this day . . . cannot be believed by any reasonable person without one'. This religion, Hume suggests, will fail in the absence of belief in phenomena now regarded as impossible.[7] These arguments have not been forgotten more than 250 years after Hume's philosophical challenge. Indeed, the ambivalent 'sacred turn' witnessed in postmodern culture has included a marked emphasis on explorations of the miraculous.

In James Robertson's *The Testament of Gideon Mack* (2006), for example, the eponymous disbelieving clergyman – named for the biblical Gideon but lacking a comparable trust in the divine – examines his necessarily secret scepticism explicitly in relation to Hume:

> The importance of evidence, the necessity of facts. Like Mr Gradgrind in *Hard Times* I believed in facts. I believed in them that day I found the Stone, which was why it disturbed me so much. I remembered Thomas called Didymus, who would not accept that Jesus had risen from the dead unless he saw and felt for himself the print of the nails in his hands. I'd have been with Thomas on that. I'd read David Hume on miracles, his argument that although a miracle was possible you'd need so much evidence to persuade you it had happened that it wouldn't be a miracle any more – and my sympathies were with him.[8]

Gideon invokes a trinity of sceptics from the Western canon: Thomas, the 'doubting' disciple of the gospels; Dickens' utilitarian theorist, Thomas Gradgrind, whose Christian name echoes that of his biblical forefather; and, finally, Hume, the debunker of miracles. Gideon's imaginative identification with this band of cynics displays the literary and religious precedents for his narrative but also signifies the contradictory instincts of the novel itself and its faith–doubt dialectic. Both of the 'doubting Thomas' figures whom he identifies with are forced to abandon their sceptical positions after destabilizing personal experiences. 'My Lord and my God!' exclaims Thomas called Didymus, following his encounter with the risen Christ (John 20.28). Similarly, Gradgrind's practical, life-denying logic is destroyed when he witnesses its deadening influence on the interior lives of his children. Dickens deploys the language of religious conversion to describe his protagonist's sudden awakening to an alternative way of reading the world. In Robertson's novel, Gideon Mack's 'testament' consciously echoes these traditions of unexpected, Pauline conversion, in a narrative that is somehow both parodic and reverent. As Gideon stumbles upon the impossible, ancient stone that miraculously appears in the woods, and is later 'saved' from a cliff-top fall by a mysterious stranger, his cool rationalism is tested. However, this minister, who received his theological education in Edinburgh, the birthplace of Hume, remains in debt to the great sceptic, and the possibility of quiescent belief is always haunted by a voice of philosophical common sense. Robertson's narrative is a complex evocation of the connections between imagination, reason and faith. Its structure, built around the Gothic trope of a discovered manuscript, appears to invite a sceptical reading since it contains evident prejudice, elision and signs of mental instability. Yet Gideon's 'testament' also questions the integrity of modern touchstones, including reason as a purely objective force, the influence of materialism – viewed as a surrogate for religion – and the stability of national identity.

Twentieth-century theology continued David Hume's sceptical trajectory but some interpretations of the miraculous resist the stark choice between supernatural agency and absolute disbelief. Although Hume's argument has been exceptionally persuasive in the progressive, post-Enlightenment West, rival accounts of the miraculous continue to proliferate. Biblical scholars, theologians and philosophers have returned to the problem of miracles and offered critical alternatives to Hume's incredulity. The miracle stories of the gospels have been reread by Rudolf Bultmann, for example, as pre-scientific fictions which ought not to preoccupy (or trouble) the faith of the modern believer. Bultmann's 'demythologization' of Jesus' miracles – emphasizing their relation to parallel pagan and Jewish narratives of the miraculous at the expense of their historical reliability – asserted that contemporary believers should seek out the message of faith encoded within the gospel reports rather than attempt to prove the unprovable. 'Bultmann did not try to eliminate or remove the myths from the Bible', notes Bernd Kollman, but rather 'he tried to unwrap the revelatory kerygma hidden in the mythological veil of the miracles'.[9] This *kerygmatic* interpretation – one that proclaims the glory of God – is not shared by everybody in a pluralistic, globalized era. Demythologization, for the atheist, is the spark that should ignite a bonfire of creedal vanities. If Bultmann's project of demythologization has gradually become the consensus understanding of Jesus' apparently miraculous acts for modern theology, particularly among liberal Protestants, it is strange to observe how many contemporary novelists, many of them writing out of an agnostic world view, continue to tell miracle stories. This chapter will consider miracle stories by a range of contemporary writers, including Don DeLillo, Nick Hornby, Jodi Picoult, David Guterson, Rhidian Brook and John L'Heureux, in novels published between 1996 and 2006. These narratives vary in mood, style, prominence and ethical complexity from DeLillo's late modernist magnum opus of the 'American century', *Underworld* (1997), to the more populist, domestic melodrama of Hornby's *How to Be Good* (2001).

Does twenty-first-century fiction offer, then, an etiolated version of the miraculous? Can realism, *pace* Rushdie's caveat, accommodate the supernatural? This chapter will explore the ways in which the contemporary novel continues to negotiate both with the idea of miracles – phenomena known in the New Testament as 'signs and wonders' – and with the legacy of Hume's scepticism towards such events. 'When life is viewed in terms of scientific cause and effect – *the* theology of the twentieth century,' argues M. Cameron Grey in the introduction to her anthology of modern miracle stories, *Angels and Awakenings* (1980), 'it certainly looks as if human affairs are being played out in a universe with either no God or, worse, a silent and indifferent one'. Yet she also asserts that the best narratives 'about angels and awakenings, Paradise, and divine intervention' are not a 'predictable or easily sentimental' panacea to this metaphysical panic.[10] Unsurprisingly, perhaps, miraculous phenomena are a commonplace of *fin de siècle* and *fin de millénium* fiction. What is less predictable, however, is the range of genres that have been infused with this resurgent fascination with the miraculous. The chapter will address the ways in which ostensibly realist writers have revived, consciously or otherwise, elements of romance to explore these unsettling, destabilizing ideas. In Paul Wilson's *Someone to Watch Over Me* (2001), Brendan Moon, a professional investigator of allegedly supernatural occurrences, claims that this supposedly rational age is crowded by a proliferation of '*new* miracles':

> The closing years of the twentieth century had seen more reports of statues moving, of visions making proclamations, of apparitions confiding heavenly secrets to a chosen few, than in the whole of the previous two centuries. People would believe anything in order to bestow upon their personal worlds a geometry and a sense of meaning which, in reality, were not there.[11]

Novelists might aspire, like the empiricist Moon, merely to report a wider cultural trend in which religion has been refigured to include, once again, a distinctively supernatural edge. Yet claims to such authorial neutrality are problematic. This chapter will consider the extent to which these narratives are able to retain a pragmatic, reasoned response to the evidence (or its lack) presented by their 'fictional' miracles. Do they attempt to demystify the miraculous, to dismiss the thought of divine intervention in human affairs as dangerous superstition? Alternatively, are there circumstances in which the texts are attracted to the recovery of a theological language that might provide a legitimate critique of such scepticism? Canonical Jewish and Christian scriptures are replete with rather different forms of miracle – stories of healing, protection, provision and punishment – all of which are read as an index of God's providence over nature and love for humanity. The chapter will address multiple postmodern iterations of these miracles but focuses on two primary, overlapping manifestations of the miraculous: visionary experiences and, secondly, the related phenomenon of miraculous healing. A coda will reflect on the transformative possibilities, or otherwise, of these fictional miracles.

Studying Wonders at 'Dot Com Miraculum'

Encounters between ordinary people and the divine are an integral part of Jewish and Christian narrative tradition. In Genesis, it is taken for granted that Noah, who 'walked with God', would also hear the unmediated voice of the deity (Genesis 6.913). In other biblical narratives, however, the divine presence is made manifest in less direct ways: Jacob, for example, famously wrestles with an angel from whom he receives a wound and demands a blessing; he later declares that he has encountered God 'face to face' (Genesis 32.22–32). Moses' encounter with the voice of God in the burning bush has also become a paradigm for imagining the otherness of divinity (Exodus 3.2). Yet, as Janet Martin Soskice argues, this strange story, 'a moment we have come to think of as a great epiphany', is rendered in rather routine, everyday language.[12] Indeed, each of these accounts of theophany – visions of God – is bound by a distinctive connection between the supernatural and the everyday.

Exemplary Jewish stories that stress the overlap between the divine and the mundane permeate elements of twenty-first-century fiction. Salley Vickers' *Miss Garnet's Angel* (2000) is not explicitly supernatural in orientation but nevertheless rewrites the myth of the angel in disguise, specifically embodied in the Book of Tobit's story of Tobias and the Archangel Raphael. Vickers' novel, an account of the gradual spiritual awakening of a middle-aged woman who prizes her strict rationalism, exemplifies the tradition of the conversion narrative, that has re-emerged in so-called 'post-secular' culture. Julia Garnet's solitary vacation in Venice, that impossible city haunted by equally strange stories in which men and angels interact, becomes a pilgrimage in pursuit of communion and, in the novel's final words, the hope of life after death ('ut mihi contingat tuo beneficio post mortem vivere').[13] The narrative is not, however, without twentieth-century precedent. In Bernard Mallamud's provocative short story, 'Angel Levine' (1955), for example, a desolate New York tailor, facing both financial and emotional ruin, is offered help by a middle-aged man who professes to be both Jewish and a member of the heavenly host.[14] The devout Manischevitz is sceptical of his uninvited guest's claim, not from a lack of religious faith but because Levine, the putative divine agent, is black. Manischevitz eventually acknowledges his visitor's angelic identity, as the spurned messenger sits drinking in a Harlem bar, and the tailor's ailing wife is swiftly restored to good health. The narrative uses a collision of undisguised prejudice and holy agency to transgress thresholds of logic and race. It also indicates that narratives of the miraculous need not be exclusively (or even primarily) concerned with an otherworldly spirituality but might confront material, political issues too. Mallamud's post-war parable reclaimed the tradition of the holy messenger to explore the limits of credulity and cynicism in modern America. Improbable agents of the divine, in the tradition of Mallamud's whiskey-drinking Harlem dweller, Angel Levine, are now more likely to be found on celluloid than on the page. Indeed, contemporary American cinema has become a veritable refuge for the heavenly host with angels, virtuous and renegade, appearing in *Michael* (1996), *The Preacher's Wife* (1996), Wim Wenders' *Wings of Desire* (1987) and its US remake *City of Angels* (1998) and Kevin Smith's *Dogma* (1999), for example.

While Hollywood is crowded with angelic beings, contemporary American fiction is similarly packed with visions and visionaries. *Underworld*, for example, Don DeLillo's vast novel of American excess, garbage and desire, spanning a half-century from the first Soviet nuclear tests to the millennium's end, turns in its own closing pages, somewhat surprisingly, to an electronic rumour of dreams and visions. Jeff Shay, the son of the novel's central character, a child of the communications age, becomes fascinated by a website 'devoted to miracles':

> There are many reports . . . of people flocking to uranium mines in order to cure themselves . . . They are trying to cure themselves of arthritis, diabetes, blindness and cancer . . . Jeff tells us this and smirks shyly, either because he thinks it's funny or because he thinks it's funny and believes it.[15]

Ironically, the World Wide Web, an upshot of a rational, scientific era, becomes a space in which the irrational and the superstitious flourish. Cyberspace appeals to magical or miraculous thinking because its 'virtual' defeat of time and space echoes the idea that a miracle constitutes a 'violation' of the natural order. 'The real miracle is the web,' reflects DeLillo's narrator: 'the net, where everybody is everywhere at once, and he is there among them, unseen' (*U*, p. 808). The online community becomes a hi-tech cloud of witnesses, rendering holy that which seems utterly mundane. If the modern mind routinely, and simplistically, regarded religion and science as utterly separate, unyieldingly conflicting rationales, postmodernity has witnessed some strange collisions between the two. 'Technology is repeatable miracles,' reflects Mo Cullin, the physicist narrator of 'Clear Island', one of the interrelated short stories in David Mitchell's *Ghostwritten* (1999).[16] Similarly, transcendence and technology are intimately related in the odd, apocalyptic ending of *Underworld*. Jeff Shay's fascination with the pages of '*dot com miraculum*' connect him to apparently miraculous events in the Bronx, the borough of New York in which his father was raised. His tongue-tied guilt in speaking of what he thinks of as 'part of the American gulag, a place ... distant from his experience' parallels the novel's difficulty in representing religious experience. Just as Nick Shay is haunted by memories of his working-class, urban origins, so too does *Underworld* unearth one more stratum of American detritus, apparently buried with the many other layers of waste. Belief in the supernatural, ostensibly dispensed with during the Cold War, an era in which humanity had the quasi-divine power of self-destruction, forces its way to the surface. In the everyday sacrament of a shared meal, Jeff tells his parents about an alleged miracle that took place in the Bronx during the early 1990s:

> A young girl was the victim of a terrible crime. Body found in a vacant lot amid dense debris ... The girl memorialized on a graffiti wall nearby. And then the miracle of the images and the subsequent crush of people and the belief and disbelief. Mostly belief, it seems ... He feels he doesn't have the credentials to relate a tale of such intensity, all that suffering and faith and openness of emotion, transpiring in the Bronx. I tell him what better place for the study of wonders. (*U*, pp. 807–8)

This self-conscious, middle-class son of a man who grew up in comparative poverty is more comfortable in the virtual realm of cyberspace than he is in addressing the flesh and blood reality of life in a blue-collar district. Yet both locations are heavily textualized – the Bronx in Nick Shay's shifting memories, and the net in its endless pages of code – and these are shimmering, metamorphosing texts in which the miraculous appears to be at work. The working-class, metropolitan community might be an ideal 'place for the study of wonders' but DeLillo's emphasis is not solely spatial; it can also be viewed as a return to a distinctively American literary theme. In *The Reign of Wonder* (1965), a groundbreaking reading of 'naivety' and 'reality' from the Transcendentalists to Saul Bellow, Tony Tanner argues that American literature has developed as a tradition of awe and transcendence. As a body of writing it 'has shown itself, perhaps, too suspicious of the analytical intellect, too disinclined to develop a complex reaction to society, too much given to extreme reactions, too hungry for metaphysics'.[17] The final pages of *Underworld* are a manifestation of this insatiable appetite for the metaphysical or greed for the unknowable.

The concluding sequence of DeLillo's novel turns away from the Shay family to the allegedly miraculous story of the Bronx that they have encountered online. Significantly, this ending focuses on a person of faith: Nick Shay, the novel's defining figure, is displaced by Sister Edgar, a nun who works with the poorest members of the Bronx, the neighbourhood of Shay's childhood. The violent death of Esmeralda, a destitute teenager found raped and murdered, has undermined Edgar's faith, her hope in transcendent and redemptive Christian truth. However, this does not signal a movement from religious piety to reason but a darker, more paranoid transformation. 'It is not a question of disbelief', reflects the narrator, but 'another kind of belief, a second force, insecure, untrusting, a faith that is spring-fed by the things we fear in the night, and she thinks she is succumbing' (*U*, p. 817). Sister Edgar's incipient paranoia echoes Tanner's claim that American literature, 'suspicious of the analytical intellect', has not been able to move 'beyond one particular syndrome of responses': 'wonder', he notes, mutates into 'horror', 'delight' becomes 'disillusion' and 'revulsion' is 'locked with awe'.[18] DeLillo's novel limns an American religious consciousness in which the separation between 'wonder' and 'horror' is fragile. Yet *Underworld* appears to reverse Tanner's sequence as scores of people claim to have witnessed an apparition of Esmeralda. The trauma of her senseless murder gives way to stories – 'word passing block to block, moving through churches and superettes ... about the same uncanny occurrence' – that an urban miracle, a sign of hope amid poverty and despair, is taking place (*U*, p. 818).

Is this vision a simple trick of the light or the product of collective hysteria, the wish-fulfilment of people desperate for a shred of the numinous in the dirty chaos of the everyday? In bringing together the incongruous categories of commerce and religious ecstasy – the ghostly phantasm of Esmeralda's face seems to emerge from a vast billboard, illuminated by a passing commuter train – DeLillo implies that American belief operates most vividly in the interstices of the sacred and the profane. Sister Gracie, who works with Edgar, embodies reason with her coolly pragmatic response to the phenomenon. 'The poor need visions, okay?' she reminds her colleague and fellow believer (*U*, p. 819). According to Gracie's common-sense view, the spectre is artificial, the manifestation of a shared longing rather than a supernatural reality. The sceptical Sister embodies the 'analytical intellect' that Tanner believed to be a defining absence in American literature. Yet Gracie's chilly logic is put to the test when she reluctantly accompanies the forlorn Edgar to one of the nightly vigils by the Harlem River, joining a vast and expectant crowd. Both of these holy women, whose 'presence' as representatives of a 'universal church' amidst this multitude of strangers 'is a verifying force', witness the apparition but disagree about what it represents (*U*, p. 822). Ironically, Sister Gracie offers an iconoclastic assessment – 'Pictures lie' – a view that resonates with traditional Puritan warnings against Roman Catholic ritual. The incident, for Gracie, can easily be rationalized whilst Edgar's response to her fleeting vision is more traditionally epiphanic:

> She sees Esmeralda's face take shape under the rainbow of bounteous juice and above the little suburban lake and there is a sense of someone living in the image, an animating spirit – less than a tender second of life, less than half a second and the spot is dark again. (*U*, p. 822)

It is a moment of sudden illumination, an instant in which this woman 'feels something break upon her'; this 'angelus of clearest joy' both renews her hope and allows her to participate in communal ecstasy (*U*, p. 822). Does DeLillo's 'miracle' – manufactured or real – perpetuate a reactionary superstition? In his 'postmodern critique' of epiphany, *The Visionary Moment* (2002),

[Margin note, handwritten:] 'belief operates most vividly in the interstices of the sacred and the profane.'

Paul Maltby argues that the literary convention of the flash of illumination is 'enmeshed in metaphysical and ideological assumptions' that are both 'theoretically untenable and ... in most contexts ... irreconcilable with progressive political thinking'.[19] Maltby focuses on epiphany as the classic moment of literary revelation, in which some previously hidden truth about the universe becomes clear, rather than on specific manifestations of the divine. But he is also unambiguous about his ultimate target: the 'postmodern challenge to the visionary moment', he states, 'will also serve as an abbreviated and allegorical way of addressing the larger question of the credibility of mystical truth claims in general'.[20] The 'visionary moment' in *Underworld* differs from many narratives of literary epiphany in that it is a collective experience and its subjective elements are muted by the commonality of the encounter. DeLillo represents the transient (and, perhaps, illusory) apparition of a murdered child – Esmeralda's ghostly face is soon replaced by a white sheet proclaiming 'Space Available' – as a sign of the times. The hunger for illumination is not, *pace* Maltby, ironized as the product of an untenable metaphysics; instead DeLillo opens up the possibility that such moments, reliant on retrospective interpretation, might remain meaningful:

> And what do you remember, finally, when everyone has gone home and the streets are empty of devotion and hope, swept by river wind? Is the memory thin and bitter and does it shame you with its fundamental untruth – all nuance and wishful silhouette? Or does the power of transcendence linger, the sense of an event that violates natural forces, something holy that throbs on the hot horizon, the vision you crave because you need a sign to stand against your doubt? (*U*, p. 824)

Ambiguity, instability and hope are integral to DeLillo's representation of the sacred: it is vital that 'the sense of an event that violates natural forces', in the novelist's distinctively Humean phrase, is not a miracle that can be proved beyond all doubt. DeLillo neither attempts to prove nor to deconstruct the event, though the narrative has constant reminders of what Maltby names the 'rhetoricity of the [visionary] moment'.[21] For Sister Edgar, facing her own death, this fleeting experience is of religious significance because it is so embedded in the senses. The recollection of jet fuel, for example, becomes the 'incense of her experience ... a retaining medium that keeps the moment whole ... the swaying soulclap raptures and the unspoken closeness, a fellowship of deep belief' (*U*, p. 824). 'Nothing is esteemed a miracle,' claimed David Hume, 'if it ever happen in the common course of nature'.[22] For Sister Edgar, by contrast, this 'fellowship of deep belief', the connection sparked between disparate individuals, city dwellers looking for a sign of grace amid violence and anomie, is a miracle that transforms Hume's 'common course of nature'.

There are echoes in DeLillo's specifically American miracles of Iris Murdoch's fascination with such irrational phenomena. For this most philosophical

of British novelists, miracle stories were necessarily ethical rather than supernatural, since she did not believe in God or in any ultimate reality outside
of the observable, day-to-day world. 'The ordinary, the untranscendent real,
the humanist world of the down-to-earth detail ... is where human truth is
uniquely,' notes Valentine Cunningham of the world according to Murdoch.
'Religion' and 'transcendence', he continues, are 'in the now of Murdoch's
novels, only realizable in the ordinary untranscendent'.[23] However, Cunningham also notes that alongside the multitude of 'pseudo-miraculous' moments
in her mythic fiction, there are also a host of other events that are less easy
to rationalize:

> On these many occasions, clearly, the devoted tracings of transcendence in
> ordinary language, the recognitions of the wonder of the world, are surpass-
> ing themselves. It's as if the nostalgia for real transcendence is getting out
> of hand, as if the ontological proof were being given something of its old
> free rein.[24]

Similarly, DeLillo's sophisticated, sceptical narrative seems to display a 'nostalgia for real transcendence' in which the disorder of history – what, on the
novel's first page, the author names the product of 'Longing on a large
scale' – might yet be subject to transcendental rules (*U*, p. 11). *Underworld* cul-
minates with a complex meditation on visionary experience but it also appears
to possess a more secular form of prescience, since its conclusion foreshadows
a visionary turn in end-of-the-century fiction exemplified by Jodi Picoult's
Keeping Faith (1999) and David Guterson's *Our Lady of the Forest* (2001), which
both focus on figures who claim to have seen and to have been spoken to by
celestial beings. These novels, animated by the complex history of spirituality
in America, become arenas for debating the validity of personal belief, the
authority of civic and religious institutions and the limits of secularity at the
fin de millennium. Do their respective explorations of the miraculous confirm
Maltby's claim that literary visions fix both 'a conservative ideology and a
logic of disempowerment', a double-bind that constitutes 'a diminished sense of
political agency and historical identity'?[25]

From a rigidly materialist perspective, one might argue that novels that
deploy supernatural phenomena simply perpetuate dangerous superstition.
Yet most contemporary miracle stories offer a more cautious, if not sceptical,
perspective on divine intervention and visions are not the only manifestation
of the miraculous in the postmodern moment. The titular protagonist in *Keeping
Faith*, for example, also appears able to heal those whom she comes into contact
with and, in the novel's most outrageous incident, seems to precipitate the resurrection of her grandmother, who has been declared dead in hospital for more
than an hour. Miracle healings are also explored in two British novels of the
period, Rhidian Brook's *The Testimony of Taliesin Jones* (1996) and Nick Hornby's *How To Be Good* (2001); the phenomenon is taken to its (il)logical conclusion in the American novelist John L'Heureux's *The Miracle* (2002), a narrative

"Occasional presence implies ordinary absence."

of a young priest's spiritual crisis in the tradition of Graham Greene's fiction. Father Paul LeBlanc, a priest who simultaneously enjoys his charismatic influence and wants to 'obliterate' all traces of ego, is transferred from his South Boston parish to a remote New Hampshire seaside town, as a reprimand for perpetuating liberal ideas.[26] He is also a rationalist for whom there 'are no miracles ... except the ordinary ones – waking, eating, speaking, sleeping – and he doesn't aspire to miracles' (*TM*, p. 2). Indeed, Father LeBlanc is haunted by the notion of the *deus absconditus*, the idea that 'God is on vacation' (*TM*, p. 22). Yet his anguished theological wrestling and view that '[t]his is not the age of miracles' is challenged when he witnesses what he believes to be the resurrection of one of his parishioners (*TM*, p. 8). This moment also raises questions about the nature of a God who might intervene in the world in such a specific, but rather random, fashion. 'The image of the created universe as an ordinarily self-sufficient whole which occasionally necessitates a little benign interference from outside is a pervasive one,' notes Mark Corner in *Signs of God: Miracles and their Interpretation* (2005). However, Corner also argues that this is a deceptive view of the relationship between divinity and the creation.

> If God 'occasionally intervenes' in the world, that implies that the Deity ordinarily stands apart from it. Occasional presence implies ordinary absence. It suggests that the universe is a self-sufficient entity which is looked down upon by a divine observer 'from above'.[27]

Do novels such as *The Miracle* imply the 'ordinary absence' of God? For Father LeBlanc, the miracle might be evidence of the efficacy of prayer but this tormented priest is also shaped by a belief that God is 'ruthless ... the God of irony. He is the God of terrible, terrifying jokes' (*TM*, p. 36). A common strand in these novels is a distinctly modern desire for proof, evidence and certainty: is the purported miracle real or fake? In L'Heureux's novel, for example, Father LeBlanc is determined to establish that Mandy's revival, after a drugs overdose, was not a blind piece of luck or an incident that might be easily and logically explained in medical terms; he wants to view it as a religious event that displays the hand of God in creation. However, LeBlanc also believes that a witness to such an event has a responsibility to 'protect' the miracle and is appalled at one of his co-witnesses, a local café owner whose excitement at the event is expressed in 'a kind of lust in his grin, as if this miracle were a superior kind of trick' (*TM*, p. 66). The same character is prepared to bear witness to the miracle but primarily as a kind of extravagant anecdote in which religious significance is beside the point: 'Miracles are from the old days with monks and the Dark Ages and, like, Saint Bernadette. But I'll tell you ... she sure as shit looked dead to me' (*TM*, p. 75). The miraculous, L'Heureux implies, can become a debased form of religious capital when spectacle or simulated sanctity displaces spiritual meaning.

Hornby's novel, though more sceptical, is similarly cautious regarding the reality of its reported miracles. *How to Be Good* is narrated by Katie Carr, a woman with a strong faith in the visible and the everyday, whose newspaper columnist husband, David ('The Angriest Man in Holloway'), goes through a sudden conversion experience after an encounter with a healer, the improbably named DJ GoodNews. This unlikely miracle worker ('a funny little man ... Thirtyish, small, astonishingly skinny' for whom 'personal hygiene might not necessarily be a priority') cures David's bad back and his daughter's chronic eczema with a simple touch.[28] Where Father LeBlanc in *The Miracle* can read miraculous intervention as evidence of divine irony, it is specifically the attitude of irony that disappears following the healing in *How to Be Good*: David is a man whose whole modus operandi thrived on irony but from whom, it seems, 'every atom of self-irony' has 'vanished' (*HTBG*, p. 72). The novel locates the collision of rationalism with the supernatural in a realist setting. Significantly, Katie is a doctor, a woman of science and reason, who is unable to accommodate the abrupt change in her habitually ill-tempered husband: 'I am a rationalist, and I don't believe in genies, or sudden personality changes. I wanted David's anger to vanish only after years and years in therapy' (*HTBG*, p. 64). In response to GoodNews's inexplicable powers of healing, Katie reflects that there is little to 'understand' about such an impossible gift but 'that everything else you have ever believed about life becomes compromised as a result' (*HTBG*, p. 68).

If disruptive miraculous events in realist contemporary fiction represent what Brian McHale has named the 'ontological dominant' of postmodern poetics, they also engender a slight return to the modernist emphasis on epistemology. For example, one of the fundamental issues at stake in Picoult's *Keeping Faith* is the authenticity of the healings and visions of the titular child protagonist. Are we expected to trust the account of her agnostic mother? Is Faith's lack of religious upbringing proof that she has not simply mistaken hallucination for desired divine consolation?

Marvels in the Mundane

Keeping Faith is both a piece of domestic genre fiction and a narrative of religious quest. The novel simultaneously traces the emotional impact of adultery and divorce and thematizes the spiritual hungers of the 1990s; indeed, its eve-of-millennium publication in America was surely no coincidence. The turn towards theological questions in both popular culture and in more abstract philosophical debate is played out in the novel's movement between private space (the painful failure of a marriage) and the public sphere (the mass media and legal system). Questions of personal belief – including devout Catholicism, radical atheism and easy-going agnosticism – are torn from their safely privatized domestic, professional or clerical spaces and forced into the public domain. The narrative hinges on the testimony of a seven-year-old child, Faith White, who suddenly experiences visions of a supernatural 'guard', recites biblical passages that she has never previously encountered and appears able to work miracles. Her mysterious religious fervour, whatever the evidence of the 'miracles', should be explicable in psychoanalytic terms as a response to the trauma of her parents' divorce. A legal case is brought to prove that the so-called visions are the product of abuse by her mother, who has a history of severe depression. The custody trial, a trope of domestic fiction, becomes an arena for debating the authenticity of Faith's 'miracles'. The novel also reso-nates with specifically American anxieties about the public role of religion, including separation of Church and State and the allegedly absolute distinction between privately held convictions and their place in political life. The court becomes an exemplary secular space that is haunted by the spectre of the sacred at the level of form and content: its hierarchical structure is quasi-religious with the judge a secular equivalent to God; Picoult also uses the court, in the novel's denouement, to stage a debate about the role of belief in contem-porary life. Faith, quite literally, is put on trial. Picoult's emphasis on testimony echoes, consciously or otherwise, Hume's critique of the miraculous. Yet the novel frustrates readerly expectations in what appears to be an otherwise realist narrative: rational explanations for Faith's experiences are simultaneously pos-ited and undermined; secular ideals, including psychoanalysis, medicine and the law are subject to the same scrutiny as the excesses of religious zeal.

Faith White herself embodies the tradition of the uncanny child in US fiction that dates back to the first novel of the American Renaissance, Nathaniel Hawthorne's *The Scarlet Letter* (1850). Like Hester Prynne's spiritually ambigu-ous daughter, Pearl, Faith is granted a disconcertingly symbolic name and regarded by her community with a fusion of superstitious awe and hostility. Their alleged associations with the spirit world – seventeenth-century Bosto-nians suspect Pearl of traffic with the Devil; Faith is hailed as a visionary and healer by her millennial disciples – distance these children from the earthly concerns of their parents. Yet both children become the locus of adult conflict regarding (appropriately enough) fidelity, psychological stability, inheritance and religious freedom. If Picoult's debt to Hawthorne's romance is less explicit than that consciously owned by John Updike, discussed in the previous chapter, and John Irving, the focus of the next, *The Scarlet Letter* nevertheless remains the urtext for all American fiction dealing with faith, freedom and sexual ethics.

Rhidian Brook's *The Testimony of Taliesin Jones* (1996) echoes Picoult's focus on a child's discovery of the miraculous amid the routine disappointments and failures of family life. It is both a rites of passage story about the loss of 'the pecu-liar gift of childhood – that ability to live completely in the present' and an evocation of faith awakened by miraculous healing.[29] Brook's first novel also shares with *Keeping Faith* and *How to Be Good* the narrative catalyst of domestic trauma to explore larger questions of religious identity and the possibility of faith in a sceptical era. Where Picoult and Hornby's novels concentrate on the consequences of adult transgression, *The Testimony of Taliesin Jones* offers a more vivid impression of the interior life of a child who rediscovers faith following his parents' separation. Taliesin Jones is an insecure, bookish eleven-year-old boy whose tranquil existence in a South Wales village has been disturbed by the sudden departure of his mother. This maternal absence, regarded by his older brother as an unforgivable betrayal, coupled with his father's depression, prompts Taliesin to ask agonized questions about the loving God whose presence in the world he has always taken for granted. Taliesin's simple faith, which he finds difficult to articulate or to defend in the crucible of the classroom, is tested by the mockery or indifference of his peers, his father's bitter doubt and the unashamed belief of his schoolmate Julie Dyer. In Taliesin's imagination, informed by the allegorical vision of George Orwell and his *Illustrated Bible*, Julie Dyer is not just a precocious schoolgirl on whom he and the entire school has a crush, but a fearless Welsh Eve who would 'definitely . . . have plucked the apple . . . And she would not have hidden her shame when God reprimanded her' (*TTJ*, p. 29).

Spirituality, as figured in Brook's novel, is a matter of risk, a challenge to authority, rather than a form of conservative consolation. The novel, like *How to Be Good*, features a faith healer who acts as a catalyst for a renewed intimation that religious belief, difficult to defend in an era that celebrates the visible, is possible. However, 'Evans the Touch' (Rhidian's piano teacher with a reputation as a gifted healer) differs from the equivalent figures in Hornby's novel and *Keeping Faith*: he has neither the casual, if naive arrogance of GoodNews, nor Faith's lack of religious background. Billy Evans is self-effacing and keen to give God the credit for any miraculous healing; where GoodNews charges for his gift, Billy refuses all offers of payment. He is a mentor figure as well as a healer: Taliesin's assumptions about faith healing are conditioned by folkloric traditions of 'the clichés of magic' but Billy demystifies his own power: his acts of healing are not a 'spell' but 'a prayer. It's simple. You could do it' (*TTJ*, p. 58). The novel rejects even a tacit Gnosticism and instead subtly draws on a theology of incarnation. 'Evans the Touch' is no guru; he neither dispenses complex spiritual formulae nor performs elaborate rituals, but is an ordinary man whose own body is growing old and frail. The narrative emphasizes that the healing acts for which Evans is a conduit take place within the everyday, amid the clutter of the mundane. In an echo of Rushdie's suggestion that the miraculous needs to emerge alongside the mundane, ordinary people are unostentatiously healed 'Right here in this stuffy bungalow . . . It is a sweet music of possibility and it is playing here in his village . . . here in this very normal, very dull place that doesn't even feature in his atlas' (*TTJ*, p. 62). The novel suggests that the miraculous is a phenomenon that quietly, barely perceptibly, persists in an age more concerned with spectacle and simulation than the sensuous reality of being incarnate.

Picoult, Hornby and Brook all draw on the tradition of literary romance. 'Romance is full of marvels,' states Terry Eagleton, 'whereas the modern novel is nothing if not mundane'.[30] *Keeping Faith*, in the tradition of romance, is replete with 'marvels' but it is also a narrative of the quotidian, 'the mundane'. Ordinary details of suburban, late-twentieth-century life vie with vatic experiences. This is also true of Hornby's *How to Be Good*: the novelist's contemporary North London landscape, the geography to which his fiction continually returns, is not typically the locus of 'signs and wonders' but, as with DeLillo's Bronx tale, the urban setting of what Katie Carr only semi-ironically names 'the Finsbury Park Miracle' heightens the sense of wonder (*HTBG*, p. 126). In this sense, Picoult and Hornby's novels undo the binary that Eagleton proposes between the 'secular, empirical world' of realist fiction and the 'mythical or metaphysical' space of romance. Indeed, though many of their characters are as 'wary of the abstract and eternal' and equally invested in the world of the senses as reasonable, modern fiction, *Keeping Faith* and *How to Be Good* refuse to close the connections between the mythic and the everyday.[31]

Robertson's *The Testament of Gideon Mack* offers a subtle critique of the traditions of literary romance. Gideon Mack's father, an unyieldingly Puritanical Church of Scotland minister, owns a complete collection of Sir Walter Scott's fiction, the pages of which remain uncut until Gideon enthusiastically takes them up in his youth. The Reverend Mack believes that Scott distorted history by defaming 'the Covenanters in *Old Mortality*'; this view was accepted as truth by subsequent generations:

> The Victorians then were like Americans now. They thought the story of the world was theirs, and that it had been written by authors like Scott. It is the great danger of romance: too many people succumb to it, and forget the one true Author.[32]

Romance, for this Puritan reader, represents an unholy, heretical challenge to divine authority. Yet for other, less theologically inclined critics, romance is problematic for aesthetic and intellectual reasons. In the early 1970s Gillian Beer noted that literary 'romance' had degenerated into a genre of 'subliterature' that included 'lightweight commercial fiction deliberately written to flatter day dreams'. However much the earlier, lofty mode of romance might have deteriorated, Beer is also quick to observe that the 'circulating libraries provided a plentiful flow of wish-fulfilment literature in the late eighteenth and nineteenth centuries'.[33] *Keeping Faith* might readily be dismissed as 'wish-fulfilment literature' – or by Gideon Mack's virulently anti-American father as irreligious – but in subtle and unexpected ways it also displays an awareness of the complexities of representing theological ideas. This novel-romance never capitulates to secular or sacred orthodoxies, but tests the limits of both discourses in a narrative that is, by turns, melodramatic, sentimental and admirably open-ended.

A 'Damascene Conversion' Without God

Picoult's liberal, agnostic approach to the representation of religious experience is shared by Hornby's narrative, though his interpretation of post-secular spiritual yearning is considerably more caustic. A significant distinction between these American and British narratives of the miraculous is the status that they grant to religious language and its continuing relevance. Where Faith's visions, depending on one's perspective, have explicitly religious connotations, David Carr's conversion from petulant cynic to born-again humanitarian is rooted in ethical questions and consciously evades questions of transcendent meaning. In fact, David and Katie are openly hostile to the possibility of supernatural experience. He describes his encounter with GoodNews as a viscerally emotional experience but one tempered by the desire to resist its spiritual implications: '[GoodNews] said it was pure love. And that's what it felt like. Do you understand how panicky it made me feel?' (*HTBG*, p. 70). This description, in which bodily sensation and spiritual yearning converge, typifies a paradigm of affective or 'affectional' religious conversion.[34] Indeed, a biblical lexis of radical personal change is extended when Katie describes the change in her husband's behaviour as a 'Damascene conversion' and David himself claims that the 'scales have fallen from my eyes' (*HTBG*, p. 120, p, 123). These allusions connect David's story of instantaneous transformation with the paradigmatic Christian conversion narrative of Saul/Paul on the road to Damascus in Acts 9. A further signifier of conversion is David's statement of repentance and the desire for personal reform: 'The first thing I thought afterwards was that I had to do everything differently. Everything. What I have been doing isn't enough' (*HTBG*, p. 70). Yet David's new-found compassion, necessitating a pious asceticism that has material implications for his family when he starts to discard their possessions, is not rooted in any particular religious creed; his conversion appears to be thoroughly post-religious. Although Katie states that her husband resembles 'someone who has undergone a religious conversion', David is clear that he has not become a Christian: 'I don't believe in Heaven, or anything. But I want to be the kind of person that qualifies for entry anyway' (*HTBG*, p. 77, p. 123).

The novel uses David's godless, rather sour conversion to test the ethical failures of the age. God might be absent from the middle-class world of *How To Be Good* but Hornby's astute novel addresses the crisis of liberal ethics in a post-ideological age. 'I'm becoming heartily sick of liberalism,' states Katie. 'I want certitude' (*HTBG*, p. 125). Is it possible to be a moral person without some clearly defined creed? What is the relationship between personal freedom and collective responsibility? For who am I responsible? In fact, Katie's narrative, her personal quest, resonates most with the biblical question: who is my neighbour? Before his sudden 'Damascene conversion', David has been writing a novel, *The Green Keepers*, a sour-sounding satire of 'Britain's post-Diana touchy-feely culture' (*HTBG*, p. 12). Is this self-parody on Hornby's part? This allusion to the emotional response to the death of the Princess of Wales – variously regarded as evidence of a new ability of the British to express emotion or final proof of the manipulative reach of the mass media – is revealing. 'Cynicism is our shared common language,' notes Katie (*HTBG*, p. 131). This echoes what Douglas Coupland, in *Generation X*, named 'Knee-Jerk Irony'.[35] Hornby's title is a reference to the book that David and GoodNews decide to write: a new secular bible that will help floundering free-thinkers such as themselves to act ethically. These ideas echo the central argument of

Alasdair MacIntyre's *After Virtue* (1981), which asserts that 'the language and the appearances of morality persist even though the integral substance of morality has to a large degree been fragmented and then in part destroyed'.[36]

Hornby's novel suggests that one of the reasons for the fragmentation of coherent morality is the decline of institutional religion. Although its narrator displays sceptical instincts about spirituality – GoodNews might be able to heal people but he is also rude, impractical and manipulative – she is also nostalgic for a faith that has never properly belonged to her. For example, David's miraculous conversion leads Katie to consider the deeply unfashionable issue of personal sin: 'When I look at my sins ... I can see the appeal of born-again Christianity. I suspect that it's not the Christianity that is so alluring; it's the rebirth' (*HTBG*, p. 181). This desire to transcend the limits of her liberalism, a world view that no longer seems adequate, prompts Katie to attend her local Anglican church. The experience both confirms her prejudices about the rather mildewed state of contemporary, non-vital religion and helps her to escape the urgent questions of faith. For example, she is unsurprised and reassured that the 'kindly middle-aged' vicar appears to be 'vaguely ashamed of her beliefs' but rather let down by the absence of anything resembling spirituality (*HTBG*, p. 186). 'It feels a long way from God,' reflects Katie, concluding that 'this may have been God's house once ... but He's clearly moved, shut up shop, gone to a place where there's more demand for that sort of thing' (*HTBG*, p. 187).

Rhidian Brook includes a similar encounter with organized religion in *The Testimony of Taliesin Jones*, in which the protagonist is also disappointed by an alienating experience of public worship. The remote Welsh chapel, like Hornby's urban Anglican church, is austere and rather colourless, a place that inspires doubt rather than faith. 'Is this really the place where God lives?' asks Taliesin (*TTJ*, p. 117, p. 112). Neither novel is particularly anti-clerical, but both reflect an enduring sense that the visible church is an unsatisfactory, even discouraging, version of what is alleged to be the body of Christ. However, the biblical passages read in these vaguely dispiriting places of worship exemplify vital issues for both novels. Taliesin hears the story of the raising of Lazarus from death (John 11.1–44), the most striking incident of miraculous healing in the gospels which in its public reading becomes emblematic of Brook's emphasis on spiritual revival. In *How to Be Good*, the sermon is clumsy and embarrassing, but its associated text from St Paul ('Charity vaunteth not itself', 1 Corinthians 13) nevertheless thematizes the novel's chief concern, the tension between superficial, visible righteousness and genuine integrity (*HTBG*, p. 189). The Pauline idea becomes a motif in the narrative, repeated in a song by Lauryn Hill and sung off-key by a child; in Hornby's world, any faint hope of the sacred is hidden in such tiny, apparently random, fragments. Big theological or ethical gestures, he implies, are likely to reflect egotism while smaller, less ambitious attempts to grasp meaning can be fragile conduits for a kind of secular grace.

Religion, however, is not easily contained in the narrative. In one of the multiple coincidences and unexpected meetings on which realist fiction of this sort has always depended, Katie later meets the rather eccentric Anglican priest in her own surgery. The bereaved female cleric is angry with God ('I hate the people I work for ... especially the boss') and her inflamed body is a sign of these normally repressed religious anxieties (*HTBG*, p. 202). What might have been a moment of mutual sympathy between two professional women struggling with similar pastoral roles becomes a gloomily comic collision between the rival stories of science and religion. Neither priest nor doctor is able to offer the comfort and assurance that they assume are integral to their respective vocations. The representative of the church even appears surprised to discover that 'doctors have spiritual crises' and the GP, rather improbably, demands that her counterpart give her unequivocal advice regarding the future of her marriage. Katie's encounter with religion is disappointing but this is partly because she wants it to grant her an absolution beyond its gift; she wants release, not from sin but from the burden of free choice. The liberalism that seems unsatisfactory to answer the multiple ills of modernity – poverty, violence, moral complacency – prompts both Katie and her husband to seek faith with conclusive, non-negotiable answers. David's new-found radical ethics have no real theological ground and his lack of specific religious belief is as clear as his unqualified moral conviction. By contrast, Katie, who appears more nostalgic for some lost era of coherent social faith, looks to the Church of England for answers. Her bitter evaluation of the 'woolly minded nonsense' that she finds merely mimics the mess of ordinary lives and reveals a longing for transcendent truths: 'It's no wonder the churches are empty, when you can't answer even the simplest questions. Don't you get it? That's what we want. Answers' (*HTBG*, p. 204). The vicar – timid, confused and faltering – is simply too human to satisfy this doctor's desire for absolute moral assurance. Katie goes looking for divine forgiveness in the established church but finds that the church itself has lost any defining sense of the spiritual.

'Seeing God'

In *Keeping Faith*, by contrast, this crisis is inverted when rational, non-religious people are haunted by an unasked for and troubling vision of God. Picoult's novel, like *How to Be Good*, focuses on characters without any particular religious commitments. Faith's given name is ironic since she has been brought up without specific religious beliefs: she is the child of a mixed marriage, with a nominally Christian father (who, we are told, is able to track his lineage back to the earliest Puritan settlers) and a non-practising Jewish mother. Faith White, whose full name appears to encode religious autonomy, should be a child of confident, secular modernity in that she has not been forced to follow a particular tradition of worship. Indeed, Faith does not even understand her (perhaps not coincidentally Roman Catholic) psychiatrist's enquiry regarding prayer as she has no inherited spiritual vocabulary. Yet the narrative offers a series of uncanny experiences that both fall short of blatant supernaturalism and undermine reductive explanations: for example, in conversation with her psychiatrist, she names specific Catholic saints ('Herman Joseph, from Steinfeld. Elizabeth, from Schonau. Juliana Falconieri') of whom her 'guard' has spoken.[37] One of the novel's most provocative devices regards the precise nature of Faith's alleged visions: her psychiatrist suggests that the phonetic similarities between the word 'guard' (the name that Faith claims her uncanny visitor gives herself) and 'God' are not coincidental. Faith, according to this representative of scientific reason, is not seeing any standard angel but divinity itself: 'Your daughter . . . I think she's seeing God' (*KF*, p. 51). Her 'guard' also appears to be female. It is this gendering of the Godhead that most upsets the orthodox religious authorities. Picoult is not only concerned with testing the secular limits of modern fiction but also with questioning the linguistic conventions that govern the representation of God. Traditional, dominantly masculine images are undermined and, though the narrative never quite fulfils its potential feminist critique of the tradition, *Keeping Faith* is energized by debates regarding incarnation, divinity and gender. Picoult affords theological discussion more room than is ordinary in contemporary fiction, not solely by the broader questions that Faith's story provokes, but in sequences such as a live Larry King television debate between a conservative Catholic theologian and a more liberal-minded rabbi. Television, a rival narrative form to the novel, is vital in the construction of American identity, both secular and sacred, and the sequence allows Picoult to test theological claims in a way that ordinary narrative might not. The debate, which ranges from the differences between Jewish and Christian accounts of Messianism, echoes DeLillo's representation of the internet as a quasi-sacred force. Technology, once more, is caught up with the language of transcendence and miracle.

Muted Millennialism

Whether or not Faith's supernatural visitor is female or merely a feminized image of Christ (as one theological sophisticate suggests), the narrative continually plays with readerly expectation. The 'guard'/'God' also allegedly prompts the visionary child to seek out a book whose author Faith names, in her childish handwriting, as 'I. I. Swerbeh'. A librarian, who conveniently has a background in early years education, recognizes the reversed lettering as Hebrews 11. 'Now faith is the substance of things hoped for . . . the evidence of things not seen', states the unnamed writer of this New Testament epistle (*KF*, p. 59). The fact that the White family 'don't even own a Bible' heightens the potential mystical charge of the moment but also exploits the ways in which such biblical ideas are deeply embedded in supposedly secular American culture (*KF*, p. 59). In *Keeping Faith*, Picoult emphasizes the simultaneous absence *and* presence of God in the public arena: Faith's unexpected knowledge of scripture cannot be a classroom discovery since such explicitly religious material has no place in the secular space of an American school. By contrast, in Brook's

Testimony Taliesin's experience of faith is shaped, in part, by a progressive Religious Education teacher who encourages her pupils to debate their personal beliefs. Both novels, however, prioritize questions of why people continue to believe in 'the evidence of things unseen' and how they choose to articulate such convictions. 'My family, well, we didn't go to church,' recalls Mariah White, 'but we didn't go to temple either'. Mariah's religious autobiography is a classically American narrative of the outsider. She cannot readily accept her own mother's pragmatic promise that their Jewish identity signified God's blessing; she is not baptized but neither does she feel 'Chosen' (*KF*, p. 247). In this rhetoric of covenant, a language deployed both in Jewish and Puritan tradition, Picoult's novel addresses a distinctively American anxiety about inclusion and segregation, the hope of a promised land and the loss of New World utopianism. The novel also limns more specifically contemporary, conservative American anxieties about the disintegration of the nuclear family and the fierce arena of sexual politics but its New Hampshire setting, replete with the ghosts of Puritan exiles, is also a clue to its more emblematic theological interests. This sense of exile is echoed in L'Heureux's more specifically Catholic narrative: Father LeBlanc, an exile in New Hampshire, is described as 'typically American' because he 'doesn't come from anyplace at all; he has no background, no roots, no parish'. The pragmatic Father Moriarty, facing a slow death and confined to bed, resentfully refers to this young, spiritually restless priest as 'Huck Finn in clerics' (*TM*, p. 37).

The spiritual geography of Guterson's *Our Lady of the Forest*, by contrast, is associated with the opposite coast of the USA. 'And of course this is happening in the American West,' reflects the novel's most cynical voice: 'Where else but the West Coast for this insane behaviour?'[38] The shared chronology of the novels – both *Keeping Faith* and *Our Lady of the Forest* are primarily set in the autumn of 1999 – is a reminder of the muted millennialism that haunts these texts. In giving specific 'real world' dates to the key events of their novels, Picoult and Guterson draw a relation between ordinary chronology and 'kairotic' time: temporality collides with eternity, any alleged miracles occur within the routine, clock-time of the everyday. Millennialism, for both novelists, is as much a matter of the mundane as it is the miraculous.

Guterson's novel also echoes Picoult's narrative in its focus on an unlikely female visionary: Ann Holmes, a homeless sixteen year old whose young life, like that of Esmeralda in DeLillo's *Underworld*, has been marred by abuse and neglect, claims to have been visited by the Virgin Mary whilst working as a piece-work mushroom picker deep in the forest of a depressed logging town in Washington State. Ann, like Faith White, has had no religious upbringing and is in a tradition of holy outsiders, figures regarded with suspicion by ecclesiastical authorities but elevated to the status of true visionary by the crowds of ordinary people who follow them. Indeed, though her bricoleur's bag of beliefs constitutes an eclectic Roman Catholicism, this adolescent visionary, a woman who claims to have been given a chastening vision of the mother of Jesus, is an echo of a celebrated seventeenth-century Puritan outcast. Anne Hutchinson

(1591–1643) was banished from Massachusetts in the late 1630s as a result of her conflict with the Puritan authorities, who accused her of propagating antinomian heresies. If Ann Holmes's name is a subtle reminder of this lineage of persecuted female American prophets so too is her escalating conflict with the authorities, both secular and sacred. For her self-styled 'disciple' Carolyn – a cynical drifter ready to exploit the visions for her own financial gain – Ann is simply 'the perfect victim of masculine authority' (*OLOTF*, p. 127). Ann, like many visionary figures, is associated not with the establishment but with those on the margins. She is no orator and with her slight, feverish frame, neither is she an imposing figure of muscular Christian belief but an embodiment of 'how the meek inherited the earth, the beggar, the thief, the whore, the dope addict, the vagabond, the pauper, the crucified' (*OLOTF*, p. 134). She also belongs to the tradition of the suffering servant – a feminized Christ figure, physically beleaguered and besieged by demands from believers and sceptics alike – a person 'inexplicably tormented by the invisible contents of the world' (*OLOTF*, pp. 135–6).

Yet *Our Lady of the Forest* is not simply concerned with the authenticity of Ann's miracles and, indeed, it is clear from the outset that her visions are likely to be the result of psilocybin trips from magic mushrooms or delusions induced by severe depression; rather, the novel focuses on the effects that the belief in these visions has on the wider community. Father Collins, for example, the town's young, liberal and idealistic priest is, in a familiar trope of religiously themed fiction, attracted by the purity of this unbaptized visionary and sexually attracted to her. He is, however, unconvinced that Ann's visions have a divine origin and requires 'hard evidence . . . facts and circumstances that appeared . . . incontrovertible' (*OLOTF*, p. 195). Ann's claims precipitate a crisis in the priest's faith since the 'hard evidence' that he demands of this homeless visionary is not even available to substantiate his Roman Catholic belief. Guterson uses this improbable saint – 'unkempt, dishevelled, incandescent' – to emblematize the spiritual hungers of the era: the town of North Fork is both economically impoverished and without a point of common reference (*OLOTF*, pp. 154–5). 'Ann of Oregon', as she reluctantly becomes, appears to renew the identity of the town, as thousands flock to encounter this new visionary.

Marketing the Miraculous

Both *Our Lady of the Forest* and Picoult's *Keeping Faith* explore a mode of religious hysteria that challenges the theory that secure secularity defines modern Western culture. In 1989 Robert Wuthnow claimed that 'the religion practiced by an increasing number of Americans may be entirely of their own manufacture – a kind of eclectic synthesis of Christianity, popular psychology, *Reader's Digest* folklore, and personal superstitions, all wrapped up in the anecdotes of the individual's biography'.[39] Written and set a decade after

Wuthnow's research, both *Keeping Faith* and *Our Lady of the Forest* are replete with such blurred religion, neither wholly privatized nor rigidly traditional. In Guterson's narrative, the forest is transformed by thousands of pilgrims who, like *Underworld*'s Jeff Shay, follow news of modern miracles online. Although the majority of these visitors are Catholic, the heavily ritualized 'apparition site' resonates with postmodern ideas of detraditionalized spirituality. The place of Ann's visions, ironically marked out with bureaucratic flags, is a site on which multiple forms of worship, not all of them Christian, converge. The organic forest, with its plural reminders of timelessness and mortality, is littered with evidence of the human desire for eternity and transcendence:

> A delirious photosynthetic rapture suffused the air of the place . . . [the apparition site] had been indicated further with a plastic crucifix propped against a tree, with votive candles, medals, chaplets, plastic water bottles, an Immaculate Heart of Mary figurine, a display of carefully separated orange segments . . . everything set in a bed of plucked ferns so that spot now looked like a holy site animists recently proselytized . . . A shrine in accord and perfectly organic; a tabernacle of totems. (*OLOTF*, p. 148)

Similarly, in *Keeping Faith*, news of Faith's visions and rumours of her ability to work miracles precipitate a vast, eclectic pilgrimage to her home which becomes both shrine and prison. Picoult uses her diverse crowd of spiritual seekers in a more explicitly polyphonic manner than Guterson. The conflict of interpretations offered by a veritable Babel of Catholic priests, evangelical atheists, mystic Jewish groups and feminist theologians resonates with the history of American religious diversity and debate. Where the novels overlap, however, is in their account of the desperate need of so many modern Americans to believe the miracle stories that surround these vulnerable young women. The absurd spectacle surrounding Faith White's home in New Hampshire, and the North Fork forest where Ann Holmes claims to have been spoken to by the Virgin Mary, echoes David Hume's withering assessment of public insatiability for the miraculous. 'The *avidum genus auricularum*, the gazing populace,' notes Hume, 'receive greedily, without examination, whatever soothes superstition, and promotes wonder'.[40] Historically, the promotion of wonder is also a good business opportunity. The fact that 'Evans the Touch' in Brook's novel, for example, refuses payment for his 'gift' is a surprise to the more sceptical people in Taliesin's world: 'Are you sure he's not one of these charlatans making a bit of money out of innocents?' (*TTJ*, p. 95). If Ann and Faith have no interest in the spiritual cash nexus, less devotional figures in their respective (but temporally parallel) worlds are ready to exploit the religious appetites of the 'gazing populace'. In *Keeping Faith*, the child becomes a viable commercial property for the mass media. Her home is surrounded by television cameras ready to snatch an image of this ready-made prophet, healer or possible messiah as a form of cultural capital. Guterson's narrative also suggests that spirituality is for sale: religious bric-a-brac is sold by opportunists in an economically gloomy town. One

Catholic character muses on the propriety of selling 'Holy Water in a Wal-Mart plastic bottle', to which he receives the pragmatic reply: 'That's America' (*OLOTF*, p. 281).

Agnostic Advocates

Although both novels, and *Keeping Faith* in particular, are able to accommodate the mystical alongside the mundane, neither narrative is a simple justification of postmodern spirituality. In fact, the mythic motifs in these narratives are subject to internal critique that defies the supposed 'evidence' of their accounts of miraculous events. In the former, Faith – both the titular visionary and in the sense of the biblical virtue that she supposedly represents – is mirrored by a sceptical antagonist in the figure of Ian Fletcher. Picoult's late-twentieth-century incarnation of Hume is no philosopher but instead 'the world's first tele-atheist', a man whose righteously anti-religious programmes aim to discredit any so-called supernatural phenomena as illusions or hoaxes (*KF*, p. 28). In Fletcher, Picoult has created a compellingly unholy hybrid: he preaches with a revivalist's charisma, offering his congregation not eternal salvation but a Richard Dawkins-style empirical unbelief schooled in Humean scepticism. This tenacious, evangelical atheist appears to embody a repressed legacy of eighteenth-century rationalism in US culture. Fletcher's doctorate in theology from Harvard connects him with a tradition of sceptical, academic thought and his aggressive approach to the supernatural ('I'm going to rip apart all these so-called miracles') ironically echoes the fervent, conversion-focused sermons of figures such as Billy Graham (*KP*, pp. 28–9). Fletcher's touring show, 'the world's first antirevival', is dedicated to exposing alleged visionaries and miracle-workers such as Faith as fraudulent. His methods, however, are less empirical and coolly objective than his public persona would suggest: he relies on ethically dubious investigative techniques but more importantly his argument is equally dependent on his viewers' faith in his own powers of persuasion. Indeed, his charisma and rhetoric are reminiscent of David Johnson's argument that the success of Hume's essay against the miraculous is entirely a product of its author's rhetorical skill:

> [T]he view that there is in Hume's essay, or what can be reconstructed from it, any argument or reply or objection that is even superficially good, much less, powerful or devastating, is simply a philosophical myth. The mostly willing hearers who have been swayed by Hume on this matter have been held captive by nothing other than Hume's great eloquence.[41]

Our Lady of the Forest has, in Carolyn Greer, an equivalent figure to Ian Fletcher. She holds similarly contemptuous views about religion, privately describing herself as a 'secular humanist' and 'material girl' who ridicules 'these Christians with their myriad insanities' including any belief in 'God's *son*, of all things': 'So what does that leave? Nothing, I guess. All I can say at Saint Peter's Gate is, I'm sorry, I went with Mexico and Science, Darwin and margaritas' (*OLOTF*, p. 317). Publicly, however, she becomes the timid visionary's spokesperson, gleefully trading on the rhetorical style of fundamentalist preachers in order to exploit the credulity of the crowd. Carolyn is, like the 'teleatheist', eloquent and financially motivated but also displays still less integrity than Picoult's arch sceptic. This burnt out traveller takes a quasi-maternal interest in Ann Holmes but her barely concealed inspiration is far from spiritual. Yet she occupies a significant position in the narrative's engagement with the postmodern religious impulse. Like Fletcher, Carolyn has a clearer critical insight into the implications of the phenomenon than any other character: the priests have their own agendas related to personal feeling or ecclesiastical duty and the pilgrims appear ready to believe in Ann's visions regardless of evidence. Carolyn's assessment of Ann's new status could be derived from a field study of postmodern religion: 'You're Madonna or somebody ... You're an all-American cult leader ... It's a completely Dada spectacle. It's Hieronymous Bosch on Budweiser' (*OLOTF*, p. 125). Ann's visions might be of the mother of Christ but for Carolyn, and for many sceptical readers, her own influence is closer to an altogether less pious iteration of the Madonna. Similarly, Ann describes holy visions but their mediation turns them into something closer to postmodern spectacle, what Jean Baudrillard describes as a simulation without authentic origin.

   Both Picoult and Guterson suggest that neither the church nor civic institutions provide an adequate home for the unpredictable spiritual yearning of post-secular culture. The secular fundamentalism and opportunistic New Age spirituality of Ian Fletcher and Carolyn Greer, respectively, are not the only sceptical positions represented in the two novels. The hierarchy of the Roman Catholic Church is similarly keen to disprove Faith's burgeoning status as an authentic visionary, particularly since her visions imply that God is female. The liberal and practical parish priest, Father MacReady, is contrasted with the supercilious theologian, Father Rampini, an emissary of the bishop, who functions as the voice of Christian orthodoxy. Ironically, this man of faith reads 'Faith' via a carefully honed version of the hermeneutics of suspicion: he asserts that her visions of God cannot be real since they contradict Church teaching ('there's no way He would appear in the form of a woman') and are more likely to be the product of 'a mild hysteria' (*KF*, p. 211). *Our Lady of the Forest* deploys a similar pairing of a sympathetic (if, in this case, sceptical) priest and an authoritarian, morally superior theologian, keen to dismiss the phenomenon of Ann's visions. In Guterson's novel, Father Collins represents a rather vulnerable, liberal version of belief, shaped by an incarnational encounter with ordinary believers, a tradition that is offset by Father Butler, who is appalled by the crowd of witnesses to 'Ann of Oregon'. Butler views the eclectic liturgy of the forest pilgrims as utterly unorthodox: 'These people are closet polytheists ... This is *not* Catholicism' (*OLOTF*, p. 255). In both novels the authoritarian instincts of institutional Christianity come into conflict with the less refined spirituality of the theological nomads who roam contemporary America and, more specifically, the pages of millennial fiction. Their shared emphasis on the return of repressed miracle stories resonates both with the narrative of secularization in the Western mind and the rival story of sacrilization. If the portrait of the Roman Catholic communion, and the priesthood specifically, is less than flattering, *Our Lady of the Forest* is no less scathing about secular opportunism.

Keeping Faith questions the rhetorics of belief and radical unbelief: the orthodox figures, Jewish and Christian, who try to determine the nature of Faith cannot arrive at a simple judgement; similarly, Ian Fletcher is unable to reconcile his experience in the company of Faith with his rigidly materialist belief system. Determined to debunk the miraculous powers of one individual and thereby to strengthen his personal crusade against religion, this antagonistic unbeliever witnesses a series of phenomena that demand he change his world view. In this sense, Picoult's narrative follows the pattern of many conversion stories as Fletcher moves from outright scepticism to something like belief. This plot is also reliant on tropes more specific to romantic genre fiction than to the Puritan conversion narrative. For example, Picoult uses the device of the family secret to test the limits of credulity and its reverse. Ian's apparently carefully reasoned atheism is revealed to be rooted in his inability to reconcile belief in a loving God with his twin brother's acute autism. Fletcher's professional, unyielding disbelief is radically altered by the 'evidence' of Faith's apparent ability to work miracles when, after a brief meeting with Faith, his withdrawn, obsessive brother is able to express himself without anger or fear. However, this shift is not a conventional religious conversion, nor a fully fledged movement from doubt to commitment, but recognition that reason itself has boundaries and limits. Indeed, Fletcher's 'conversion', if we can call it that, is to a much earlier model of American civic values. He, like the Enlightenment-influenced signatories of the Declaration of Independence, offers a privatized version of religion: 'I'm up here going out on a limb to tell you that God is nobody's business but your own', he tells a crowd of journalists (*KF*, p. 418). This volte-face by a modern-day Hume presents an ambivalent defence of religious freedom that might also be read as an argument for the privatization of belief. Ultimately, the novel is able to 'keep faith' only by making a clear distinction between secular and sacred and private and public spheres.

Conclusion: Transformative Miracles

'To be a miracle an event must contribute significantly toward a holy divine purpose for the world,' argues Richard Swinburne.[42] Do any of these twenty-first-century fictions of the miraculous contribute to such a purpose? Or might they be read as further evidence of the impossibility of reading the world in religious terms? The ending of each novel encodes a particular attitude toward the meaning of their 'miracles'. In L'Heureux's *The Miracle*, the resurrected Mandy dies for a second time, this time in a road accident but without resurrection. Father LeBlanc, who struggles to understand the nature of these events, falls in love and leaves the priesthood. This romantic resolution is not entirely faithless, however: the narrative suggests that LeBlanc will continue to wrestle with his faith, but will no longer create an idol of his own holiness. *Keeping Faith* and *How to Be Good*, by contrast, both feature what we might read as anti-epiphanies, moments in which meaning disappears or mutates from a sense of wonder to one of blankness and grief. Their similarly ambiguous endings encode an agnostic refusal to commit to belief. In Picoult's novel, Faith, the child visionary, afflicted by stigmata and close to death, is restored to health – and to her the care of her mother – but the omniscient narrator unambiguously reveals her to be feigning conversation with her 'guard': 'Faith continues to talk to no one at all ... until she is certain that nobody is listening' (*KF*, p. 422). This manufactured or performed theophany might be evidence that the 'guard'/'God' was simply the product of an unhappy child's imagination, a cry for attention. Yet it is also a reminder of the dominant traditions of prayer in the major world religions, conducted as acts of faith, that persist without the convenient reassurance of a visible embodiment of the divine by one's side. Hornby's novel ends with an image of domestic connection, as the reunited Carr family attempt to fix the roof in a storm. It is a sweet moment, an epiphanic 'spark' but one that is subverted when 'just at the wrong moment' Katie catches 'a glimpse of the night sky' and sees 'that there's nothing out there at all' (*HTBG*, p. 244). The divine reassurance that Katie sought in church and in ethical action is negated in the novel's final words.

The end of *Our Lady of the Forest* also plays on the tradition of ambivalent epiphany. Tom Cross, a violent misogynist whose cruciform surname is a sign of his family's acute suffering, is the novel's counterpoint to its teenage female visionary. He demands a miracle from this frail visionary, a request she is unable to grant. Guterson creates a tableau of Ann and Cross together in the church, the visionary and the desperate criminal side by side, like the two thieves at Calvary, as a statue of Christ on the cross hangs above them (*OLOTF*, p. 328). In a parody of the conversion of Saul/Paul, Tom is blinded by a pepper spray (*OLOTF*, p. 331). This crisis moment fuses what Maltby views as two entirely distinct modes of 'visionary moment': 'redemptive' and 'catastrophic' revelation. In his 'postmodern critique' of epiphany, Maltby argues that these categories of vision share key characteristics including suddenness, brevity, an emphasis on mystical 'insight' and a belief that such a moment represents 'the communication of pure and transcendent knowledge'. The distinction that he draws between 'redemptive' and 'catastrophic' visions is that the former 'signifies a transfiguration or regeneration of the subject' while the latter 'is marked by a sense of spiritual desolation'.[43] However, in the ambiguous ending to Guterson's narrative, Tom, violently 'introduced to illuminating blindness', is both utterly bereft and witness to an inward change:

He flailed in search of the visionary's presence but the ordinary world had abandoned him . . . What did all his suffering mean? Imprisoned as he was behind his eyelids he beheld a light as thorough as darkness. Mother of God, he prayed silently. Be inside me now. (*OLOTF*, p. 331)

Tom's penitence coincides with Ann's sudden death: Guterson exploits the Christian narrative of personal sacrifice and vicarious suffering. In an epilogue, set twelve months after the principal narrative, a church has been built to honour the dead visionary. Commerce and religion continue to collide in this conclusion as the economically revived town now bears the 'marketing slogan The Lourdes of the Northwest Rain Forest' (*OLOTF*, p. 338). Indeed, Carolyn Greer, the novel's most cynical voice, returns to comment that the church itself, like the alleged miraculous visions, is a sacred simulation, final evidence that the real has been overtaken by artifice: 'Phenathol's behind this massive spectacle. This multimillion-dollar film-set church. That's what you're presiding over, Father. A Phenathol trip' (*OLOTF*, p. 344). Carolyn's commentary seems to confirm the most sceptical elements of the narrative. Yet this Humean voice is undercut by the novel's final image, a tableau of thousands of 'pilgrims' standing outside the forest church, drenched by a biblical downpour, simultaneously telling dirty jokes and praying. The miraculous, in Guterson's novel as in DeLillo's *Underworld*, takes place in the vividly coarse reality of the everyday, where secular and sacred narratives intertwine and blur.

The ground of most writers working within a continuum of 'realism' is materialist. This does not mean that realist writers never have a personal belief in the supernatural – faith in God, for example, or the hope of an afterlife; it implies, rather, that the shape of such fiction is dictated by the tangible facts of the everyday. Since miracles, apparent violations of the natural order, are regarded as exceptionally rare even by believers, such supernatural phenomena are unlikely to be a part of the realist landscape. For most writers working within a confidently secular culture, however, a version of Hume's argument is normative: miracles, like all supernatural incidents, are a pure fiction, a remnant of a pre-critical, irrational age. However, none of these novels presents its alleged 'miracle workers' as charlatans; neither do they offer easy explanations, drawn from theology or psychology, as to how these phenomena came about. *The Testimony of Taliesin Jones* might encode an explicitly Christian response to the miraculous but it is also the least essayistic of the novels considered in this chapter. 'Can the supernatural be so unexceptional?' wonders Taliesin (*TTJ*, p. 105). This, in a sense, is the question that informs each of the novels discussed. In comparison to the controlled debates regarding the ground for belief or scepticism in *How to Be Good* and *Keeping Faith*, for example, Brook's novel privileges experience, incarnation and testimony above analysis. Taliesin is able to accept that belief in God emerges only in a personal encounter with the numinous – a numinous, however, that is rooted in the experience of the everyday. His experience of God is mediated by a dying old man, a figure regarded as a harmless eccentric by the community and with cold suspicion by the local church authorities. Taliesin's religious awakening is born from both rational debate and intimate encounter with a mysterious God. Fiction cannot 'prove' the reality of miracles – indeed, its instincts seem to undermine any such absolute claims – but, like Taliesin's 'testimony', it might offer a space of witness to the miraculous amidst the mundane.

5

Little Wonder: John Irving's Modern Miracles

The fiction writer, according to John Irving, is burdened with a miraculous mission both to destroy and to save.[1] This apocalyptic hypothesis is offered in 'Trying to Save Piggy Sneed' (1982), a characteristically uncanny short story that describes the alarming events of how its narrator became a writer: he begins by telling the reader that the story 'is a memoir' but immediately qualifies absolute trust by claiming that 'all memoirs are false' (*TTSPS*, p. 9). In this evocation of childhood cruelty, the speaker recalls his friends' terrible taunting of a man they called Piggy Sneed, the local dustbin collector, who lived on a pig farm and spoke only in a series of grunts and squeals. The children in this memoir/story are not innocent or even playful: they echo the indeterminate, postlapsarian images of childhood represented in the nineteenth-century American Gothic fictions of Nathaniel Hawthorne, Edgar Allan Poe and Henry James. Irving does not sanitize or seek to explain their abhorrent mocking of this unfortunate man. The story reaches its crisis with the unexplained incineration of his small home. The narrator tells us that he was a teenage member of the voluntary fire service: even as they attended the blaze, jokes and stories about Piggy Sneed continued. When the man fails to emerge from his burning home after repeated calls, the narrator recounts his sudden desire to rationalize the fire and the apparent disappearance: Mr Sneed was not dead; he had simply retired and fled to Florida or Europe, starting the fire as an act of vengeance for the years of persecution he had suffered in this small American town; his friends collaborate in these imagined improbabilities and even speculate that the man was a European émigré. The truth is more prosaic and brutal: the persecuted man died and the writer tells us that it was he who was required to remove his charred remains from the cinders of the home.

A sequel to the fire affords the tale a more explicitly parable-like quality. The narrator states that he originally told his grandmother 'the *plain* truth' but years later Piggy Sneed makes a kind of spectral return as Irving is forced to reinterpret these events in response to his sceptical grandmother's desire to know why he ever became a writer:

> so I told her everything about the night of the fire, about how I imagined that if I could have invented well enough – if I could have made up something truthful enough – that I could have (in some sense) saved Piggy Sneed. At least saved him for another fire – of my own making (*TTSPS*, p. 24)

His grandmother suggests that this sophisticated justification of his creative motivation would not have been necessary had he 'only treated Mr Sneed with a little human decency when he was alive'. Irving's response and the conclusion of this disturbing narrative is ambiguous: 'Failing that, I realize that a writer's business is setting fire to Piggy Sneed – *and* trying to save him – again and again; forever' (*TTSPS*, p. 25). Henry Jansen's lucid interpretation of the story concludes that a 'writer's task . . . is to find a happy ending to this (kind of) story to find a plot where things do turn out well in the end, even though reality contradicts this kind of ending'.[2] Yet Irving's vision of writing as an eternal act of creation, salvation and destruction is more ambivalent than Jansen suggests. The god-like novelist is, in this sense, a terrifying figure ('lawless' is how Irving's grandmother viewed it), with a self-bestowed power either to recreate or bring to an end their fictional world; the promise of literary resurrection is coupled with the fear of judgement. Storytelling, for Irving, has an implicitly theological dimension in that it is a transformative, near miraculous act: a storyteller can make the dead rise and the mute speak; he can also afflict his world with suffering, trial and tears.

For Frederick Buechner, novelist, Presbyterian minister and one of Irving's mentors at Phillips Exeter Academy in New Hampshire, all acts of narration struggle in vain to communicate truths; in particular, Buechner, as a Christian, argues that language cannot contain the voice of the divine because God speaks to individuals thorough event and experience: 'they are ultimately always incarnate words. They are words fleshed out in the everydayness no less than in the crises of our own experience'.[3] This recognition of the limits of language, shared by critical theorists who reject the transcendent worldview evinced by Buechner, is confronted by Irving. The novelist takes the flesh of 'experience' – even the imagined 'memory' of the burnt flesh of Piggy Sneed – and turns it into words. The potent, uncertain events of personal history that play themselves out in memory are given shape to by the creative writer and, however shadow-like they may be, Irving seeks to give these narrative fragments a kind of coherence.

In common with the majority of his contemporaries, Irving is not an avowedly 'religious' novelist; he writes without a doctrinal or institutional agenda. Indeed, his eleven novels, from *Setting Free the Bears* (1968) to *Until I Find You* (2005), are the product of a defiantly individualist sensibility: they are distinctive, strange, magical and represent a morally complex, if not chaotic universe. Irving is unhappy with the assertion that his work is self-consciously attracted to the absurd. In a 1997 interview the writer claimed that 'one of the silliest things I read about myself is that I'm bizarre'. Indeed, he claims that the inclusion of events that ostensibly appear abnormal and characters who behave in a way that seems peculiar or artificially out of the ordinary are merely the result of paying close attention to the textures of 'real' life: 'I don't go out of my way to find or invent things that are bizarre. It just seems to me that I notice more and more how commonplace the bizarre is'.[4] Irving, like his most frequently acknowledged literary forefather, Charles Dickens, writes about people who live on the margins of society; his characters, he has confessed, tend to be individuals whose lives are characterized by incongruity, people who are 'on the edge or beyond the edge': 'I like people who have sort of staked out a margin, an existence at the periphery of where most humans live, and yet have to go through the same kind of common everyday existence that the rest of us do.'[5] Yet these characters who are 'on the edge or beyond the edge' are perpetually seeking to integrate themselves into mainstream society, to navigate their way from the periphery to a stable centre, even if they discover that this secure social core is mythic.

The worlds that Irving has chosen to narrate, including, in *The Cider House Rules* (1985), an illegal abortion clinic hidden within an orphanage, a series of brothels in *The World According to Garp* (1978) and *A Widow for One Year* (1998) and the hallucinatory underworld of Bombay/Mumbai in *A Son of the Circus* (1994) confront the religious reader with an uncomfortable sense of otherness. They are spaces more easily erased or evaded than confronted by the Christian consciousness. However, Irving's fictive worlds often revolve around an axis of sin, repentance and redemption rooted in the Christian metanarrative. Although Irving is no apologist for doctrinaire Christianity, his work draws on a body of spiritual language and tradition mourned by later generations of North American writers. Douglas Coupland, for example, writes of an era apparently beyond religious belief, 'the life of children of the children of the pioneers – life after God – a life of earthly salvation on the edge of heaven' which becomes 'a life lived in paradise' that leaves 'any discussion of transcendental ideas pointless'.[6] John Irving, unlike Coupland, was raised in the still lively Christian traditions of New Hampshire; although he has distanced himself from the explicit and exclusive truth claims of Christianity, Puritanism, with its emphasis on knowledge of scripture and austere morality, is a crucial part of Irving's cultural history. Where Coupland's characters seek spiritual truth in the absence of religious schooling and are almost always free from a history of familial piety, Irving's protagonists are often burdened with a specific framework of belief with which they must negotiate. 'Even at our most believing', argues Buechner in *A Room Called Remember*, 'we have our serious reservations just as even at our most unbelieving we tend to cast a wistful glance over our shoulders.'[7] The space between the 'serious reservations' of doubt and the 'wistful glance' of faith might be used accurately to describe the spiritual position of Irving's fiction.

John McClure has identified the 'post-secular' fictional strategies of Don DeLillo and Thomas Pynchon, contemporaries of Irving, as characterized primarily by their post-Christian spiritual motifs. DeLillo, notes McClure, narrates the 'homeless spiritual impulses' of people 'mesmerized by new religious movements' while Pynchon's writing is replete with 'paranormal events ... that reflect the disparate ontologies of gnosticism, spiritualism, Native American and African traditions, the martial arts traditions, and American transcendentalism'.[8] These detraditionalized, eclectic spiritualities are not part of Irving's landscape, though he does explore elements of Hindu belief in *A Son of the Circus*. Early in *A Prayer for Owen Meany* (1989), Irving's most explicitly theological work, the narrator's grandmother reflects, even in the post-World War II years in which the novel's action begins, that 'Puritanism had never entirely relinquished its hold on us Wheelwrights'.[9] Similarly, Irving is wrestling with a Puritan legacy that has not 'entirely relinquished its hold' on his storytelling. Its traces are visible in the rather brutal myth of origin narrative, 'Trying to Save Piggy Sneed', which delineates a world in need of redemptive intervention. His fiction is, to borrow Graham Ward's diagnosis of much postmodern critical theory, 'haunted by the Christian imaginary'.[10]

This chapter explores the Christian haunting of the world according to John Irving, with particular reference to his exploration of miracles in *A Prayer for Owen Meany*. This sustained examination of Irving's novel develops the argument of Chapter 4 with its wider focus on postmodern literary miracles. These phenomena, read in the wide Christian tradition as evidence of God's authority and presence in the material universe, disturb the worlds of Irving's novel and frame his engagement with crucial religious questions regarding free will, redemption and divine judgement. Similar ideas also preoccupy *A Son of the Circus*, though with less explicit focus on Christian theology. Irving's fiction, even when attending to more secular concerns, has a sacramental quality and is animated by forms of pilgrimage, conversion and a serious engagement with morality. Stephen R. Haynes has offered the most acute and comprehensive 'religious reading' to date of *A Prayer for Owen Meany*.[11] Haynes elucidates crucial aspects of the novel's theological argument, religious context and what he argues is 'the book's providential structure'; the article is particularly strong on the Puritan histories that Irving re-awakens and on its debt to tropes of the New Testament. He defends the Christological framework of Owen's story as more than a casual, immature flirtation with biblical mythology and believes that the novel is littered with clues that in conjunction build a powerfully persuasive novel of religious experience. Haynes also offers a compelling analysis of the importance of Frederick Buechner's influence on the novel, tracing the origin of specific theological ideas discussed by some of its principal characters (Johnny Wheelwright, Owen and the elusive Pastor Merrill) back to the writings of Irving's former teacher. This chapter builds on Haynes's analysis of the novelist's exploration of theological ideas and locates Irving in an evolving tradition of postmodern Anglophone writers whose novels test the secular status of the novel and continually explore the purpose of storytelling for religious belief.

'The capability of reverence': Puritan Origins and Biblical Intertexts

'Have no anxiety about anything, but in everything by prayer and supplication with thanksgiving let your requests be known to God' (Philippians 4.6). *A Prayer for Owen Meany* begins with this epigraph taken from the apostle Paul's letter to the Philippians and ends, perhaps inevitably, in an act of supplication. In fact, John Wheelwright, the novel's damaged, near despairing but garrulous narrator, concludes the apparently miraculous story of Owen Meany with two prayers: he intercedes for his late friend ('INTO PARADISE MAY THE ANGELS LEAD YOU') and, finally, out of overwhelming grief, he makes a psalm-like plea for Owen's resurrection, not in heaven, but on earth, in the here and now (*APFOM*, pp. 636–7). This devotional ending, in which hope for eternal salvation exists in tension with the routine joy and pain of life in a fallen world, is indicative of the quasi-theological quest that informs Irving's fiction in general and this powerful twentieth-century parable in particular. John Ruskin, the visionary Victorian critic, once claimed that the 'capability of reverence' is 'the most precious part of the human soul'.[12] Serious contemporary fiction is more often associated with justified contempt for a corrupt, hopeless world; in Irving's work, however, the need to cultivate the 'capability of reverence', both for human endeavour and divine possibility, transcends his sometimes bitter, satirical vision. As John Sykes claims, it is a novel that, with its strata of biblical allusion and refiguring of the Christ story, 'virtually demands theological assessment' and one that takes religious belief very seriously.[13] However, like its narrator, the novel is unflinching in its portrayal of abusive piety, wherever it might be found: Johnny Wheelwright objects not to God but to 'the screamers who say they believe in Him and who claim to pursue their ends in His holy name!' (*APFOM*, p. 563). Despite this anger with the political abuse of religion, the novel is perhaps the most biblically allusive mainstream novel of the 1980s. The Pauline epigraph foreshadows a narrative crowded with references to the Jewish and Christian scriptures, including citations from the gospels, the psalms and a variety of epistles. In this sense, Irving's highly political vision of contemporary American life is rewritten in an apparently antiquated scriptural mode that has more in common with the Puritan world than it does with the detraditionalized, postmodern era in which it was published. 'When the Pilgrims first set foot ashore at Plymouth,' notes David Lyle Jeffrey, 'their Bibles arrived with them, not just in the physical sense of many well-worn copies but as a conscious and vividly developed mythography.' What meaning, beyond historical interest, can such a world view have for a sceptical and comic contemporary novelist? In fact, the prominent position of the Bible, this 'foundational cultural text', both in the nascent Puritan imaginary (vital for the novel's sense of American history) and in a living 'mythography' defines the novel's critique of contemporary American culture.[14]

Philippians, the source of the quotation with which the novel, but not John Wheelwright's narration, begins, resonates with the anxieties that animate the novel. Paul's letter was written in thanksgiving to the local church and, as commentators have noted, is 'outstanding as the N[ew] T[estament] letter of joy'.[15] Yet the apostle wrote these words of encouragement while incarcerated: his exhortation emerges from persecution, his prayer from suffering. Similarly, John Wheelwright's story is prompted by a desire to communicate a startling, and, to the non-believer, outrageous religious conviction forged in sorrow.

Composed by a self-imposed exile, a voluntary stranger in a strange land, Wheelwright's narrative paradoxically parallels Paul's prison letters. If this strange religious tale has an implied reader apart from God (and to whom else would a prayer be offered?), unlike Paul's epistle, it is not a body of believers, but rather a faithless United States; a country that has, in the eyes of John Wheelwright, abandoned its covenant and sacred duty towards both God and its citizens. None of this is to argue that his creator is writing with the zealous agenda of the apostle; *A Prayer for Owen Meany* is, in part, an account of a conversion but it is always fiction, never a tract designed to elicit Christian belief in the reader. There is a rupture between the novel that Irving has written and the story that his narrator is telling: Wheelwright's righteous complaint against his country of origin amounts to what David Lyle has named a 'Postmodern Jeremiad'; Irving, by contrast, is able to awaken sympathy for Wheelwright while maintaining an ironic detachment from his wilder judgements.

Owen Meany is not just saturated with a religious vocabulary but is also structured around defining Jewish–Christian themes of sacrifice, transcendence and divine calling. It narrates the life of a boy who, after accidentally killing his best friend's mother during a little league baseball game in the Summer of 1953, believes that he is a messenger of God who must identify and carry out a sacred duty. Owen is unusually small and, though fiercely articulate, speaks with a 'wrecked' voice that is impossible to imagine, and is represented on the page with capitalized letters. His bereaved friend, John Wheelwright, becomes another of Irving's Dickensian orphans: succeeding the eponymous hero from *The World According to Garp* (1978), and Homer Wells of Saint Clouds orphanage in *The Cider House Rules*, Wheelwright too has never known the identity of his real father. Indeed, Irving uses the detective story of John's search for the truth regarding his biological father as one of the novel's defining quests, which itself takes on theological implications. He describes how his eccentric, perplexing childhood friend challenged a variety of unjust institutions in their hometown of Gravesend, New Hampshire, experienced a sequence of terrifying prophetic dreams and eventually, as he believed he would, became a martyr in 1968, an indirect casualty of the Vietnam War. Wheelwright's Christian name might be viewed as a piece of metafictional self-reference: the narrator of *The Hotel New Hampshire* (1981) is also called John and the novel playfully draws on some elements of the author's biography. However, the narrator's given name is also an echo of 'the disciple whom Jesus loved', the supposed author of the Gospel of John (13.23). John Wheelwright's story is, then, not just a 'prayer', but a form of testimony, an act of witness to a life and its extraordinary impact. I concur with Haynes's view that *A Prayer for Owen Meany* is a Johannine novel: its narrator, like the ascribed author of John's Gospel, offers a highly theological reading of a holy man's life.[16] John Wheelwright is certainly no fictively pious saint: he is an angry, disillusioned and grief-stricken individual. Indeed, one of the most sophisticated elements of Irving's narrative is its mediation between biblical allusion and a clear sense of contemporary political reality and its potentially damaging distortions of religious faith.

The 'present' of *A Prayer for Owen Meany* is almost precisely contemporaneous with its date of publication: the non-linear, retrospective narrative, focusing on the years between World War II and the United States' calamitous intervention in Vietnam, is recounted by Wheelwright in the late 1980s in Toronto, the Canadian city to which he escaped, with some disgust, during the latter military campaign. The deployment of this retrospective framework echoes Frederick Buechner's reflection, mediated from Paul Tillich, on the relationship between past and present:

> It is more than just memory, I think, that binds us to the past. The past is the place we view the present from as much as the other way around, and nothing I heard Tillich say about eternity was as eloquent as what was said by such times as those, where past, present, and future are all caught up together in a single timelessness.[17]

For Wheelwright, the present is both shaped by the dreadful, astonishing past and judged according to its values: his contempt for Ronald Reagan's administration, for example, as intemperate and emotional as it might be, is ordered by his formative years in New Hampshire and, in particular, by the life and death of Owen Meany. The integrity embodied by this extraordinary character has become an absolute for the narrator; by contrast, the moral decadence he sees in contemporary American culture is the inverse of Owen Meany's authentic spirituality. The 'single timelessness' represented by Wheelwright's meditative movement between past and present, however, is far from the liberating eternal or *kairotic* moment envisaged by Buechner and Tillich. Instead, Wheelwright is incarcerated by memory, 'doomed to remember a boy with a wrecked voice' (*APFOM*, p. 13). His act of narration is framed by Irving as an act of supplication: but the prayer is not simply for Owen Meany, it is also a desperate attempt to redeem the narrator's memory, to free him to move into the third phase of time named in Buechner's trinity: Wheelwright has been unable to envisage a future without his friend.

Sacvan Bercovitch argues that 'the Puritan legacy to subsequent American culture lies not in theology or logic or social institutions, but in the realm of the imagination'.[18] Irving's novel is one of the strange flowers of this Puritan imagination. At the time of the novel's publication, Irving told *The New York Times*, 'I've always asked myself what would be the magnitude of the miracle that could convince me of religious faith.'[19] The novel is predicated on a conversion narrative as Wheelwright recounts his movement from scepticism to a melancholy faith but it is not crudely designed to elicit a religious response in its reader. Irving is more interested in the ways in which individuals find to move beyond the cynicism of a materialist age than in engendering faith per se. John Wheelwright's anger towards the politics of the United States in a post-Vietnam age finds expression and structure in the rituals of his Anglican spirituality. Wheelwright has his origins literally and figuratively in the history of Puritan New England: at the level of metaphor, he, like the Pilgrim and Puritan founders of America, finds himself in conflict with the corruption of the contemporary world, and abandons his country of origin in order to live with spiritual and moral integrity. In more literalistic terms, the narrator can trace his ancestry to the first Pilgrims as his grandmother's family arrived in America onboard the *Mayflower*. The inheritance from his grandfather is similarly crucial: his ancestor, the original John Wheelwright, exiled from the original Massachusetts colony for preaching heterodox ideas regarding the holy spirit in 1638, is the founder of the fictional town of Gravesend, where John and Owen Meany are born in 1942 and live until their early adulthood. In this genealogical narrative, Irving, using a trope that reiterates many of his more avowedly postmodern contemporaries, confounds the relationship between reality and fiction as the 'real' John Wheelwright, whose religious biography parallels that of his imagined counterpart, actually founded Exeter, New Hampshire, the town in which Irving was, like his narrator, born in 1942, where he was raised; he makes clear in his acknowledgements that Gravesend is based on his place of origin.[20] Philip Page has observed that Irving is playful with 'the pseudo-biographical connections between John Wheelwright, the narrator/ character, and John Irving, the author', using his own life as further fictional intertext and, implicitly, demanding the reader to consider the complex relationship between storytelling and reality.[21] One of the non-fictional Wheelwright's namesake-descendants in the mid-twentieth century echoed his forefather's religious radicalism: John Wheelwright, a minor but fascinating Boston poet, outraged conservative New England society with his heretical synthesis of Christian and Hindu creeds.

Irving's rather conservative narrator shares more than a patronymic and a Christian name with his controversial ancestors. John inherits their propensity for religious dissidence: in childhood and adolescence, he is a sceptic, unable to believe unequivocally in the God in whom his friend, Owen, has an unshakeable faith that he created all things; more specifically, he does not share the belief that his friend's life has a unique divine purpose. John's religious education includes two competing Christian traditions: after the marriage of his mother to Dan Needham, John reluctantly moves from a Congregational fellowship, a direct heir of New England Puritanism, led by the charismatic but doubting Pastor Merrill, to the town's Episcopalian church, ostensibly in deference to his generous stepfather's upbringing (though we later discover that this was another red herring, as Needham had no specific institutional affiliation). Ultimately, as he announces on the novel's first page, he has become a member of the Anglican Church of Canada. This is a symbolic return, in a country that remains part of a Commonwealth, which is, notionally at least, governed by the British monarchy, to the church that was forsaken by Puritans in their pursuit of an Edenic new world. Irving creates a cyclical version of American history in his narrator's emblematic affront to his spiritual ancestry; it is an insult, however, which is shaped by the defiant spiritual independence of his forebears. The Puritan intention was never to secede from the Church of England but to reform it from within; Wheelwright's return is a sort of homecoming, a ritual of transformation or healing in which the old and new worlds are unified.

A Prayer for Owen Meany has a number of potent literary intertexts, and its highly allusive style includes multiple citations from classic novels such as F. Scott Fitzgerald's *The Great Gatsby* (1925) and Thomas Hardy's *Tess of the D'Urbervilles* (1891).[22] Like John Updike's *Roger's Version* (1986), published only three years earlier, however, the narrative explicitly reworks themes and motifs from Nathaniel Hawthorne's *The Scarlet Letter* (1850). As John Sykes has observed, this rewriting is at its most overt in the subplot that involves a 'frail and doubt-racked New England minister' whose 'unrepentant lover (known to some only as the lady in red) bravely rears their child and goes her independent way'.[23] Irving also makes use of the Gothic tradition with which Hawthorne is now retrospectively associated to re-imagine elements of the original's narrative. Although Tabitha Wheelwright is a re-imagined, twentieth-century version of Hester Prynne, so too, obviously, is John's cousin, Hester. This subversive, sensual adolescent embodies the impulsiveness of her nineteenth-century counterpart: we might say that while Tabitha most resembles the self-restraint of Hester Prynne in the 'marketplace', Hester (who as a rock star is later known as 'Hester the Molester') is closer to Hawthorne's heroine when she enters the unregulated space of the forest. Hester and Tabitha are not the only Gothic doublings in the novel: though Owen, as Sykes notes, is closest to Hester's 'uncanny' daughter, Pearl, this identity is shared with Johnny. Owen is convinced that he has no earthly father, while Johnny finds, to his disappointment, that he is the son of the Reverend Lewis Merrill. This spiritually hesitant pastor is a stuttering, doubting Dimmesdale for the era of Vietnam and Kennedy. Even the town itself, the fictional Gravesend, becomes a double of Hawthorne's simulated seventeenth-century Boston and of the Exeter, New Hampshire of Irving's youth.

A Prayer for Owen Meany might be read as a powerfully political indictment of the degeneration of American values in the second half of the twentieth century. The years in which the novel's engendering crisis (the accidental killing of Tabitha Wheelwright) occurs were once deprecatingly named the 'tranquillized fifties' by Robert Lowell, another writer at odds with a personal legacy of New England Puritanism; for Lowell, the wryly self-named 'fire breathing', conscientious objector to World War II, the United States had no narrative tradition that could give shape to a dynamic, questing art or spirituality.[24] Lowell's poetry of dissent, ironically echoing the Puritan tradition that he viewed as no great inheritance, found structure in his conversion to Roman Catholicism in 1940. Irving, by contrast, creates a small, 1950s New England town in which the people, despite their manifest weaknesses, failures and casual bigotries, have a distinctive imaginative narrative with which to celebrate the commonplace and the transcendent, in both religious and secular sacraments. The marriage and burial of Tabitha Wheelwright are separated by a year but within the novel they are narrated side by side; Irving explores the potency of sacred rites and, in dislocating the novel's chronology, he causes his reader to see such regular customs in an estranging and re-enchanted light. The novel is also a Dickensian fiction about the power of personal sacrifice (with an echo of

A Tale of Two Cities) and the persistent presence of goodness in an apparently absurd world. In the acknowledgements to *A Prayer for Owen Meany*, Irving emphasizes his intellectual debt to the Reverend Frederick Buechner. This novelist and Presbyterian minister was chair of the religion programme and, later, school minister at Exeter Academy, New Hampshire, from 1958 to 1967, where he taught Irving. His theology, indebted to the diverse influences of Karl Barth and those who taught him at the more liberal Union theological seminary is crucial in Irving's novel.[25] In his memoir, Irving writes of his regard for Buechner's ideas even in the most sceptical days of adolescence:

> We were a negative lot of students at Exeter, when it came to religion. We were more cynical than young people today; we were even more cynical than most of us have since become – that is to say that my generation strikes me as *less* cynical today than we were. (Is that possible?) Anyway, we didn't like Freddy Buechner for his sermons in Phillips Church or in our morning chapel, although his sermons were better than anyone else's sermons I've ever heard or read – before or since. It was his eloquence about *literature* that moved us.[26]

Before the tragic experience that compels John Wheelwright to faith, he has strong adolescent disdain for the Episcopalian minister. This unconsciously echoes the disillusion of seventeenth-century Puritans who abandoned English shores when they recognized that reforming zeal alone would renew neither the Anglican Church nor the state as a whole. Irving ironically inverts this cultural resonance: Puritans and Separatists were angered by the worldly and ritualistic nature of the established church; John, however, prefers the Congregational church not because it represents a holier religious space but because it is one in which honest doubt is prized. Lewis Merrill is 'infinitely more attractive' than his energetic but simplistic Episcopalian peer because 'he expressed *our* doubt in eloquent and sympathetic ways':

> In his completely lucid and convincing view, the Bible is a book with a troubling plot, but a plot that can be understood: God creates us out of love, but we don't want God, or we don't believe in Him, or we pay very poor attention to Him. Nevertheless, God continues to love us ... Pastor Merrill made religion seem *reasonable*. (*APFOM*, p. 124)

This 'lucid and convincing view' is derived directly, and with very little modification, from *Now and Then*, the second volume of Frederick Buechner's autobiography:

> For all its vast diversity and unevenness, [the Bible] is a book with a plot and a plot that can be readily stated. God makes the world in love. For one reason or another the world chooses to reject God. God will not reject the world but continues his mysterious and relentless pursuit of it to the end of time.[27]

The relationship between the source of Christian belief and narrative is vital to Buechner's theology, as it will be for Owen Meany, who interprets his life in terms of a 'plot' that has been scripted by God and one which he will relentlessly pursue 'to the end of [his own] time'. *Now and Then* is a 'memoir of vocation', in which the minister-novelist reflects on the years that he spent at Exeter immediately following his ordination. Haynes has commented on this and other allusions to Buechner's biography and theology, noting that Irving cites a number of works by his teacher but, in some strange Bloomian move, fails to include the memoir that is most explicitly present in the work. He also outlines the very close similarities between Buechner and Lewis Merrill: both were Princeton literature majors before training for the ministry at Union Theological Seminary where they were taught by such major figures as Paul Tillich, Rienhold Niebuhr and James Muilneburg.[28] Merrill's doubt is not, primarily at least, in God but rather in mankind's ability to comprehend the love of God; neither is he, as one might superficially suggest, so theologically vague that he has no real faith in the transcendent. Rather, he confesses the frailty of the human condition and the persistence of divine love for a humanity that constantly stands in need of redemption. The Reverend Merrill, as we shall see, is no exception to this creed. Owen Meany, described by the narrator as 'a natural in the belief business', castigates Merrill for his rational wrestling with faith. 'BELIEF IS NOT AN INTELLECTUAL MATTER', proclaims the unconventional, troubling child (*APFOM*, p. 126).

As a teenager, Owen Meany believes in an imminent, political restoration of American virtue; although this hope, thrown into relief by Irving's historical scope, is ruined by successive political failures and continuing violence, he comes to embody an idealized American innocence. One of the most provocative elements of Irving's novel is its representation of Owen Meany as a contemporary Christ. In fact, as distinctive a creation as he is, Owen echoes a tradition described by Theodore Ziolkowski in *Fictional Transfigurations of Jesus* (1972) as the '*imitatio Christi*', a genre that he argues gained popularity at the end of the nineteenth century following a renewed fascination with Thomas a Kempis's *The Imitation of Christ*. Ziolkowski describes these novels as narratives 'in which the hero makes up his mind to live consistently as Jesus would have lived had he been born into our world. Here we are dealing not with the resurrected historical Jesus, but with modern heroes who act out their own conception of Christ.'[29] Owen Meany, like his fictional forefathers, is similarly appalled by the parlous state of his era (in this case, America in the 1950s and 60s) and his idealistic challenge to crooked authority (ecclesiastical, educational and political) resonates with this specifically secular mode of 'literary transfiguration'. The narrative contrasts the moral integrity of Owen with the insidious corruption of US political life, culminating in John Wheelwright's astringent response to the Reagan administration of the 1980s. Irving plays on the tradition of Jesus as modern hero, the man of unimpeachable integrity, but his strange saviour is too distinctive to be one more superman. Indeed, the novel also raises the altogether less comfortable, indeed, the impossible suggestion that Owen may be a twentieth-century Christ in more than deed. Indeed, Sykes suggests that the 'Christ pattern' of the novel 'invoked in support of the supernatural . . . is re-figured in a way that diverts our attention from the Jesus Christ of Christian scripture'.[30]

Irving and his narrator make a series of parallels between the titular hero and the Jesus of the Gospels: as an eleven-year-old, the tiny Owen is chosen to represent the Christ child in the church nativity play; he, like, Jesus, has modest origins as the son of a craftsman who learns his father's trade of stonemasonry; there are further signs in his constant battles with secular and religious authorities but also in more supernatural terms. Owen experiences visions and dreams that foretell the sacrificial nature of his future death; more controversially, he believes that he is the product of a virgin birth. This uncanny child-man believes his parents' outrageous story that his conception was miraculous rather than natural, for example, and Owen, like Christ, displays prescience regarding the manner of his death. Irving uses, in particular, the parallel retelling of two Christmas stories as a means of exploring Owen's uncanny Christ-like identity: Owen takes on the roles of the infant Jesus in the church's nativity play and as the Ghost of Christmas Yet to Come in a stage production of Dickens' *A Christmas Carol*: 'Thus did Owen Meany remodel Christmas', recalls John (*APFOM*, p. 215). In these twin set-pieces, simultaneously comic and frightening, an uncanny and, perhaps, holy child recasts two stories of divine warning and incarnation in his own, wilful design.

Before the nativity of 1953 Owen had been regularly cast, appropriately enough, as the 'Announcing Angel'; by giving him a similarly supernatural prophetic role in Dickens's spectral tale, Irving reinforces the concept of Owen's prescience and the ominous nature of his warnings. However, his performance as a 'little lord Jesus' who is neither meek nor mild is more theologically challenging. A conservative reader might, on a superficial level, interpret this nativity as a heretical appropriation of the biblical account of Christ's birth, in which a twentieth-century novelist casually borrows the old, old story to give emotional depth to his own profane narrative. Indeed, in adult life, Johnny reflects that this simulated nativity 'has replaced the old story' (*APFOM*, p. 240). The performance is littered with standard technical failures and forgotten lines but is marked by Owen's sudden anger at the arrival of his parents to the pageant. His fierce demand that they leave ('IT IS A *SACRILEGE* FOR YOU TO BE HERE!') is interpreted by one non-Christian spectator as part of the narrative ('this is no ordinary baby. You know, he's the *Lord!* Jesus) (*APFOM*, p. 234, p. 243). However, neither Irving nor his complex, beguiling eponymous hero truly wish to arrogate Owen Meany to the status of Christ child. But this radical reshaping of the story is not one that simply allows the people of Gravesend to view Owen Meany as supernatural. More significantly, Owen's strange presence, coupled with the accidents that surround him, forces the spectators, including, one suspects, the most religious members of the audience, to reassess a story that they believe they know. What Owen Meany and John Irving do here is to restore the wonder and, literally, the terror at the heart of the original

Christmas story. As the narrator reflects, his friend's performance left him with an unforgettable and unforgiving 'vision of the little Lord Jesus as a born victim, born raw, born bandaged, born angry and accusing' (*APFOM*, p. 241). Irving's comic nativity effectively deconstructs the 'fantasy' of sentimental accounts of Christ's birth and, like Jim Crace's sceptical interpretation of the desert temptation in *Quarantine*, a biblical story regains its power to shock. The miraculous is not sweet and reassuring but alienating and strange.

Owen belongs to what John Schad in *Queer Fish* (2004), an alternative account of religious impulses in the modernist moment, has named the ' "tradition" of holy idiocy' or, in a phrase borrowed from Michel Foucault, 'Christian unreason'. For Schad, the strangeness of Christianity somewhat ironically re-emerged with the advent of the so-called 'death of God', amid such 'masters of suspicion' as Nietzsche, Freud and Darwin. 'Christianity's ancient, inherent disposition to unreason', he argues, 'was redoubled by a new, cultural positioning as the other of secular modernity. It was now – or rather, now and again – something eccentric, odd, even queer'.[31] Owen, a stranger in his own country, a prophet without honour, might well be one of Schad's disparate body of 'losers, the unreasonable Christians' who 'have *no* official history' and who belong to 'a "tradition" that refuses tradition . . . that emerges when and where it is least expected. Above all, it is often a church invisible, even to itself'.[32]

Owen's emphasis on the ascendancy of personal faith over the authority of the hierarchies of the church echoes the charges of antinomianism for which Anne Hutchinson, sister-in-law to the original John Wheelwright and a figure discussed in Chapter 4 of this study, was exiled from Massachusetts. From infancy he is in conflict with religious authorities across the spectrum of Christian tradition. In fact, he is Roman Catholic by birth, but his parents have abandoned the Church because of an 'UNSPEAKABLE OUTRAGE', an insult that both Owen and Irving are careful to conceal for much of the novel; similarly he causes havoc in his reordering of the Episcopalian church pageant. Yet, in his determination to follow what he believes to be God's will, Owen is close to the most orthodox of New England Puritans and the narrator wryly notes that 'on the subject of predestination, Owen Meany would accuse Calvin of bad faith'. This born Catholic, in other words, is a pious rival to Jean Calvin (1509–64), the most cherished theologian of the Puritan world. The novel's interest in predestination and the question of free will versus determinism brings together questions of narratology and theology. Indeed, *A Prayer for Owen Meany* self-consciously explores the tropes of coincidence, accident and contingency on which realist fiction depends. For Owen, '[t]here were *no* accidents' (*APFOM*, p. 115). Owen's literalism echoes the understanding of the Bible offered in Eric Auerbach's celebrated study of 'the representation of reality in western Literature', *Mimesis* (1953). In one frequently quoted passage Auberbach contrasts Homer's *Odyssey* with biblical writing, and specifically those books now only controversially referred to as the 'Old Testament': 'Far from seeking, like Homer, merely to make us forget our own reality for a few hours, it seeks to overcome our reality: we are to fit our own life into its world, feel ourselves to be elements in its structure of universal history'.[33] Similarly, Owen reads the world entirely in terms of its relationship with the purposeful teleology of scripture. Indeed, Auerbach's analysis reads like a template for Owen Meany's unshakeable belief that his life is subject to the structures of a providential design: 'Everything else that happens in the world,' observes Auerbach of the scriptures, 'can only be conceived as an element in this sequence; into it everything that is known about the world ... must be fitted as an ingredient of the divine plan'.[34] For Owen, all other narratives (including those of American political hubris, the legends of small town life and the experience of personal humiliation) are subordinate to a 'divine plan' that has 'overcome' his 'reality'. Irving confronts this uncomfortably unscientific form of belief in the most audacious element of the novel: its representation of the miraculous.

Miracles of design: Wrestling with Graham Greene

'YOU CAN'T TAKE A MIRACLE AND JUST SHOW IT!' claims an indignant Owen Meany, in response to an Easter screening of Cecil B. de Mille's final film, *The Ten Commandments* (1956). He also strongly disapproves of the 'magic' performed by TV evangelists (*APFOM*, p. 326). The adolescent prophet is especially irritated by the parting of the Red Sea: 'YOU CAN'T PROVE A MIRACLE – YOU JUST HAVE TO BELIEVE IT' (*APFOM*, p. 288). Although motivated by a piece of cinematic narrative, this iconoclastic approach to a fictionalized nature-defying event raises questions regarding the rectitude of literary representations of the miraculous. Do fictional miracles cynically trade on what Graham Ward has named the 'charismatic past' of religion, together with its comforting 'illusions or simulations', rather than engage with its theological implications?[35] Chapter 4 of this volume discussed the ways in which secular fiction has indicated a movement from the miraculous as 'special effect' to a more substantially theological reappraisal of 'signs and wonders'. *A Prayer for Owen Meany* is more than unusually sensitive to the major questions regarding the purpose of such supernatural events. Are such phenomena enough to persuade a rational individual to believe in God? Is it possible to believe without the 'evidence' of a miracle? In an echo of Dostoyevsky's Ivan Karamazov, one of the secular saints on his religion and literature course, Pastor Merrill argues that 'Faith itself is a miracle ... The first miracle that I believe in is my own faith itself' (*APFOM*, p. 325).[36] This idea is put under pressure later in the narrative when the privately sceptical Merrill is revealed to be John's father. He refuses to believe that Owen's prediction of his own death was a supernatural revelation: 'real miracles don't m-m-m-make faith out of thin air; you have to *already have faith* in order to believe in real miracles' (*APFOM*, p. 542). Yet when his angry, estranged son manufactures a miracle that seems to bring Tabitha Wheelwright back to haunt him, Merrill's faith is saved and he once again becomes a brilliant preacher. John's simulation of the supernatural was, in fact, designed to terrify his erstwhile father but this revival of faith suggests that even 'rational' individuals might be vulnerable to spectacular 'supernatural' events.

Irving explores similar ideas in *A Son of the Circus*, the immediate successor to *A Prayer for Owen Meany*. Although this riotous narrative of transsexual serial killers, circus performers and Bollywood iconography has a very different tone to its forerunner, one subplot in the novel is concerned with a 'miracle'. Dr Daruwalla, a man of science who is married to a Roman Catholic, experiences a religious conversion following the 'evidence' of his encounter with what he believes to be 'the ghost of the pilgrim who dismembered St Francis Xavier'. His discovery, many years later, that this supernatural experience and 'the source of his conversion to Christianity was the love bite of a transsexual serial killer . . . diminished the doctor's already declining religious zeal'.[37] This comic narrative seems to emphasize the contingency, even the arbitrariness of religious belief. However, Irving sets up a theologically rich debate when Daruwalla meets a Jesuit priest, Martin Mills: 'I'm not trying to take your miracle away from you. I'm only trying to make you see the *real* miracle. It is simply that you believe – not the silly thing that made you believe' (*ASOTC*, p. 617).

Significantly, on his religion and literature course, Merrill introduces the Catholic fiction of Graham Greene (specifically his 1940 novel, *The Power and the Glory*) to the class that Johnny Wheelwright describes as 'an atheistic mob' and, excepting Owen Meany, he recalls that 'we were such a negative, anti-everything bunch of morons' (*APFOM*, p. 325). This is another biographical echo: Irving's earliest encounter with Greene was on a Religion and Literature course taught by Frederick Buechner.[38] Although the imaginative legacy of Puritanism is vital to the world of Owen Meany, there are also signs of engagement with Roman Catholic thought. In fact, Irving's narrative has strong echoes of perhaps the most famous twentieth-century Catholic novel to explore miraculous, divine purpose and grief. Greene's *The End of the Affair* (1951), one of the writer's sequence of sombre, strongly theological novels, and described by Irving as both the first novel to shock him and as 'the most chilling antilove story I know', has been somewhat overlooked as perhaps the most significant precursor for the shape and themes of *A Prayer for Owen Meany* (*TIG*, pp. 36–7). The similarities between these God-haunted novels, however, are striking: for example, both are structured around conversion narratives premised on apparently miraculous events during a time of war and its aftermath; both are narrated by sour, rather reluctant believers incapable of reconciling their sad personal histories with blissfully rational, godless world views. Similarly, the novels share an emphasis on determinism, delusion, the power of storytelling, the irrationality of religious sacrifice, and both end with prayers. In the final lines of Greene's novel, Bendrix demands to be left alone by God; in Irving's novel, also addressed to the divine 'You', it is a request not for annihilation or desertion but for the resurrection of his friend. They are connected, too, by a shared source for their epigraphs. Greene's novel is prefaced by a solitary, oblique quotation from Léon Bloy (1846–1917), the idiosyncratic late nineteenth-century writer: 'Man has places in his heart which do not yet exist, and into them enters suffering in order that they may have existence.' Bloy, who is viewed as a herald of the French Catholic Revival, was, like Greene, both a serious writer and a committed Roman Catholic. One critic describes the defining aim of Bloy's work as the transformation of dissatisfaction with his own life into 'the redeeming language of Crucifixion and Apocalypse'.[39] This thematic emphasis on religious suffering foreshadows *A Prayer for Owen Meany* and it is not surprising that one of the epigraphs to Irving's novel should be attributed to the French writer: 'Any Christian who is not a hero is a pig'.[40] This theological maxim sets up the heroic sacrifice at the heart of the novel and the narrator's grimly determined faith but its rather obscure source also foreshadows the connections between Irving's narrative and the religious ambiguities of Greene's melancholy story of 'an odd sort of mercy'.[41]

   The End of the Affair inverts Lukács' claim that the novel is 'an epic of a world abandoned by God'. Indeed, T. R. Wright has argued that the narrative represents Greene's 'most powerful challenge to rational liberal humanism and its exclusion of God both from the real world and the "realistic world" of fiction'.[42] Greene's post-war fable is narrated by Maurice Bendrix, a bitter agnostic who has come to believe in God but who desperately wishes to escape the cruel reality of his new-found faith. He certainly cannot reconcile faith with reason, viewing the former as a sign of decadent excess: 'When we get to the end of human beings we have to delude ourselves into a belief in God, like a gourmet who demands more complex sauces with his food' (*TEOTA*, p. 145). Belief in divinity has not conferred peace or religious ecstasy on this obsessive narrator, but a renewed sense of hate. Indeed, for Bendrix, God is no benign redeemer but a Satan-like tempter: 'It's You who take us up to a high place and offer us the whole universe. You're a devil, God, tempting us to leap' (*TEOTA*, p. 191). The origins of such self-conscious blasphemy are traced back to Bendrix's wartime liaison with Sarah Miles, the wife of an intellectually dry civil servant. Just as Johnny Wheelwright confesses, on the opening page of his account, that Owen Meany is the 'reason I believe in God', so Maurice Bendrix coyly alludes to 'that other, in whom in those days we were lucky enough not to believe' (*TEOTA*, p. 7). For Irving's protagonist, as for Bendrix, the life of faith is not one of reassuring answers: 'For although I believe I know what the *real* miracles are, my belief in God disturbs and unsettles me much more than *not* believing ever did' (*APFOM*, p. 591). Wheelwright and Bendrix are both, to borrow a phrase, victims of a miracle: Johnny Wheelwright has witnessed the fulfilment of his best friend's anticipated martyrdom, while Greene's protagonist was apparently granted a reprieve from an aerial bomb by the prayer of his lover. Both Sarah and Owen keep journals and write letters which are later used by the grieving narrators to make sense of the lives and faith of their dead companions.

   Bendrix, notes Wright, learns 'that grace is irresistible, that God's mysterious plot, like those of his own novels, is moving inexorably to a predestined end'.[43] The novel begins with a reflection on the apparent contingencies of narrative action: 'A story has no beginning or end,' claims Bendrix, 'arbitrarily one chooses that moment of experience from which to look back or from which to look ahead ... but I do in fact of my own will *choose* that black wet January night' (*TEOTA*, p. 7). Irving has a similar interest in the structure of narrative and, as Debra Shostak argues, the majority of his novels 'explore the nature of plotting' and interrogate what she calls 'extrafictional structurings of experience'.[44] Irving's eleventh novel, *Until I Find You* (2005), another narrative in which a missing father and spirituality collide, is similarly drawn to the issue of narration and memory. The novel is prefaced with a quotation from William Maxwell's *So Long, See You Tomorrow*:

What we ... refer to confidently as memory – meaning a moment, a scene, a fact that has been subjected to a fixative and thereby rescued from oblivion – is really a form of storytelling that goes on continually in the mind and often changes with the telling ... in talking about the past we lie with every breath we draw.[45]

Does Irving represent story as purely fictive, an artificial counter to randomness and chaos? '[M]an is in his actions and practice, as well as in his fictions, essentially a story-telling animal', claims Alasdair MacIntyre in *After Virtue* (1981; 1985). The human being, he argues, is not just 'a teller of stories' but a storyteller whose narratives 'aspire to truth'. 'Life's narrative structure reveals the human desire for a *telos*', notes Mark Ledbetter, in response to MacIntrye. 'The desire for completion, a sense of emotional and intellectual wholeness to life, is what gives lived narrative its religious sense'.[46] This is certainly true for the painful pilgrimage of Johnny Wheelwright. Both *The End of the Affair* and *A Prayer for Owen Meany* are concerned with versions of what MacIntyre defines as the ethical question that, he argues, can only be answered appropriately in the light of a 'prior question': 'Of what story or stories do I find myself a part?'[47]

In Greene's novel, Bendrix connects narrative purpose with the life of faith: 'The saints', he suggests, 'in a sense create themselves. They come alive. They are capable of the surprising act or word. They stand outside the plot, unconditioned by it' (*TEOTA*, p. 186). Such figures, like Sarah Miles or Owen Meany, seem to be more than a function of plot. This idea echoes Lukács' claim that the novel, unlike earlier forms of epic, 'tells of the adventure of interiority'. A 'hero' like Owen Meany believes that the universe has a coherent design, but this is based on a leap of faith rather than an absolute guarantee structured into the genre. Lukács, following Goethe and Schiller, contrasts the necessary 'passivity of the epic hero' whose 'destiny-forming event' is 'only ... a profound and dignified ceremony' with the 'adventures' of the novel's protagonist.[48] For Shostak, Irving's reliance on 'a miracle that portends providential design ... necessarily erases the possibility of fully autonomous choice'.[49] Yet the wagers of faith taken by Owen, and by Sarah in *The End of the Affair*, amplify rather than diminish their sense of agency. For Bendrix it is the faithless who, like the most recalcitrant figures in his own fiction, 'have the obstinacy of non-existence':

We are inextricably bound to the plot, and wearily God forces us, here and there, according to his intention, characters without poetry, without free will, whose only importance is that somewhere, at some time, we help to furnish the scene in which a living character moves and speaks, providing perhaps the saints with the opportunities for *their* free will. (*TEOTA*, p. 186)

Johnny Wheelwright, like Bendrix, experiences plot as one on the periphery. In fact, he is always conscious of his identity as a reader – one who always comes late to the text – rather than as a creator. The act of reading, however, becomes emblematic in the novel: Owen castigates John for belittling his own 'gift' of reading and this, too, is a textual trace of the novel's religious purpose (*APFOM*, p. 521). The narrator is not, as he reflects at one point, 'just a Joseph', the marginal, apparently passive earthly father of Jesus (*APFOM*, p. 221). His role is also that of the apostle John, 'beloved' of Christ; he too is engaged in reading and writing the life of his holy friend; his responsibility is one of interpretation, itself a 'gift', 'learned' from or given by Owen, and left for John to wrestle with. Indeed, Page has argued that the novel is dominated by a 'hermeneutical dialectic' as the principal characters 'are confronted with a rich array of signs – objects, events, texts, other characters – which they have difficulty interpreting'.[50]

Echoing other narratives of encounters with the divine, Johnny's (interpretative) relationship with Owen Meany is both a blessing and a curse, wound and healing: he is damaged by it, literally, in the trigger finger lovingly severed by his friend, and, following the apparently miraculous fulfilment of Owen's dream, is transformed by his sudden inability to read the world in simple, materialist terms. Like Jacob after he wrestles the angel, Johnny is scarred by his experience of divinity and, to use Valentine Cunningham's terms, continues to limp in his act of interpretation.[51] In later life, when he becomes a literature teacher, Johnny Wheelwright is professionally concerned with the nature and purpose of narrative: his slightly irritable pedagogic reflections on Hardy's *Tess* and Fitzgerald's *Gatsby*, for example, are part of the novel's interrogation of fiction and fate. Greene's narrative also emphasizes the vital role of interpretation in both literature and religion: 'If we had not been taught how to interpret the story of the Passion,' reflects Bendrix, 'would we have been able to say from their actions alone whether it was the jealous Judas or the cowardly Peter who loved Christ?' (*TEOTA*, p. 27). Similarly, John's 'prayer' for Owen Meany is reliant on a pre-understanding of the salvific role that his dead friend believed that he was born to enact.

Where John Wheelwright is primarily a 'reader', Maurice Bendrix defines himself by his profession as writer. The fact that Greene's cynical narrator is also a novelist is an allegorical as well as an autobiographical device: as a creator of plots, the hidden hand behind every accidental meeting and catastrophe to befall character, the author is widely recognized as an analogue for the creator God. In his anti-hero, Greene creates a post-war Promethean rival to the God in whom he can no longer disbelieve. Indeed, the reluctantly religious dimension of Greene's metafiction anticipates Roland Barthes' revolutionary essay 'The Death of the Author' (1968). For Barthes, reading itself after this symbolic 'death' becomes an 'anti-theological activity, an activity that is truly revolutionary since to refuse to fix meaning is, in the end, to refuse God and his hypostases – reason, science, law'.[52] Yet Bendrix's resistance to 'God and his hypostases', including narrative itself, is defeated by the discovery of a plot beyond his own interpretative control. Like Bendrix, John is also preoccupied by the problem of freedom and providential control. In the final page of his narrative, he recalls the Sunday School ritual of lifting Owen Meany into the air. This image of ascension is also one of 'forces' outside of ordinary human agency: 'they were the forces we didn't have the faith to feel ... and they were also lifting up Owen Meany, taking him out of our hands' (*APFOM*, p. 637).

This final allusion to the 'lifting up' of Owen Meany's sacrifice – the act of divine courage that he believes God has always intended him for – takes place in Phoenix, Arizona. This allusion to the mythical bird, often read as a symbol of the bodily resurrection in Christ, underscores Irving's exploration of the redemptive schema integral to Christian theology. Owen's diary, the literary space within which the 'miraculous' hero wrestles with his terrifying sense of vocation, includes a pencil drawing of a phoenix, accompanied by a note describing its associations with rebirth and immortality (*APFOM*, p. 576). Indeed this diary extends the motif of resurrection as it literally allows Owen to speak from beyond the grave, to be revivified in words; the narrator reads these private writings, delineating an agonizing struggle to understand and to accept the will of God, only after the heroic death of his best friend. The diary, another of the novel's fictional intertexts, subverts and problematizes the narrative which frames it: Haynes claims that 'if death is Owen's emblem, resurrection increasingly becomes his hope'.[53]

The prophecy of self-sacrifice that so scars and shapes Owen's life is fulfilled not, as he assumed, during active service in Vietnam but in the liminal space of a United States airport: the airstrip is a place of exchange from which soldiers depart for war and to which they return, dead or alive. The heroic act, which Owen had witnessed in a dream some years before, is played out almost exactly as he had foreseen: in this dream/nightmare he saves a group of Vietnamese children. This vision is realized without Owen ever leaving the USA; the children he saves are refugees attacked by a disturbed American teenager, Dick Jarvits, who is obsessed by the war in which his similarly violent older brother was killed; Jarvits throws a stolen grenade into the makeshift bathroom that the children are using. As in the vision, Roman Catholic nuns are present and the 8 July 1968 date also corresponds with the inscription Owen believed he had seen on Scrooge's grave in the Gravesend Players' production of *A Christmas Carol*. Similarly, as Owen predicts, John is crucial to this ending; the sub-four-second 'slam dunk' basketball shot that the two had obsessively practised throughout school gains meaning as it allows Owen to dispose of the grenade through a high window.

This apparent confirmation of Owen's prophecy, which seems uncannily precise, allows Irving to confront a sceptical, postmodern (and, indeed, post-Vietnam) readership with a miracle. Irving's fictional universe is dominated by the unusual and, as Henry Jansen has rightly observed, grotesque accidents and personal suffering engender remarkable transformations in the majority of his novels; in Jansen's view, Irving does not simply accept that life is replete with meaningless 'tragic consequences' but rather seeks to 'affirm life and the value of human life'.[54] Yet *A Prayer for Owen Meany* is Irving's first and, to date, only novel so dependent on a series of events with an explicitly supernatural dimension: the human origins of the manufactured 'miracles' in *A Son of the Circus* are eventually exposed to their beneficiaries; *The Fourth Hand* (2001) explores the concept of intuition and dream-prophecy but Irving's emphasis is less explicitly theological in this novel. We do not have to accept John Wheelwright's belief in his friend's divine calling. The 'miracle' by which the previously sceptical John – the doubting Thomas to Owen's twentieth-century Jesus – is converted might also be read as a simple act of human courage, desperately sought out by an extraordinary but deluded individual.

There are, after all, good psychological and material reasons for both characters to make their leaps of faith: Owen, traumatized by the cruel accident on the baseball field that caused the death of Tabitha Wheelwright, the mother figure whom he idealized, would surely have been compelled to find an explanation for such an event, one that might redeem the apparently random nature of the universe. Indeed, Shostak notes that Irving 'leaves [the] possibility open through much of the novel' that 'psychological necessity alone lies behind Owen's search for the sacred'.[55] Owen's messiah-complex is further rationalized by his parents' destructive fantasy that he is the product of a virgin birth and by his subsequent altercations with religious and secular authorities. Similarly, John, bereaved for a second time, is faced with a choice between an absurdist/nihilist world view and the Christian literalism of Owen Meany. In choosing the latter, a sceptical reader might reasonably conclude that the narrator has chosen a comfortable fiction, one that offers hope of reunion with the departed, instead of confronting the disquieting truth. This rather reductive psychoanalytic reading is also substantiated by John's failure to mature, even in middle age: he never marries and rejects the possibility of a romantic relationship. Rather than remain in the United States and fight for its moral and political rebirth after Vietnam, John simply escapes to Canada, where he remains a perpetual exile, unable to integrate himself fully into his new national identity. The allusions to F. Scott Fitzgerald's *The Great Gatsby*, taught by John to his aloof, bored pupils, inform this reading: John Wheelwright's belief in Owen Meany echoes Nick Carraway's devotion to his own late friend; both are enchanted by a character more dynamic, wayward and ambiguous than themselves and both are gravely embittered by a youthful encounter with a violent, fallen world. Page argues that the conscious invocation of an ostensibly trustworthy narrator who, as one of Wheelwright's cynical students reminds him, is less reliable than he consistently claims to be, subtly undermines John's 'reliability as a narrator, especially as a witness who claims Owen's divinity'.[56] Irving's novel does not evade these questions – indeed, they are questions demanded by a plot that seems designed to provoke both faith and doubt, uncertainty and hope, ambivalence and conviction – but it suggests that commonplace, logical answers are not always satisfactory.

Conclusion

Few writers of literary fiction in the early twenty-first century will claim, as did the late Flannery O'Connor, with whom Irving has been compared, that '[b]elief . . . is the engine that makes perception operate'.[57] *A Prayer for Owen Meany* is dependent on its readers trusting a narrator whose own 'perception' depends on the 'engine' of belief. However, as its author distances himself from such certainty, how do we interpret the novel's religious dimension? Is it a sceptical novel in the guise of a religious tract or a piece of sentimental Christian narrative masquerading as serious literary fiction? For Shostak, the novel is 'a prayer for meaning, for events to add up into a purposeful design.'[58] *A Prayer for Owen Meany* certainly resonates with McClure's claim that postmodern fiction 'maintains and revises a modernist tradition of spiritually inflected resistance to conventionally secular constructions of reality'.[59] Are any of his literary miracles genuinely salvific? In his study of the 'eclipse of biblical narrative', Hans Frei argues that in serious 'realistic narrative . . . the sublime or at least serious effect mingles inextricably with the quality of what is casual, random, ordinary, and everyday'.[60] Irving's novel tests the boundaries of realistic fiction: its titular hero does not believe in 'what is casual' or 'random' and his understanding of the 'ordinary' and 'everyday' is shaped by a stern providentialism. A resolute defence of the reality of the novel's defining miracle might miss the point and, from a Christian perspective, risk undermining the mystery of revelation. As William C. Placher argues, the modern claim

> that God does some things but not others forces theologians in a secular age into defensive efforts to find some things for God still to do and negotiations between too much limit on God's power and too much limit on human freedom. It leads to explanations of what God does and does not do, and these explanations lose the mystery of radical transcendence.[61]

Not all critical readings of *A Prayer for Owen Meany* have evaluated the implications of Irving's engagement with Christianity favourably. Most recently, Henry Jansen's reading of the 'postmodern comic' approach to suffering, in the fiction of Irving and others, defends the novel's moral seriousness but concludes that *Owen Meany* is ultimately 'unsatisfactory theologically'.[62] For Jansen, the tension between 'the fundamental chaos or plotlessness of the world' evinced in Irving's earlier novels and the form of belief demanded in *Owen Meany*, itself informed by a sense of determinism, undermines a coherent, truly Christian argument.[63] Yet Jansen seems to miss some of the seriousness with which Irving treats belief, in spite of his simultaneous wish to parody aspects of it. Irving's approach to the world as a place of chaos, demonstrated most explicitly in *The World According to Garp* and *The Hotel New Hampshire* (1981), is revised by his encounter with Christianity.

What a number of critics have missed, Haynes argues, is that *Owen Meany* 'stands apart from Irving's other novels because it evinces eschatology. What our narrator renders is not a cycle in a repeating pattern, but a linear history finding ultimate resolution in a triumphant act of redemption.'[64] Johnny Wheelwright's retrospective narrative is caught between eschatological hope – one that will result in the resurrection of his dead friend – and an intuitive pessimism regarding western culture: 'I will tell you what is my overriding perception of the last twenty years: that we are a civilization careening toward a succession of anticlimaxes – toward an infinity of unsatisfying and disagreeable endings' (*APFOM*, p. 562). At the end of James Wood's *The Broken Estate* (1999), a collection of essays on 'literature and belief', the ambivalent, disbelieving critic throws a final question to believers: 'why, before heaven must we live? Why must we move through this unhappy, painful, rehearsal for heaven . . . this foreword written by an anonymous author, this hard prelude in which so few of us can find our way?'[65] For Owen, the 'anticlimaxes' of US history, including the disappointments of the politics and the failures of everyday fallen existence, are transfigured by the hope of a future resurrection.

6

'How Clear is Your Vision of Heaven?':
Douglas Coupland at the End of the World

Yes, the world is over. It's still *here* but it's . . . *over*. I'm at the End of the World
. . . The end of the world as we know it . . . It sounds glamorous but it's not.
It's dreary and quiet and the air always smells like there's a tire fire half a mile
up wind . . .

Douglas Coupland, *Girlfriend in a Coma* (1998)[1]

Few contemporary novelists seem as prepared for the end of the world as
Douglas Coupland. Indeed, for a writer without ostensible religious affilia-
tions, he is unusually absorbed by questions of the world to come. An uneasy
expectation of a rapidly approaching end coupled with inevitable judgement
dominates Coupland's fiction: culture is ephemeral, individual lives are danger-
ously fragile, and the long-term future of the planet is in doubt. The latter concern might simply be an upshot of the legacies of cold war paranoia, lurid
catastrophes imaged in disaster movie spectacles and an escalating awareness
of ecological crisis if it were not for the persistent rumours of grace that punctu-
ate his novels. Indeed, a distinctively theological hope for a better world gives
shape to these apocalyptic narratives. Coupland's novels resonate with Paul
Fiddes' claim in *The Promised End* (2000) that 'eschatology [is] the basic mood'
not just of theology but also of 'literary creation'.[2] They belong to what Frank
Kermode, in his path-finding work on the apocalyptic aspect of literature, *The
Sense of Ending* (1967) – a crucial text for Fiddes – names 'end-determined fictions'. What kind of ending does Coupland's fiction anticipate? Are his narratives, like Kermode's examples of Genesis and Virgil, 'placed at what Dante
calls the point where all times are present . . . [giving] each moment its fullness'?[3] Conversely, do they anticipate an end that will obliterate, rather than
fulfil, the human desire for divine meaning?

Jared, the adolescent, ghostly narrator of *Girlfriend in a Coma*, becomes a
kind of spectral guide to a future '[that] doesn't exist yet' but one that may
await an unthinking, acquisitive humanity (*GIAC*, p. 5). He is the sole 'witness'
to an exhausted and abused future that is littered with the remains of human
endeavour and excess. In Christian thought, as Fiddes observes, this end-
focused emphasis falls on four particular 'last things': 'the final advent of the
Lord of the cosmos, the last judgement, heaven and hell'.[4] Postmodern narrative, though frequently tormented by more straightforwardly secular fears of

annihilation, is rarely animated by the specifics of creedal Christian hope for the future life. A notorious non-theological form of apocalyptic ending materialized in the publication of, and response to, Francis Fukuyama's famous study, *The End of History and the Last Man* (1992). In this epoch-making – or era-ending – work, the conservative social theorist claimed that the larger struggles of human history had been resolved in the ascendancy of Western liberal democracies such as the USA. Published shortly after the apparent final failure of Marxist ideology – embodied in the fall of Communist states – the thesis was viewed by theorists still inflected by socialist thought as perilously reactionary and complacent. Indeed, Jacques Derrida, in *Spectres of Marx* (1993; trans. 1994), argued that the vogue for 'eschatological themes' was itself, like so much postmodern thinking, somewhat belated: '[these ideas] were, in the '50s, that is, forty years ago, our daily bread'.[5] '[T]hey look like latecomers', added Derrida before defiantly admonishing this sluggish, postmodern eschaton: 'How can one be late to the end of history?'[6]

In *Blank Fictions* (1998), James Annesley writes of 'Endism' – a term he borrows from a *New York Times* article on Fukuyama – or 'the culture of the end'.[7] G. P. Lainsbury, who reads Coupland's fiction as a response to Fukuyama's theory, notes that one manifestation of an 'end'-focused culture is the 'loss of a sense of the possibility of the meaningfulness of a commitment to something larger than the self or economic extensions of the self'.[8] Perhaps most importantly, Lainsbury identifies the 'anticlimactic end of history' that has been signified by the 'end of the cold war' for the characters in *Generation X* (1991): the threat of nuclear annihilation meant that 'the end of history and the end of the human species would be synchronous events.' In short, the horizon of mutually assured destruction seemed to confer meaning on death whereas, in the post-historical moment, death will 'signify nothing'.[9] Similarly, Annesely suggests that the apocalyptic atmosphere of much youth-oriented, late-twentieth-century fiction, offers 'no relief, no real revelation or redemption, only a profoundly depressing sense of impending destruction'.[10] However, Coupland's ambiguous, experimental and theologically-charged fiction is marked by a wrestling not only with the pervasive fear of extinction but, more distinctively, with the promise of apocalypse as revelation. There is a distinctive 'Adventist' turn in Coupland's writing; many of his narratives are concerned with what Derrida, again in *Spectres of Marx*, named 'the future-to-come'.[11] The possibility of a strange remaking of human history, in which the future might be more than an enhanced, faster and more productive consumer-driven fantasy (in short, more than Fukuyama's version of the 'end of history') is at play in Coupland's visionary writing. Indeed, it also implicitly demands a revaluation of post-modern culture as one defined entirely by desire, faithlessness and anomie. 'Postmodernity abolishes conceptual idolatry', argues the theologian Kevin Vanhoozer, 'in order to make room for faith'.[12] Similarly, a quiet, idiosyncratic and religionless – that is non-institutional – faith is crucial in Coupland's imagining of this 'future-to-come'. Is this future dependent on the coming of a Messiah figure? Vanhoozer's theological gloss on Derrida's distinction between foreclosed 'messianism', in which a messiah is supposedly already present, and an open, undetermined 'messianic' idea, in some ways illuminates Coupland's ambivalent sense of expectation: 'The messianic is the unforeseeable, the beyond that is always desired but never attained. On this view, the postmodern condition is essentially, that is structurally, messianic: constitutionally open to the coming of the other and the different'.[13] *Girlfriend in a Coma*, for example, is a strikingly 'messianic' novel from this perspective: Karen McNeil, the novel's titular heroine, becomes a kind of redemptive, messiah-figure – her coma is a symbolic atonement for the sins of her generation – but the novel configures her suffering and divine visions as participating in a bigger sacred story. Karen's actions anticipate, rather than limit, the interrelationship between the present and the transcendent. She is not literally divine, and her courageous willingness to suffer – a version of vicarious sacrifice – does not become a religious fetish. Instead, a challenge is offered to her surviving friends to wake up and to 'change the world' (*GIAC*, p. 276).

Although Coupland, who, in the early 1990s, became a reluctant prophet of the so-called 'Generation X' – a term re-energized by the famous title of his debut novel – has never identified himself with any particular religious community or faith position, his work is now widely identified as theologically dynamic and open to competing religious readings.[14] In one review of Coupland's unsettling, experimental tenth novel, *JPod* (2006), for example, Matthew Reynolds recognizes the 'reverent tone and persistent Christian echoes' of much of his fiction; the frequent motifs of 'baptism, the Last Day [and] the Garden of Eden', he argues, suggest that the novelist is 'serious about his mysticism, in a shy sort of way'.[15] Ali Smith has described Coupland as 'a postmodern transcendentalist', and Alan Bilton suggests that the novelist's defining subject matter, 'the longing to escape an overly complex and materially corrupt civilization [and to] rescue a sense of selfhood amongst the solitude of Nature' is, indeed, '*the* great American theme'.[16] While Coupland's search for the sacred does not begin and end in the wilderness, Smith's epithet provides a useful connection between this contemporary Canadian writer and the restless spirituality of the nineteenth-century New England Transcendentalists Ralph Waldo Emerson and Henry David Thoreau. Alternatively, Gordon Lynch, a British theologian and pioneer in research on patterns of Generation X religiosity, has observed that 'one researcher looking at emerging trends in the Christian Church said to me that young people he had met as part of his research were more likely to cite Coupland's novels as important influences for them than the writing of any traditional or mainstream Christian theologian'.[17]

Coupland becomes a crucial paradigm for Lynch's study, which develops into 'a set of personal reflections on how his novels might help those of us with a "Generation X" view of the world in our own pursuit of meaning'.[18] The appropriation of a contemporary novelist to illuminate this search for a twenty-first-century spiritual identity might appear rather reductive, diminishing complex narrative art into little more than a superior self-help guide.

However, in identifying the emergence of Coupland as an influential theological voice – both within and outside of institutional religion – Lynch limns a primary way in which contemporary spirituality is experienced. Pop culture, in the forms of music, fashion, film and even literary fiction, has become a revitalized space for theological debate. In *Virtual Faith* (2000), Tom Beaudoin, another self-styled 'Gen X theologian', argues against a simplified consensus that suggests religious belief is no longer available to a materially driven, ideologically blank, youth culture: 'Far from residing in a cultural wasteland devoid of spiritual symbols, Generation X matured in a culture of complex and contradictory signs, some of them religious. Some currents within that Gen X pop cultural stream carry more than mere microbes of an inchoate GenX spirituality'.[19] Coupland's fiction, littered with allusions to music and television of the 1970s, 1980s and 1990s – *Girlfriend in a Coma* is also the title of a song from The Smiths' final album, *Strangeways Here We Come* (1987), for example – embodies this threshold between pop culture and piety. His protagonists – with the exception of the central characters of *Hey Nostradamus!* (2003) – are rarely religious according to most traditional standards. In common with most writers of Coupland's generation, organized faith traditions do not play even a peripheral role in the majority of his novels. As Richard W. Flory has argued, one strand of so-called Generation X culture is a revitalized approach to spirituality in which the emphasis is placed on 'authentic religious experience' rather than doctrine: 'authenticity', in Flory's terms, is 'identified by experience, narrative, creativity and example, not by rational argumentation for the truth claims of a particular religious belief system'.[20] Yet orthodox spiritual subjects, related to salvation and the presence/absence of God in human suffering, for example, explicitly or implicitly stimulate most of his characters. Their quests, however, are much more likely to be conducted outside of traditional, collective arenas of religious truth: churches, mosques, temples and synagogues are replaced by hospitals, forests, bars, automobiles and, with an echo of mystic traditions, desert spaces. Coupland's most spiritually engaged fiction, including the quasi-confessional *Life After God* (1994) and *Hey Nostradamus!*, does not monumentalize a specific mode of spiritual experience or creed but suggests that human identity, in its multiple incarnations, is diminished without a sense of the sacred.

An explicitly apocalyptic strand of Coupland's fictional universe is established in one of the oral fictions uttered in *Generation X: Tales for an Accelerated Culture* (1991) and explored further in a number of his later novels. When Dag, the most anarchic of the novel's trinity of taletellers, proclaims, 'I've got an end-of-the world story', Coupland's narrator, Andy, observes that '[t]he end of the world is a recurring motif in Dag's bedtime stories'. Dag regularly offers 'eschatological You-are-There accounts of what it's like to be Bombed, lovingly detailed, and told in deadpan voice'.[21] In retrospect, Andy's assessment reads like an uncanny anticipation of the next decade of Coupland's creative life: both a muted millennial anxiety and a more generalized foreboding of entropy have been a persistent theme since this zeitgeist-defining debut. Visions of apocalypse are not only the subject of his most explicitly theologically themed novels, but also preoccupy more conventionally secular characters in *Shampoo Planet* (1992), *Microserfs* (1995), *Polaroids from the Dead* (1996) and *Eleanor Rigby* (2004). Coupland seems to share Dag's concern that '[t]ime was (and is) running out' (*GX*, p. 36). This anxiety does not always manifest itself in improbable 'end time' narratives but frequently surfaces in Coupland's representation of mortality: many of his key characters experience either the death of the person closest to them or die themselves and, in three key instances, narratives are related from beyond the grave.

The impossible prospect of a time *without* the linear progress of standard clock time is crucial to Coupland's fiction and shapes its complex sense of spirituality. It would be inaccurate to suggest that these novels simply enact Christian eschatology – they are not religious tracts and, indeed, problematize aspects of traditional religious thinking – but both the thematic 'sense of an ending' and the temporal scheme of the novels frequently echo ideas of biblical eschatology. This chapter traces alternative representations of time – chronological and apocalyptic – and examines the creative tensions in Coupland's use of biblical images and religious thought. How do these images of end times compare with Jewish and Christian beliefs about God, creation and eternity?

Out of Time: Coupland, Chronos and Kairos

'One of my big problems is time sickness', reflects Liz Dunn, the lonely narrator of Coupland's *Eleanor Rigby*.[22] This peculiar malaise, in which present unhappiness seems to destroy both past pleasures and the promise of time future, typifies a railing against the limits of linear, clock time in Coupland's fiction. 'I wish modern science would invent a drug that causes time to feel much longer', Liz reflects later. The problem is not that time crawls, but that it seems empty; this 'miracle drug' would allow 'adulthood [to] feel long and full instead of like some out-of-control carnival ride' (*ER*, p. 73). Liz's account mediates between the three clock times: the present tense of the narrative; the pivotal change that precipitates the central plot of the novel (a sudden encounter and transformative relationship with her adopted son, seven years previously); and finally, Liz's anticipation of an ambiguous, indeterminate future, which she knows promises both the premature end of her own life and the birth of a second, unexpected child. During her years of depression, Liz is in thrall to what Theodor Adorno named 'the realm of the eversame'.[23] Adorno's reflections on 'Free Time' conclude that supposed leisure time in a consumerist economy 'is shackled to its opposite ... free time depends on the totality of social conditions, which continues to hold people under its spell'.[24] Liz does not possess the resources – either personally or culturally – to find a way beyond this stultifying 'realm of the eversame'. Pop culture, in the form of sentimental movies and TV dinners, acts as a temporary palliative but cannot cure 'time sickness'. However, *Eleanor Rigby*, in many ways Coupland's most melancholy and spiritually ambivalent novel, ends with a recovered sense of the miraculous nature of life: 'Will wonders never cease?' asks Liz, at once invoking a bland truism and re-appropriating a sense of openness to awe (*ER*, p. 249). Roger Lundin suggests that 'the dread of cosmic loneliness . . . haunts so much of the music, art, poetry, and fiction of the modern West. Are we alone in what Pascal called "the eternal silence of these infinite space"?'[25] This fear is crucial to *Eleanor Rigby* and Liz Dunn's loneliness is redeemed only when she gains a transfigured sense of both space and time.

The tension between different time schemes in Coupland's fiction enacts Frank Kermode's distinction between *chronological* and *kairotic* time. Drawing on enduring theological debates, Kermode notes that '*chronos* is "passing time" or "waiting time" – that which, according to Revelation, "shall be no more" – and *kairos* is the season, a point in time filled with significance, charged with a meaning derived from its relation to the end'.[26] *Eleanor Rigby* turns on the delicate interplay between these alternative modes of time. Liz reflects on her frustration with the boredoms of a lonely, work-driven life – the sense of endless, empty routine that engenders 'time sickness' – and is also able to recount how this pathology was healed through a new experience of time. The transformation occurs when Liz is witness to a rare astronomical phenomenon that takes on the character of epiphany:

> [a] comet . . . passed earth seven years ago, back in 1997 – Hale-Bopp, a chunk of some other demolished planet hurtling about the universe. I saw it just past sunset while standing in the parking lot of Rogers video . . . Sure, I think the zodiac is pure hooey, but when an entirely new object appears in the sky, it opens some kind of window to your soul and to your sense of destiny. No matter how rational you try to be, it's hard to escape the feeling that such a celestial event portends some radical change. (*ER*, p. 3)

The moment is characterized by scepticism and faith: Liz refuses to collude with vague astrological speculation (superstition is often derided in Coupland's fiction) but she remains open to the possibility of 'radical change'. Indeed, her perception of time shifts from an overwhelming sense of futility to one of pattern and purpose. Time is transformed, from one theological perspective, by a belief that eternity is figured in the present. When Liz meets her estranged son, Jeremy, for the first time since birth, as he awakes from a coma in the Lions Gate Hospital – a recurrently visited space in Coupland's fiction, as Nicholas Blincoe has observed – she notes that it feels like 'the fulfillment of a prophecy' (*ER*, p. 31).[27] *Kairotic* time permeates the narrative and Liz gains a defamiliarized perspective on the significance of her superficially undistinguished life. The phenomenon known as 'eternal life', Keith Ward suggests, should first and foremost be regarded as 'a life lived in relation to the eternal' rather than merely as 'life going on forever'.[28] When Liz is later confronted with the reality of her own mortality, it is unclear whether she anticipates the bodily resurrection promised in certain Christian interpretations of scripture. However, she does experience a powerful intimation of timelessness, a sense that an element of ordinary human life might transcend the painful process of routine decay and ruin.

Chronological time does not simply evaporate in Coupland's writing, how-ever. He is concerned with the ways in which culture takes its place in the broader sweep of history. In the introduction to the *Polaroids from the Dead* (1996) anthology – an experimental fusion of essays, postcards and short fic-tion – Coupland reflects that '[t]he pieces in this book reflect a 1990s world-view that seems time-expired now': '[it] explores the world that existed in the early 1990s, back when the decade was young and had yet to locate its own tex-ture'.[29] Coupland's sensitivity both to *kairos* and *chronos* is partly a response to an awareness of deep geological time represented by the vast tracts of uninhabited land that are rather hesitantly named 'Canadian'. In *Souvenir of Canada 2* (2004), for example, the author notes that the vast rock formation known as the Cana-dian Shield – 'a massive U-shaped chunk of central and eastern Canada ... 8 million square kilometres (3 million square miles) in all' – generates difficul-ties for human conceptions of time:

we are utterly unable to envision a future – any future – that exists maybe more than a hundred years beyond our individual predicted year of death ... Knowing this, the Canadian Shield, to Canadians, is a lot of inescapable intellectual hard work. It's 4.5 billion years old, covers 40 per cent of the country and fully challenges our mortal notions of when time and history began, and how we fit into it. The Shield rudely and undeniably posits that time – of some sort – will continue long beyond when we humans exit this granite chip that orbits our sun.[30]

Physical geography, an empirical discipline, has unexpectedly spiritual con-notations in Coupland's evocation of the long chronological perspective. Although this example includes no biblical allusion, the writer's emphasis on the near incalculable antiquity of Canada's geology echoes David Lyle Jeffrey's contrast of the use of the Bible in Canadian literature with its typological appli-cation in US writing. In the United States, he argues, a national mythology emerged explicitly in relation to a typological reading of scripture, allowing 'authors ... to invest immediate and local experience with eternal significance'. The Canadian use of scripture, he suggests, is 'more tentative, less schematic' and more 'personal', partly as a result of a 'wilderness' that 'seemed more resis-tant to subjugation'.[31] Coupland's salutary recognition of mortality tacitly reiterates the wisdom of Ecclesiastes: 'Generations come and generations go, but the earth remains for ever' (1.4). This twenty-first-century writer's response to landscape, culture and belief is shaped by his perception of the brevity of human life in comparison with the vast sweep of geological time and the unthinkable implications of eternity. In fact, his narration of West Coast experience in particular, the notion of being at the 'end of the world', both lit-erally and figuratively, intensifies a sense of apocalyptic time, of temporality invested with meaning. As Robert McGill argues in an exceptional article on the 'geography of apocalypse' in Coupland's writing, 'it is a human tendency to inscribe geography with temporal qualities, to give space a beginning and an end'.[32] This manifests itself in *Girlfriend in a Coma*, in particular, in the lives of characters who, McGill notes, 'have inherited a space-time model that conflates end times with end spaces' and that 'postulates a new heaven and a new Earth that perpetually slip out of reach, and habitually situates itself on the brink'.[33]

In a sense, Coupland records time more obsessively than almost any other contemporary author: specific dates are logged meticulously in many of the novels. *Generation X* uses dating in a quasi-visionary sense – the last chapter of a work published in 1991 is entitled 'Jan. 01, 2000' – while in *Microserfs*, the electronic journal begins in 'Early Fall, 1993' and ends, very specifically, on Tuesday 17 January 1995. This precise dating opens Coupland's fiction up to the ravaging processes of history. A narrative of the particular working conditions of one multinational company in a specific historical moment is likely to 'date' quickly. Consciously or otherwise, the novelist renders his fiction radically temporal, for all of its longing for transcendence and the eternal moment.

Coupland also uses this compulsive desire to locate narrative in the normal flow of time as a way of producing a kind of aperture between times past, present and (an unknown) future. The deaths of his major characters – some of whom deliver ghostly narratives – are all given dates: Jared 'died on January 14, 1979' (*GIAC*, p. 3); Cheryl Anway, the first narrator of *Hey Nostradamus!*, is murdered on 'a glorious Fall morning' in 1988; and Kelly Harding, who in *School Spirit* haunts her Californian high school, 'died on [her] birthday, April 14, 1984, the day [she] turned sixteen'.[34] In death, these characters reach beyond the limits of chronology or, to use Coupland's term, 'time expired'. Kelly, for example, tells her listener that eternity has an entirely different logic: 'You'd think I'd be lonely here, but no – boredom is something you get when you live in linear time. Eternity isn't linear, so therefore there's no boredom' (*SS*, p. 48).

Why should contemporary fiction anticipate eternity? Does this yearning for the infinite suggest an inability to engage with the politics of the everyday? The paradox of an apparently confident, liberal West, dependent upon advanced technologies that also nurture a wholly irrational desire for a transcendent realm, energizes Coupland's narration of the postmodern experience. One character in *Polaroids from the Dead* reflects on the strange experience of an airline pilot asking his 'passengers to pray for rain – an odd intrusion of the mystical world into the secular' (*PFD*, p. 45). Moments of sacred 'intrusion', in which the ordinary pattern of history is interrupted by an appeal to the miraculous, are vital to Coupland's representation of an everyday spirituality. These moments echo what the cultural theorist Walter Benjamin, in his elliptical modernist fragment 'Theses on the Philosophy of History' (1940), named as a ' "time of the now" which is shot through with chips of Messianic time'.[35]

In Coupland's fiction, characters experience a form of 'Messianic time' in moments of epiphanic revelation and this perception of timeless time also figures when individuals are drawn into personal, frequently unexpected acts of worship.[36] *Life After God* (1994) ends with a private forest baptism, for example: this secret rebirth is a surprising moment of redemptive change in a sequence of stories about spiritual loss and it signalled a shift in Coupland's representation of acts of faith. In his subsequent fiction, private spirituality re-emerges in unexpected public spaces. *Microserfs*, the immediate successor to *Life After God*, narrates the lives of brilliant but exploited young minds working for Microsoft in the mid-1990s, then viewed as the most successful and technologically progressive company in the world. Yet Coupland's themes of spiritual longing permeate even this scientific and highly competitive, commercial sphere. When Dan, Coupland's narrator, reflects on the death of his brother, Jed, he longs for 'pictures of the afterworld': he lacks these because he, like other characters in Coupland's work, was raised 'without any beliefs'.[37] Images of the future life and questions of spirituality, he observes, are diligently avoided by his peers. He even wryly notes that the cult of Bill Gates, the company's CEO and icon for IT geeks everywhere, might even constitute 'the subconscious manufacture of God' (*MS*, p. 16). 'The premise of the novel', argues Jefferson Faye, 'is that people can no longer separate commercial and religious icons, that wealth can indeed substitute for humane qualities', but that this is coupled to a sense of the redemptive possibilities of new technology.[38] One of Dan's colleagues, Michael (a Bill Gates style entrepreneur and scientific mystic), is fascinated by the connections between technophilia, magic and spirituality. 'Do you think humanoids *people* – will ever design a machine that can pray?' asks Michael. 'Do we pray *to* machines or *through* them? How do we use machines to achieve our deepest needs?' (*MS*, p. 183). One of the novel's defining anxieties is that technology has altered the human perception of time and space to such an extent that a vivid interior life has become impossible. In such an era beyond eras, known as the 'post-historic' age, the religious impulse is, like so much else, simply obsolete. However, later in the narrative Dan learns that his mother has suffered a paralysing stroke and in this moment he participates in a spontaneous, religious act:

> Right there and then, Todd and his parents fell down on their knees and prayed on the Strip, and I wondered if they had scraped their knees in their fall, and I wondered what it was to pray, because it was something I have never learned to do, and all I remember is falling, something I have talked about, and something I was now doing. (*MS*, p. 360)

Dan's experience of prayer is both visceral and unrepresentable: the subsequent pages in his laptop journal is an incoherent sequence of images, supposedly embodying the unconscious life of the narrator, that moves through a series of appellations including 'Skywalker', 'Codebreaker' and 'Godseeker' (*MS*, p. 363). Significantly, this devotional moment happens neither in the Canadian wilderness nor in the barren American desert but on the Strip in Las Vegas, the most postmodern and secular of cities: 'it's like the subconsciousness of the culture exploded and made municipal' (*MS*, p. 339). The instinct to perform a sacred and irrational act materializes in a space that ostensibly contradicts all such impulses.

The image of a figure in an attitude of prayer by a roadside is now a recurrent trope of Coupland's fiction. Indeed, in *Hey Nostradamus!*, Cheryl Anway and

Jason Klaasen, en route to their secret wedding in Las Vegas, stop in the 'exotic lifeless nothingness' of the desert between 'the airport and the Strip' (*HN*, p. 29) and, in this liminal space, both kneel and pray. Las Vegas, which, to Cheryl, '[i]nstead of feeling brand new ... felt thousands of years old' again becomes witness to an act of spontaneous worship (*HN*, p. 29). Later in the narrative – a decade after the horrifying murder of Cheryl, as she sits in an attitude of prayer, alongside dozens of her school friends – Jason coolly watches his unyieldingly religious father, Reg, praying 'in a wrinkled ... and sinless black suit' by a roadside in Vancouver (*HN*, p. 74). For Jason, alienated by the unforgiving, suspicious nature of other believers, '[t]his was about as interested as I'd been in praying since 1988': 'The absence of any other car on the highway made his presence seem like that of a soul in pilgrimage' (*HN*, pp. 74–5). Despite Jason's estrangement, from both father and faith, this incongruous image takes on a *kairotic* charge – time becomes connected with a greater sense of purpose in the concept of 'a soul in pilgrimage'. The motif of unlikely pilgrimage is repeated in *Eleanor Rigby* with another character on his knees by a Vancouver highway. Liz finds her eccentric, semi-mystic son crawling along the Trans-Canada Highway 'toward the sun' because '[i]t's humble' (*ER*, p. 51). Even Ethan Jarlewski, the detached, rather morally indifferent narrator of *JPod*, offers a half-prayer 'that God would shake my Etch-a-Sketch clean overnight'.[39] Unlike Dan Underwood or Linus from *Girlfriend in a Coma*, Ethan is emphatically not a spiritual seeker; yet even this blithe, affable hedonist yearns for spiritual absolution. These moments of absurd devotion – interruptions to the constitution of rational human behaviour – suggest that Coupland's fiction operates like an eccentric collection of postmodern biblical parables rather than as standard contemporary narrative.

In a 2002 article on the emergent and evolving postmodern spirituality of Coupland's early fiction, I explored the quasi-sacred function performed by a series of interpolated tales that both disrupt and give structure to the deliberately disconnected narrative arc of his debut novel, *Generation X: Tales for an Accelerated Culture*.[40] Coupland's disaffected protagonists, exiles from the relentless pursuit of wealth in early-nineties America, seek holy solace in a daily ritual of 'bedtime stories', a fertile assortment of personal anecdotes and allegorical fables from their shared imaginary world, 'Texlahoma ... a mythic world which we created ... where the year is permanently 1974' (*GX*, pp. 45–6). For these 'new human beings', storytelling becomes an act of healing and communion, signifying the possibility of redemption through narration (*GX*, p. 63). In the 'Brentwood Notebook', a chronicle of a single day in the curious, bland suburb of Los Angeles included in *Polaroids from the Dead*, Coupland returns to the theme of story – or its absence – as vital to belief in any kind of timeless human identity:

> It has been said that as animals, one factor that sets us apart from all other animals is that our lives need to be stories, narratives, and that when our stories vanish, that is when we feel lost, dangerous, out of control and susceptible

to the forces of randomness. It is the process whereby one loses one's life story: 'denarration' (*PFD*, p. 179).

For Coupland, the 'sense of living within a historic continuum' became forfeit with the 'deluge of electronic and information media into our lives' (*PFD*, p. 180). The age of mass communication – sometimes a synonym for postmodernity – alters our experience of time and erodes the common, humanist belief in a continual, accelerated movement towards perfection. Time becomes a series of instants – crammed with pleasure or pain – described in *Generation X* as 'isolated little cool moments' (*GX*, p. 10). In a culture fixated on mass consumption, meaning is deferred by the pursuit of sensation. 'Postmodernism', argues Elizabeth Deeds Ermarth, 'transforms the historical construction of temporality that took shape in the Renaissance and that informs the humanistic tradition'.[41] Coupland's fiction is neither straightforwardly nostalgic for the loss of this 'historic continuum' nor optimistic about the exposure of the Renaissance-myth of linear, logical time.

Apocalyptic visions of history, predicated on catastrophic rather than gradual change, are not necessarily religious. The arbitrary, possibly violent 'forces of randomness', in Coupland's terms, that preoccupy Western culture in the early twenty-first century, sometimes feed into equally dangerous fictions of secret conspiracy and fear of the stranger. 'Denarration' might become a brutal renarration when new stories of threat and foreign menace are deployed to replace the 'vanish[ed]' stories. Coupland's narrative drive, his search for a viable and benign spiritual metanarrative, necessarily negotiates with the contingencies of the bloody, frequently corrupt atmosphere of a globalized era.

The predicament represented by a distorted, postmodern temporality has implications for any theological reading of culture. In 1996 Gerard Loughlin observed that '[t]he close of our century is potent with the sense of ending':

> The grand narratives human beings used to tell themselves – about how tomorrow would not only follow today but be better than anything that had gone before – have become incredible. The idea of human progress has suffered one set-back too many. It is as if history had used up time and we are now counting the days on the world's last calendar. In a sense the eschaton has already been realised: and this realisation, a *delighted* realisation, is postmodernism.[42]

For Loughlin, the emergence of 'textual nihilism' – a rejection of a larger, purposeful pattern to human history – has estranged individuals and communities from participation in an older, more hopeful 'eschaton': the story of God's participation and fulfilment of creation in and through the life, death and resurrection of Jesus Christ. This tradition of narrative theology provides a useful context for reading Coupland's novels but, to borrow a phrase popularized by Larry Kreitzer, we might also 'reverse the hermeneutical flow', and explore this sense of divine story via his fiction.[43] Coupland's novels have a theological shape that is explicitly related to a sense of purposeful metanarrative: the phobia of 'denarration' identified in 'The Brentwood Notebook' is also expressed by many of his characters who long for the salvation of their own stories. Dag, in *Generation X*, rationalizes his decision to drop out of a conventional career because his 'life had become a series of scary incidents that simply weren't stringing together to make for an interesting book' (*GX*, p. 36). This melancholy moment is echoed in *Eleanor Rigby* when Liz observes that '[l]ike anybody, I wanted to find out if my life was ever going to make sense, or maybe even feel like a story' (*ER*, p. 3). Similarly, the frustrated, Hollywood-dwelling former celebrities of *Miss Wyoming* feel alienated from their personal histories, as they walk away from the town: 'They crossed San Vincente Boulevard, passing buildings and roads that once held stories for each of them, but which now seemed transient and disconnected from their lives'.[44] Postmodern anomie seems to dissolve the potential to tell meaningful stories and obviate the possibility of becoming part of a more significant narrative in the process. One of the random, subconscious thoughts transcribed by the narrator of *Microserfs* might be a kind of appeal to the reader to recuperate their own sense of sacred narrative: 'We generate stories for you because you don't save the ones that are yours' (*MS*, p. 349). The stories 'generated' by Coupland – drawn from his act of witness to a world that seems to have sacrificed its sense of sanctity whatever its superficial piety – frequently turn to visions of destruction, death and a possible ending of human history. How might this recurrent, almost obsessive 'sense of an ending' confront a contemporary negation of story, purpose and ultimate meaning? The final section of this chapter evaluates the type of eschatology offered in Coupland's writing and considers his representation of death and resurrection.

Dry Bones Dancing: Coupland, Apocalypse and Resurrection

'Bad visions are better than no visions', states Liz Dunn, reflecting on the presence of medical miracles at the opening of *Eleanor Rigby* (*ER*, p. 2). Liz's son, Jeremy, is haunted by strange images of the future: 'Omens. Things we see when we're near end times' (*ER*, p. 42). Liz herself later inherits – and in interpretation completes – her dead son's strange gift. On the novel's penultimate page, Liz takes a painkiller that facilitates a vivid continuation of her son's recurrent vision of prairie farmers whose world has become a wilderness. However, Liz is not simply a mute witness in this analgesic hallucination; this lifelong sceptic becomes a prophetic voice:

> They asked me, 'What is our choice?'
> And I said, 'You have to decide whether you want God to be here with you as part of your everyday life, or whether you want God to be distant from you, not returning until you've created a world perfect enough for Him to re-enter' (*ER*, p. 248)

This peculiar dream, in its embrace of pastoral and apocalyptic imagery, reflects Coupland's ongoing interest in the way God is imagined in contemporary culture. Should God, if believed in at all, be considered to be part of 'everyday life' or as a reserved and remote creator? Tom Wright argues that Jewish and Christian cosmology emphasizes that 'God's space' and human space, though distinct, 'interlock'; 'heaven', in this set of overlapping traditions, 'is not miles away up in the sky, but is, so to speak, God's dimension of the cosmos'.[45] The fear that God might have deliberately absented himself from the universe is addressed in *Hey Nostradamus!*, Coupland's most theologically solemn novel. As the murdered Cheryl Anway narrates her last day on earth from an indeterminate place in the afterlife ('I'm no longer a part of the world and I'm still not yet a part of what follows'), she recalls writing the odd binary 'GOD IS NOWHERE/GOD IS NOW HERE' repeatedly across her binder (*HN*, p. 9). This theological conundrum emblematizes the novel's focus on the possibility, or otherwise, of belief in a benevolent, loving and powerful God in a world in which evil persists and random violence thrives. As Brian Draper observes, Cheryl's overinterpreted gnomic epigram not only 'relies on a space for its linguistic impact' but also symbolizes the 'gap between God's seemingly random presence and absence in a hurting world' that seems most to interest Coupland.[46] Although *Hey Nostradamus!* avoids tidy answers to such a complex problem of theodicy, it presents a powerful narrative of a fallen world that is nevertheless crowded with fragile signs of grace. Cheryl describes the world as 'unbearably pretty' but views humanity as defined by its 'capacity at any moment to commit all possible sins' (*HN*, p. 3). Coupland's oblique return to these themes in *Eleanor Rigby*, the novel's immediate successor, underlines a concern with the theological problem of pain. The wilderness dwellers in Liz's dream are caught between a despairing theology of divine alienation and one that might recuperate a relationship with God. Her vision differs from many of the other moments of revelation in Coupland's fiction because it appears to transcend time rather than to represent a dream of a time to come. Visions of the future, frequently represented as a less than joyful prospect, pervade *Polaroids from the Dead* and *Girlfriend in a Coma*. Indeed, all manner of visions, prophecies, predictions, omens and anticipations of an imminent end saturate Coupland's novels. These visions are not exclusively granted to the most spiritually sophisticated characters in his oeuvre. Indeed, Tyler Johnson, the materialistic but naive young narrator of *Shampoo Planet*, a character whose 'memories begin with Ronald Reagan', is perhaps the least obviously spiritually oriented of Coupland's protagonists.[47] Yet, as he drives on what he names 'a pilgrimage to Apple Headquarters' and through the San Francisco Bay area, he experiences an odd vision of a decayed civilization:

[C]ities so big and so dead as to have their own complete cosmologies of the afterworld ... I envision screaming housewife mummies in pearls dog-paddling in the molten coke lakes of the anti-Pittsburgh. I picture eyeless ghost engineers huddled above the blueprints of iron machines that will eat the sky in slow motion. I imagine skeleton passengers on a BOAC prop flight that will never land, their bones clad in smart wool suits, lifting cocktails to grinning skull faces, rattling and chanting with rage at their eternal damnation, gleefully clacking their fibulas together and toasting the black-and-white industrial landscapes below – the anti-Bremen, the anti-Portsmouth, the anti-Hamilton, the anti-Yokohama, and the anti-Gdansk – the plane puncturing the fluffy clouds of smokestacks – billowing gray tufts of dioxides and burning time. (*SP*, p. 217)

Tyler's daydream vision, as vivid as any religious painting in the history of western art, is both offhand and secular. As a child of the cold war, Tyler's death-filled post-industrial landscape is shaped by the ideology of a triumphant capitalism but it is also unconsciously steeped in a language of apocalypse that he does not have the religious background to contextualize. The busy roads of the west coast are a popular space for such end-time visions in Coupland's fiction: in *Microserfs*, Dan Underwood also indulges in a moment of Californian dreaming when 'locked' in traffic:

I saw visions of the Valley and snapped out of my daydream jealous of the future. I saw geranium in the groundwater and dead careers. I saw venture capitalists with their eyes burned out of their sockets by visions of money, crashing their Nissans on the 101 – past the big blue cube of NASA's Onizuka Air Force Base, their windows spurting fluorescent orange blood. (*MS*, p. 192)

Whereas Tyler's vision is of failed European communism, Dan's reverie combines enthusiasm for the near future with a punitive envy of those who will be given access to such a world. Neither dream is explicitly theological but they both affirm the argument that even 'secular' literature cannot escape apocalyptic ideas. For Paul Fiddes '[a]ll texts are eschatological, both in being open to the new meaning which is to come to them in the future, and also in being "seriously" open to the horizon which death gives to life'.[48] In *Microserfs*, Dan, who is neither a theologian nor a literary theorist, makes a strikingly similar observation in response to the potentially unlimited arcs of multimedia storytelling: 'Narratives (stories) traditionally come to a definite end (unlike life); that's why we like movies and literature – for that sense of *closure* because they *end*' (*MS*, p. 139). What kind of 'closure' does Coupland's fiction favour? Dan and his friends are fascinated by the spectacle of catastrophic endings: their shared predilection for disaster movies, watched on a VCR 'frame-by-frame', are a way of containing their fears of an imminent end; these motifs of civilization in ruins also anticipate the apocalyptic dreamscape of *Girlfriend in a Coma* (*MS*, p. 232). Yet, in spite of these anxieties, the 'microserfs' broadly share Tyler Johnson's optimism regarding the future. Indeed, Michael suggests that the 'belief that tomorrow is a different place from today is certainly a unique hallmark of our species' (*MS*, p. 242). Significantly, this default anthropological confidence in 'tomorrow' has evaporated in *JPod*, Coupland's thematic sequel to *Microserfs*. 'I don't believe in the future. I think we're all doomed', comments one character who is convinced that civilization will soon end as a result either of global warming, terrorist activity or deadly virus or as a fatal melange of all three (*JP*, pp. 329–30). *JPod* explores the disappointments of living in an era in which the idea of the future has failed. Where the characters in the morally dazed and confused world of *JPod* can find no genuine alternative to this melancholy, many of Coupland's protagonists are confronted with alternative ways of thinking about the future.

Two of the three storytellers in *Generation X*, for example, are accidentally brought together as the result of an end-of-the-world forecast. Claire meets Andy in a Palm Springs resort on 'on the hot, windy Mother's Day weekend that Nostradamus (according to some interpretations) had predicted would be the end of the world' (*GX*, p. 37). Claire rejects the superstitions that have brought together her entire family – who believe that they might avoid the last judgement by escaping Los Angeles – and sees this New Age apocalyptic as evidence of a deeper malaise: 'I mean, when people ... get all misty-eyed about the Last Days, then it's about as striking a confession as you're ever likely to get of how upset they are that life isn't working out the way they thought it would' (*GX*, p. 42). Similar apocalyptic fears are pursued in 'The Wrong Sun', one of the short stories in *Life After God*. Coupland explores the fear of nuclear annihilation common to people who grew up in the 1960s, 70s and 80s and in a surreal section entitled 'The Dead Speak', he ventriloquizes multiple witnesses to the end of the world. The descriptions of burning skies, exploding bodies and melting furniture typify late-twentieth-century fictions of disaster but the story becomes distinctive in its sudden evocation of an afterlife:

> It is much later on, now. Please, take your breath, for breath is what *you* require – oxygen, light and water. And time. But not us. We are no longer with you. We are no longer part of the living. The birds are here with us now this is where they went. And the fish in the sea – and the plants and all of God's fine animals.
>
> It is cooler here, too, and it is quiet. And we are changed souls; we don't look at things the same way anymore. For there was once a time when we expected the worst. But then the worst happened, did it not? And so we will never be surprised ever again.[49]

This picture of heaven might be regarded as audacious or as an evasion of reality. Is Coupland's fascination with the apocalyptic evidence of an escapist urge or does it signify something more spiritually complex? Bilton maintains that Coupland's narratives 'deploy ... sentimentality to counter soullessness' and that his 'sincerity ... can be seen as apolitical, anti-intellectual and twee'.[50] Similarly, Matthew Reynolds observes that 'the switch from satire to bearing witness' in Coupland's fiction 'has always felt uneasy'.[51] In fact, his novels demonstrate a distinct antipathy for convenient, commitment-free spiritualities or what he implies is hazy, easily exploited, New Age religion. Just as the narrator of *Eleanor Rigby* dismisses 'the zodiac [as] pure hooey', the title of *Hey Nostradamus!* is derived from one of its characters railing against the apparent limits of the legendary prophet's foresight. Heather, the novel's penultimate narrator, is also cruelly manipulated by a fraudulent psychic who claims to be able to mediate messages from the missing, presumed dead, Jason. The implication of Coupland's narrative is not that the transcendent itself is a fiction, but that it has become debased in gross materialism: 'How could you use extortion when you were doing something so . . . *sacred*?' (*HN*, p. 228).

An urgent lack of authentic spirituality provides the context for *Girlfriend in a Coma*. For Robert McGill, this strange fable is 'not apocalyptic' but rather is 'a response to apocalyptic literature'.[52] Yet, for all that the novel parodies 'end-time' fantasies, prevalent in the final years of the twentieth century, it is also dependent on a tradition of Christian apocalyptic to challenge its readers. As Jason Cowley notes, the novel taps into 'the longing for a great cleansing act that may redeem humanity and allow us all to start again, unchained from history'.[53] In 1979 Karen McNeil experiences vivid but fragmentary visions of a future world, stripped of meaning and beauty, without redeeming illusions or hope. Shortly afterwards, she slips into a coma and awakens many years later, in time to witness the final – in her eyes – bewildering days of the twentieth century. The novel takes on a fable-like quality as the last days of humanity are precipitated by an appalling plague that, in an echo of Karen's coma, induces sleep and death. This trope of global catastrophe resonates with what Robert Detweiler, in identifying the 'theological trends' of postmodern narrative, has described as the 'point at which science fiction joins serious literature, where evocations of other worlds or future versions of our world are employed to provide the substance and presence lacking in our experience'.[54] Similarly, *Girlfriend in a Coma* confronts the spiritual deficiencies of the present world in its image of a blank, forsaken future landscape. Karen's immediate group of friends are the only survivors of this sleep-plague, and they are haunted by Jared, one of Coupland's three high-school spectres, who confronts them with the truth about their own lack of spiritual hunger. As a kind of divine witness, one who bears testimony to the heaven that he has seen, Jared offers them the opportunity to restore the world that was apparently exhausted and at an end: 'Ask questions, no *screech* questions out loud – while kneeling in front of the electric doors at Safeway . . . Ask: *Having become human, what is it that we are now doing or creating that will transform us into whatever it is that we are slated to next become?*' (*GIAC*, pp. 269–70). In a novel that explores the blurred distinction between the ideas of 'the future' (the upshot of human progress) and the 'afterlife' (a concept beyond conceptualization), this wayward angel shares a vision of eternal paradise:

> Heaven's like the world at its finest. It's all natural – no buildings. It's built of stars and roots and mud and flesh and snakes and birds. It's built of clouds and stones and rivers and lava. But it's *not* a building. (*GIAC*, p. 230)

This image recalls both the vision of paradise shared in 'The Wrong Sun' and the epiphanic (but not supernatural) ending of *Shampoo Planet*, in which Tyler Johnson, suddenly drenched in the peculiar baptismal waters of a neighbour's pond, proclaims that '*the world is alive*' (*SP*, p. 299). Similarly, Jared's account of heaven as both thoroughly corporeal and organic is a significant counterpoint to Coupland's focus on the suburban world. Indeed, it rewrites the utopian notion that he identifies in the 'Brentwood Notebook' as vital to postmodern municipal space: '*Heaven is manufacturable*' (*PFD*, p. 164).

Jared also grants Linus a brief 'glimpse of heaven' which, in an echo of Saul's Damascene conversion, temporarily blinds him (*GIAC*, p. 237). Jared, this strange angel, echoes a figure from Benjamin's mystical theses on history: the Angel of History, derived in turn from a Paul Klee painting and narrated so hauntingly in Benjamin's prophetic essay:

> Where we perceive a chain of events, he sees one single catastrophe which keeps piling wreckage upon wreckage and hurls it in front of his feet. The angel would like to stay, awaken the dead, and make whole what has been smashed. But a storm is blowing from Paradise; it has got caught in his wings with such violence that the angel can no longer close them. This storm irresistibly propels him into the future to which his back is turned, while the pile of debris before him grows skyward. This storm is what we call progress.[55]

Jared, like Benjamin's angel, watches the woeful spectacle of a decadent, 'progress'-focused humanity, but he is able to revive and transform the self-satisfied lives of his peers. Coupland's protagonists are symbolically awakened to the necessity of connection with a broader community and forced to see beyond the present to a world beyond personal gratification and the grave. The bodies of the 'countless leathery skeletons' are made whole again and in an echo of Ezekiel 37.7 – 'and as I prophesied, there was a noise and behold a shaking, and the bones came together, bone to his bone' – the 'dry bones' of an apparently dead culture are given new life. Jared becomes an unlikely angel – one who is able to impart a renewed *eschaton* to a lethargic and complacent culture – and embodies an irreverent, postmodern whisper of divine judgement.

The Christian hope of bodily resurrection is played out in the extraordinary, miraculous conclusion to *Girlfriend in a Coma*. Not all critics are enthusiastic about Coupland's exploration of the transcendent. Mark Forshaw, for example, notes that the 'spectral otherworldliness' of the final section of the novel 'seems bound to disappoint Coupland's less transcendental, more materialist readers'.[56] However, this turn to theological narrative, and particularly to the miraculous, has become crucial to Coupland's exploration of materialism. A motif of the relationship between mortality and eternity is enacted in 'How Clear is Your Vision of Heaven?', one of the interpolated short stories in *Polaroids from the Dead*. The framing narrative is set at a Grateful Dead outdoor concert in California and is spoken by a bohemian mother to her children. It is a story with a counter-cultural matrilineage, told to its narrator by her own mother in a 1960s commune. The parable, however, has earlier origins and, like the revivification of the dead in *Girlfriend in a Coma* it alludes to Ezekiel's vision (indeed the prophet's name is given to one of the characters in the framing story). In Columbia's story of the 'enchanted city', a wealthy king and his people pray for rain and are visited by a skeleton with a prophetic message:

> While you live in mortal splendor – with glass elevators and silk shirts and grapes in December – the price you pay for your comfort is a collapsed vision of heaven – the loss of the ability to see pictures in your heads of an afterlife. You pray for rain, but you are also praying for pictures in your heads that will renew your faith in an afterlife. (*PFD*, p. 59)

The skeleton is cast from the city three times before the king repents, acknowledges his own mortality and realizes the need to envision a future beyond the present, material world: rain falls on the city, the skeleton departs, and the children, in listening to this strange, troubling parable, become part of a bigger tradition of apocalyptic storytelling. The skeleton, whose dry bones dance, is an intimation of eternity, the promise of resurrection. In *The Promised End*, Fiddes argues that '[o]urs is a society that evades death, by shutting it away ... Death has been packaged as virtual reality, as a media event'.[57] The spirituality of Coupland's fiction is dependent on its fierce wrestling with death: yet the many reminders of mortality in his work – the number of deaths in adolescence, for example – are not signs of morbidity or a collusion with a culture that has made a fetish of death as 'media event'. 'Neither the artistic imagination nor religious faith can really offer us visions of alternate worlds as a substitute for this one,' argues Detweiler, 'for what they show us is simply a fuller, more affirmative vision of our own present world'.[58] Coupland's emphasis on mortality leavened by the hope of a future life also echo Alasdair MacIntyre's analysis of the connection between futurity and narrative:

> We live out our lives, both individually and in our relationships with each other, in the light of certain conceptions of a possible shared future, a future in which certain possibilities beckon us forward and others repel us, some seem already foreclosed and others perhaps inevitable. There is no present which is not informed by some image of some future and an image of the future which always presents itself in the form of a *telos* – or of a variety of ends or goals – towards which we are either moving or failing to move in the present. Unpredictability and teleology therefore coexist as part of our lives.[59]

The resurrection imagery of 'How Clear is Your Vision of Heaven?' is pursued in the conclusion to *Hey Nostradamus!*: the novel begins with an epigraph from Paul – 'Behold, I tell you a mystery; We shall not all sleep, but we shall all be changed' (1 Corinthians 15.51–2) – and concludes with the expectation of a miracle. A novel that has witnessed mass murder in the motiveless slaughter of students by three of their peers – ends with a rewriting of the parable of the Prodigal Son as narrated in Luke 15.11–32 : 'Rejoice! All of you! Rejoice! You must! My son is coming home!' (*HN*, p. 244). The hope expressed by a penitent father, in a reversal of the biblical narrative, might be regarded as wholly irrational. His son's disappearance is unexplained and it is likely that he has perished, or been murdered, in the wilderness outside Vancouver. Yet it is a redemptive ending, not based on fairy-tale superstition, but in an *eschaton* that insists on faith in bodily resurrection. In the miraculous realism of Douglas Coupland, a wild hope in an impossible future is staked and our collective 'collapsed vision of heaven' is challenged.

7

Conclusion: Miraculous Realism

'The theologian and the artist alike', maintains Peter C. Hodgson, 'are engaged in a creative act, a *poiésis*, an envisionment of a possible world in which human beings might dwell humanly'.[1] If this is the case, does fiction need to be outwardly religious to speak meaningfully of spiritual matters? Literature, alongside art and music, as Philip Sheldrake observes, has become a medium 'for an inchoate and non-thematic exploration of spirituality and human meaning'.[2] From a more conservative position, the God-talk of contemporary culture risks undermining the specifics of religious belief: in such an era God loses a unique identity. As one theologian argues, God 'has become pluralized into a general spirituality and identified with virtually anything whatsoever.'[3] Yet a fundamental claim of this book is that ostensibly secular novels can be profoundly theological. The religious dimension of contemporary fiction is, as discussed in previous chapters, partly a product of a wider 'sacred turn' or what one theologian has described as 'the amazing return of religion'.[4] It is also an outcome of an era in which theological ideas and beliefs at a popular level, as Christopher Deacy has argued, 'traditionally expressed in the Christian religion in the language of sin, estrangement, atonement and redemption, are being articulated through radically different vehicles of expression and outside traditionally demarcated boundaries of religious activity.'[5] This is not to suggest that religiously inclined readers should expect all good fiction to be covertly theistic. I concur with Paul S. Fiddes' contention that literature and doctrine should not simply be conflated in the continuing, productive dialogue between the two. However, what Fiddes describes as literature's emphasis on the 'playful freedom of imagination' certainly illuminates belief in surprising, dislocating ways to which orthodox, doctrinal statements do not aspire.[6]

The contemporary novel has become a space in which sacred and secular concerns converge in surprising ways. Towards the close of Jon McGregor's outstanding debut novel, *If Nobody Speaks of Remarkable Things* (2002), for example, a father listens patiently to his daughter's questions about angels and other inexplicable phenomena. His non-doctrinaire answer is energized by a sensation of wonder that emphasizes the importance of bearing witness to the 'remarkable':

> He says this is a very big world and there are many many things you could miss if you are not careful. He says there are remarkable things all the time,

this study's preceding chapters, many novelists who are hostile to the traditions of Christian belief continually return to its claims as a source of imaginative inspiration or as an arena for debate.

The relationship between the categories of the sacred and the secular is far less secure than believers or sceptics sometimes claim. John Updike, for example, is a serious theological novelist with professed Christian beliefs whose fiction often seems more despairing and certainly more vividly worldly than the fiction of many of his faithless peers. Indeed, in *The Theology of Culture* (1959), Paul Tillich reminded his readers that alongside the 'glory' of religion that 'gives us the experience of the Holy, of something which is untouchable, awe-inspiring, an ultimate meaning' lies its 'shame' in the way in which it 'despises the secular realm'. In losing humility and by making its traditions into idols, religion 'forgets its own emergency character'.[14] Novels by atheists, agnostics and itinerant spiritual seekers such as Jim Crace, John Irving, Michèle Roberts and Douglas Coupland (and, indeed, the scores of other established and emerging writers whom it has not been possible to explore in a single volume) prompt their readers to remember the 'emergency character' of religious belief. Their fiction, particularly when it addresses, explicitly or otherwise, the central moment of the Christian metanarrative, the life, death and resurrection of Jesus Christ, is capable of challenging both religious and secular complacency. As Fiddes argues, the story of incarnation, in particular, is 'a journey of identification with the human situation, drawing together the scattered and broken pieces of life' and 'a movement of both revelation and divine imagination.'[15] Fiction is a poor substitute for faith in such an incarnation but faith itself is weakened without the imaginative resources of its (provisional) fictions. The novel, that most polyphonic of literary spaces, continues to bear witness to 'remarkable things'.

Notes

1.   Introduction: Re-enchanted Fictions

1. Douglas Coupland, *Life After God* (London: Simon & Schuster, 1995), p. 359.
2. Yann Martel, *Life of Pi* (Edinburgh: Canongate, 2002), p. x.
3. E. L. Doctorow, *City of God* (London: Abacus, 2001), p. 16.
4. See, for example, Steve Bruce, *Religion in the Modern World: from Cathedrals to Cults* (Oxford: Oxford University Press, 1996) and *God is Dead: Secularization in the West* (Oxford: Blackwell, 2002).
5. Callum Brown, *The Death of Christian Britain: Understanding Secularisation, 1800–2000* (London: Routledge, 2001), p. 32, p. 30.
6. William E. Connolly, 'Refashioning the Secular', Judith Butler, John Guillory and Kendall Thomas (eds), *What's Left of Theory? New Work on the Politics of Literary Theory* (New York: Routledge, 2000), pp. 157–91 (p. 157). These ideas are developed in more detail in Connolly's book, *Why I Am Not a Secularist* (Minneapolis: University of Minnesota Press, 1999).
7. Peter L. Berger, 'The Desecularization of the World. A Global Overview', in Peter L. Berger (ed.) *The Desecularization of the World: Essays on the Resurgence of Religion in World Politics* (Washington: Ethics and Public Policy Center; Grand Rapids: William B. Eerdmans), p. 2. Also cited in *Religion in Modern Times: An Interpretive Anthology*, Linda Woodhead and Paul Heelas (eds) (Oxford: Blackwell, 2000), p. 434.
8. Harvey Cox, 'The Myth of the Twentieth Century: The Rise and Fall of Secularization' in *The Twentieth Century: A Theological Overview*, Gregory Baum (ed.) (New York: Obis/London: Geoffrey Chapman, 1999), pp. 135–43 (p. 143).
9. Graham Ward, *True Religion* (Oxford: Blackwell, 2003), p. vii.
10. Sarah Coakley, 'Fresh Paths in Systematic Theology', in Rupert Shortt, *God's Advocates: Christian Thinkers in Conversation* (London: Darton, Longman and Todd, 2005), pp. 75–6.
11. Zygmunt Bauman, 'Postmodern Religion?' in *Religion, Modernity and Postmodernity*, Paul Heelas (ed.), with David Martin and Paul Morris (Oxford: Blackwell, 1998), pp. 55–78 (p. 74).
12. John D. Caputo, *On Religion* (London: Routledge, 2001), p. 66.
13. Graham Ward, Introduction: 'Where We Stand', *The Blackwell Companion to Postmodern Theology*, Graham Ward (ed.) (Oxford: Blackwell, 2001), xii–xxvii (p. xv).
14. Ward, *op. cit.*, p. xxi.
15. Kevin Hart, *The Trespass of the Sign: Deconstruction, Theology and Philosophy* (New York: Cambridge University Press, 1989); Graham Ward, *Theology and Contemporary Critical Theory*, second edition (Basingstoke: Macmillan, 2000); Hent de Vries, *Philosophy and the Turn to Religion* (Baltimore: Johns Hopkins University Press,

1999); E. M. Mazur and K. McCarthy (eds), *God in the Details: American Religion in Popular Culture* (New York and London: Routledge, 2001); Luke Ferreter, *Towards a Christian Literary Theory* (Houndmills: Palgrave, 2003); Arthur Bradley, *Negative Theology and Modern French Philosophy* (London: Routledge, 2004).

16.   See, for example, the editors' prefatory essay, 'Introduction – Apology for the Impossible: Religion and Postmodernism' in John D. Caputo and Michael J. Scanlon, *God, the Gift and Postmodernism* (Indiana and Bloomington: Indiana University Press, 1999), pp. 1–19. 'Let us say that what brought the participants in this conference together is a desire to *experience the impossible*, to go where we cannot go, as Angelus Silesius said, where the 'method' prescribed by modernity prohibits; to cross these limits, to defy the border patrol, to think the unthinkable' (pp. 2–3).

17.   de Vries, *op. cit.*, p. 3.

18.   Georg Lukács, *The Theory of the Novel: A Historico-Philosophical Essay on the Forms of Great Epic Literature*, trans. Anna Bostock (London: Merlin, 1971), p. 88. For recent discussions of this influential claim see Terry Eagleton, *The English Novel: an Introduction* (Oxford: Blackwell, 2005), p. 16; Mark Knight and Thomas Woodman, 'The Word in the Word: An Introduction', *Biblical Religion and the Novel, 1700–2000* (Aldershot: Ashgate, 2006), pp. 1 ff.

19.   J. Hillis Miller, *The Disappearance of God: Five Nineteenth-Century Writers* (Cambridge: Belknap Press, 1975 [1963]), p. 1.

20.   Hillis Miller, *op. cit.*, p. 2.

21.   Peter Fuller, *Images of God: Art and the consolation of lost illusions* (London: Hogarth, 1993), p. 189.

22.   Fuller, *op. cit.* , p. 190.

23.   Paul S. Fiddes, *The Promised End: Eschatology in Theology and Literature* (Oxford: Blackwell, 2000), p. 7. See also Fiddes, *Freedom and Limit: A Dialogue between Literature and Christian Doctrine* (Basingstoke: Macmillan Press, 1991), pp. 15, 33–5.

24.   James Wood, *The Broken Estate: Essays in Literature and Belief* (London: Jonathan Cape, 1999), pp. xiii, xiv.

25.   Salman Rushdie, Imaginary Homelands: Essays and Criticism, 1981–1991 (London: Granta, 1992), p. 427.

26.   Ralph C. Wood, The Comedy of Redemption: Christian Faith and Comic Vision in Four American Novelists (Notre Dame: University of Notre Dame Press, 1988), p. 280.

27.   Stephen R. Haynes, 'Footsteps of Ann Hutchinson and Frederick Buechner: A Religious Reading of John Irving's *A Prayer for Owen Meany*', *Religion and Literature*, 27.3 (1995), 73–98 (p. 73).

28.   Robert Detweiler, *Breaking the Fall: Religious Readings of Contemporary Fiction* (Louisville: Westminster John Knox Press, 1995), pp. 48–9.

29.   Sara Maitland, 'Religious experience and the novel: a problem of genre and culture', *The Novel, Spirituality and Modern Culture*, edited by Paul S. Fiddes (Cardiff: University of Wales Press, 2000), pp. 77–96 (p. 79).

30.   Maitland, *op. cit.*, pp. 77–8.

31.   Blake Morrison, 'God and Me', *God's Own Countries*, pp. 183–4 (p. 184).

32.   James Wood, 'The Celestial Teapot', *The New Republic*, 18 December 2006, pp. 27–32 (p. 27).

33.   For a nuanced reading of Hardy's fiction in relation to nineteenth-century religious discourse, including its debt to debates regarding both blasphemy and Evangelical

faith, see Mark Knight and Emma Mason, *Nineteenth-Century Religion and Literature: an Introduction* (Oxford: Oxford University Press, 2006), p. 143, pp. 180–1.

34. Henry James, 'The Art of Fiction' (1884), reprinted in *The Portable Henry James*, Morton Dauwen Zabel (ed.) (London: Penguin, 1977), pp. 387–414 (p. 389).
35. Terry Eagleton, *The English Novel: An Introduction* (Oxford: Blackwell, 2005), p. 3.
36. John Updike, 'Religion and Literature' in *The Religion Factor: An Introduction to How Religion Matters*, William Scott Green and Jacob Neusner (eds) (Louisville: Westminster John Knox Press, 1996), p. 239.
37. Paul Maltby, *The Visionary Moment: A Postmodern Critique* (Albany: SUNY, 2002), p. 1.
38. John D. Caputo, *On Religion* (London: Routledge, 2001), p. 17.
39. Head is discussing what he sees as the 'anachronistic' spiritual crisis in Pamela Hansford Johnson's 1959 novel *The Humbler Creation*. Dominic Head, *The Cambridge Introduction to Modern British Fiction, 19502000* (Cambridge: Cambridge University Press, 2002), p. 18.
40. Donna Tartt, 'The Spirit and Writing in a Secular World', in *The Novel, Spirituality and Modern Culture*, Paul Fiddes (ed.) (Cardiff: University of Wales, 2000), pp. 25–40 (p. 25).
41. Brown 2001, p. 193.
42. Brown 2001, p. 36.
43. Brown 2001, p. 193.
44. James Robertson, *The Testament of Gideon Mack* (London: Penguin, 2007), p. 51.
45. 'Interview with James Robertson: The Testament of Gideon Mack', www.booksfromscotland.com/Authors/James-Robertson/Gideon-Mack-Interview (8/2/2007).
46. Robertson 2007, p. 37.
47. David Jasper, *The Study of Literature and Religion: An Introduction* (Houndmills: Macmillan, 1989), p. ix.
48. Richard Swinburne, 'Introduction' to *Miracles*, Richard Swinburne (ed.) (New York: Macmillan, 1989), pp. 1–17 (p. 2).
49. T. R. Wright, *Theology and Literature* (Oxford: Blackwell, 1988), p. 111.
50. Douglas Coupland, *Microserfs* (London: Harper, 2004), pp. 142–3.
51. Gillian Beer, *The Romance* (London: Methuen, 1970), p. 10.
52. Ward 2003, p. 32.
53. For an authoritative analysis of Magic Realist traditions in literature and film see Maggie Ann Bowers, *Magic(al) Realism* (London: Routledge, 2004).
54. John Updike, 'Hawthorne's Creed', *Hugging the Shore: Essays and Criticism* (Harmondsworth: Penguin, 1985), p. 78.
55. John L'Heureux, *The Miracle* (New York: Grove, 2002), p. 4.
56. Jonathan Coe, *The Rotters' Club* (London: Penguin, 2002), p. 15. All subsequent references to the novel will be given parenthetically to this edition, as *TRC* followed by the page number.
57. Hans W. Frei, *The Eclipse of Biblical Narrative: A Study of Eighteenth and Nineteenth-Century Hermeneutics* (New Haven: Yale University Press, 1974), p. 14.
58. Knight and Woodman 2006, p. 5.
59. David Maine, *The Flood* (Edinburgh: Canongate, 2005), p. 83.
60. Valentine Cunningham, 'Introduction: The Necessity of Heresy', in *Figures of Heresy: Radical Theology in English and American Writing*, Andrew Dix and Jonathan Taylor (eds) (Brighton: Sussex Academic Press, 2006), pp. 1–18 (p. 2).

61. Cunningham, *op. cit.*, p. 1, p. 12.
62. Harold Fisch, *New Stories for Old: Biblical Patterns in the Novel* (Basingstoke: Macmillan, 1998); Jo Carruthers, 'Literature', *The Blackwell Companion to the Bible and Culture*, John Sawyer (ed.) (Oxford: Blackwell, 2006), pp. 253–67 (p. 256).
63. See David Lyon's use of the 'haunting phrase of Berger, Berger, and Kellner' who write of the 'homeless minds' of the 'moderns', *Jesus in Disneyland: Religion in Postmodern Times* (Cambridge: Polity, 2000), p. 31; Peter L. Berger, Brigitte Berger and Hansfried Kellner, *Homeless Minds* (Harmondsworth: Penguin, 1974).
64. Jeanette King, *Women and the Word: Contemporary Women Novelists and the Bible* (Houndmills: Palgrave, 2000), p. 123.
65. James Wood, *The Book Against God* (London: Vintage, 2004), p. 16. All subsequent references will be given parenthetically to this edition as *TBAG*, followed by the page number.
66. Flannery O'Connor, 'The Church and the Fiction Writer', *Mystery and Manners: Occasional Prose* (London: Faber, 1972), pp. 151–2.
67. Michael Edwards, *Towards a Christian Poetics* (London: Macmillan, 1984), p. 12.
68. Douglas Coupland, *Girlfriend in a Coma* (London: Flamingo, 1998), p. 90.
69. David Lodge, *Paradise News* (London: Penguin, 1992), p. 352.
70. Lodge, *op. cit.*, p. 352.
71. Robert Detweiler, 'Theological Trends of Postmodern Fiction', *Journal of the American Academy of Religion*, 44.2 (1976), pp. 225–37 (p. 234).
72. Zygmunt Bauman, *Intimations of Postmodernity* (London: Routledge, 1992), p. x.
73. Bauman, *op. cit.*, p. x.
74. Terry Eagleton, *The Meaning of Life* (Oxford: Oxford University Press, 2007), p. 30.
75. John A. McClure, 'Postmodern/Post-Secular: Contemporary Fiction and Spirituality', *Modern Fiction Studies*, 41.1 (1995): 141–63 (p. 143). Also cited in Brian D. Ingraffia, 'Is the Postmodern Post-Secular?', in *Postmodern Philosophy and Christian Thought*, Merold Westphal (ed.) (Bloomington: Indiana University Press, 1999), pp. 44–68 (p. 44).
76. Martyn Percy, *The Salt of the Earth: Religious Resilience in a Secular Age* (London and New York: Sheffield Academic Press, 2001), p. 65.
77. Stuart Rose, 'Is the Term 'Spirituality' a Word that Everyone Uses, But Nobody Knows What Anyone Means By it?', *Journal of Contemporary Religion*, 16.2 (2001), 193–207.
78. Rose, *op. cit.*, p. 202.
79. Alister E. McGrath, *The Future of Christianity* (Oxford: Blackwell, 2002), p. viii.
80. Philip Sheldrake, *A Brief History of Spirituality* (Oxford: Blackwell, 2007), p. 2.
81. Ingraffia 1999, p. 45 ff.
82. Brian D. Ingraffia, *Postmodern Theory and Biblical Theology: Vanquishing God's shadow* (Cambridge: Cambridge University Press, 1995), p. 14.
83. Ingraffia 1995, p. 6.
84. Phillip Blond, 'The primacy of theology and the question of perception', in Heelas, Martin and Morris (1998), pp. 285–313 (p. 285).
85. Roy M. Anker, *Catching Light: Looking for God in the Movies* (Grand Rapids: William B. Eerdmans, 2004), p. 11.
86. Rhidian Brook, *The Testimony of Taliesin Jones* (London: Flamingo, 1997), p. 49.
87. Salman Rushdie, *The Ground Beneath Her Feet* (London: Vintage, 2000), p. 99, p. 242.
88. N. T. Wright, *The Challenge of Jesus* (London: SPCK, 2000), p. 70.

89. Martin Amis, *Heavy Water and Other Stories* (London: Vintage, 1998), pp.1867. Updike's emphasis on the 'longing' for God is a key part of *Roger's Version* (1986), discussed in Chapter 3 of this book.
90. Amis, *op. cit.*, p. 187.
91. Martel 2002, p. x.
92. Martel 2002, p. 50.
93. Wright 1988, p. 111.
94. Rushdie 2000, pp. 82–3.
95. Martel 2002, p. 28.
96. Wood 1999, p. xiv.
97. Kevin J. Vanhoozer, 'Scripture and Tradition' in *The Cambridge Companion to Postmodern Theology*, Kevin J. Vanhoozer (ed.) (Cambridge: Cambridge University Press, 2003), pp. 149–69 (p. 167).
98. Keith Ward, *Christianity: A Short Introduction* (Oxford: Oneworld, 2000), p. 179.

2. This Other Christ: Jesus in Contemporary Fiction

1. William C. Placher, *The Domestication of Transcendence: How Modern Thinking about God Went Wrong* (Louisville: Westminster John Knox Press, 1996), p. xi.
2. N. T. Wright, *The Challenge of Jesus* (London: SPCK, 2000), p. x.
3. Pat Barker, *Double Vision* (London: Penguin, 2004), p. 9, p. 7. All subsequent references will be given parenthetically to this edition as *DV*, followed by page number.
4. Rupert Shortt, *God's Advocates: Christian Thinkers in Conversation* (London: Darton, Longman and Todd, 2005), pp. 22–3.
5. Mieke Bal, 'Postmodern Theology as Cultural Analysis', in *The Blackwell Companion to Postmodern Theology*, Graham Ward (ed.) (Oxford: Blackwell, 2001), pp. 3–23 (p. 4).
6. Jim Crace, 'Introduction to *Quarantine*'. This short essay was published by amazon.com, and may now be accessed via a link at www.jim-crace.com.
7. John Updike, 'Religion and Literature' in *The Religion Factor: An Introduction to How Religion Matters*, edited by William Scott Green and Jacob Neusner (Louisville: Westminster John Knox Press, 1996), p. 239.
8. Crace, 'Introduction to *Quarantine*'.
9. Philip Tew, *Jim Crace* (Manchester: Manchester University Press, 2006), p. 117.
10. Jim Crace, *Quarantine* (London: Penguin, 1998), p. 22. All subsequent page references will be given parenthetically in the text as *Q*, followed by page number.
11. Tew, p. 116.
12. Patrick Sherry, *Images of Redemption: Art, Literature and Salvation* (London: T&T Clark, 2003), p. 17.
13. Richard J. Lane, 'The Fiction of Jim Crace: Narrative and Recovery', in *Contemporary British Fiction*, Richard J. Lane, Rod Mengham and Philip Tew (eds) (Cambridge: Polity Press, 2003), pp. 27–39 (pp. 32, 28) (2nd edn London: Continuum, 2006).
14. Crace, 'Introduction to *Quarantine*'.
15. Shortt 2005, pp. 22–3.
16. Graham Ward, 'Suffering and Incarnation' in *The Blackwell Companion to Postmodern Theology*, p. 193.
17. Kenosis has been a major theme of Ward's theological negotiation with postmodern culture since his first monograph, *Barth, Derrida and the Language of Theology*

(Cambridge: Cambridge University Press, 1995): see, in particular, pp. 158–60. It is also a feature of his interdisciplinary survey, *Theology and Contemporary Critical Theory*, (2nd edn; Basingstoke: Macmillan Press, 2000). The conclusions of Ward's extensive explorations in Christology are developed in his monograph, *Christ and Culture* (Oxford: Blackwell, 2005).

18. Ward 2005, p. 2.

19. Karl Barth, *Dogmatics in Outline* (London: SCM, 2001), p. 59.

20. Zygmunt Bauman, 'Postmodern Religion?', in *Religion, Modernity and Postmodernity*, Paul Heelas (ed.), with David Martin and Paul Morris (Oxford: Blackwell, 1998), p. 55.

21. John A. McClure, 'Postmodern/Post-Secular: Contemporary Fiction and Spirituality', *Modern Fiction Studies*, 41.1 (1995), pp. 141–63. For an extended discussion of McClure's work, see the introduction to this book.

22. Graham Ward, 'Introduction: "Where We Stand" ', in *The Blackwell Companion to Postmodern Theology*, pp. xii–xxvii (xxi).

23. Brian D. Ingraffia, 'Is the Postmodern Post-Secular?', in *Postmodern Philosophy and Christian Thought*, Merold Westphal (ed.) (Bloomington: Indiana University Press, 1999), p. 64. See also *Ingraffia's Postmodern Theory and Biblical Theology: Vanquishing God's Shadow* (Cambridge: Cambridge University Press, 1995).

24. Barth 2001, p. 58.

25. Kevin J. Vanhoozer, 'Theology and the condition of postmodernity: a report on knowledge (of God)', in *The Cambridge Companion to Postmodern Theology*, ed. Kevin J. Vanhoozer (Cambridge: Cambridge University Press, 2003), pp. 3–25 (p. 24).

26. Michel de Certeau, 'How is Christianity Thinkable Today?' (1971) in *The Postmodern God: A Theological Reader*, edited by Graham Ward (Oxford: Blackwell, 1997), pp. 145–6. See Graham Ward's discussion of this essay in the context of de Certeau's other writing in *Theology and Contemporary Critical Theory*, p. 150.

27. John Schad, ' "These Are My Bodies": An Introduction', in *Writing the Bodies of Christ: The Church from Carlyle to Derrida*, John Schad (ed.) (Aldershot: Ashgate, 2001), pp. 1–7 (p. 3).

28. Wright 2000, p. 2.

29. Slavoj Žižek, 'Christ's Breaking of the 'Great Chain of Being', in *Writing the Bodies of Christ*, pp. 105–10. The phrase 'fighting materialist' is used in Žižek's more detailed exploration of Christianity, *The Fragile Absolute or, Why is the Christian Legacy Worth Fighting For?* (London: Verso, 2001), p. 1.

30. Theodore Ziolkowski, *Fictional Transfigurations of Jesus* (Lawrenceville, NJ: Princeton University Press, 1972).

31. Norman Mailer, *The Gospel According to the Son* (London: Abacus, 2000), p. 3. All subsequent references will be given parenthetically to this edition as *TGATTS*, followed by page number.

32. Michèle Roberts, *The Wild Girl* (London: Methuen, 1985). See 'Author's Note', p. 7. All subsequent references will be given parenthetically to this edition as *TWG*, followed by page reference.

33. See Wright's discussion and critique of the 'alternative' gospels controversy in *Simply Christian* (London: SPCK, 2006), pp. 82–5. Jeanette King explores Roberts's use of these gospels and a variety of Gnostic texts in her impressive study, *Women and the Word: Contemporary Women Novelists and the Bible* (Houndmills: Palgrave, 2000), pp. 105–17.

34. King 2000, p. 5.

35. Francis Watson, 'The quest for the real Jesus', in *The Cambridge Companion to Jesus*, Marcus Bockmuehl (ed.) (Cambridge: Cambridge University Press, 2001), p. 156.

36. Ulrich Mauser, 'Temptation of Christ', in *The Oxford Companion to The Bible*, ed. Bruce M. Metzger and Michael D. Coogan (eds) (New York and Oxford: Oxford University Press, 1993), pp. 735–6.

37. Justin Cartwright, 'After the Plague' (Review of Jim Crace's *The Pesthouse*), the *Guardian*, 17 March 2007, p. 16.

38. Tew 2006, p. 6. For an extended examination of the relationship between Crace's fiction and landscape see, in particular, the opening chapter of Tew's study, 'Exploring Craceland', p. 1–34.

39. David Jasper, *The Sacred Desert: Religion, Literature, Art and Culture* (Oxford: Blackwell, 2004), p. 100.

40. Hugh S. Pyper, 'Desert', in *The Oxford Companion to Christian Thought*, Adrian Hastings, Alistair Mason and Hugh S. Pyper (eds) (Oxford: Oxford University Press, 2000), p. 161.

41. Douglas Coupland, *Life After God* (London: Simon and Schuster, 1994), p. 167, pp. 182–3. All subsequent references will be given parenthetically to this edition as *LAG*, followed by page reference.

42. Pyper, *op. cit.*, pp. 161–2.

43. Miyahara Kazunari, '*Quarantine:* Jim Crace's Anti-Christ', *English and English-American Literature*, 35. This useful and thorough article is available via a link at www.jim-crace.com.

44. Marcus J. Borg and N. T. Wright, *The Meaning of Jesus: Two Visions* (San Francisco: Harper Collins, 1999), p. 39.

45. Frederick Buechner, *A Room Called Remember: Uncollected Pieces* (San Francisco: Harper Collins, 1992), p. 61.

46. Yann Martel, *Life of Pi* (Edinburgh: Canongate, 2002), p. 50, p. 55.

47. Martel, *op. cit.*, p. 54.

48. Martel, *op. cit.*, p. 58.

49. John Macquarrie, *Jesus Christ in Modern Thought* (London: SCM/Philadelphia: Trinity Press International, 1990), p. 245.

50. Ibid., pp. 245–6.

51. Macquarrie also identifies 2 Corinthians 8.9 as important for kenotic theology: 'For ye know the grace of our Lord Jesus Christ, that, though he was rich, yet for your sakes he became poor, that ye through his poverty might be rich.' See *Jesus Christ in Modern Thought*, p. 246.

52. Charles Gore, *Dissertations on Subjects Connected with the Incarnation* (1895). Quoted in Macquarrie, *Jesus Christ in Modern Thought*, pp. 249–50.

53. Colin E. Gunton, *Yesterday and Today: A Study of Continuities in Christology* (London: SPCK, 1997), p. 221.

54. Cited in John Polkinghorne, 'Introduction', in *The Work of Love: Creation as Kenosis*, John Polkinghorne (ed.) (Grand Rapids: Wm. B. Eerdmans, 2001), p. xiii. From the same volume, see also Keith Ward, 'Cosmos and Kenosis', pp. 152–66.

55. Graham Ward, 'Kenosis and Naming: Beyond Analogy and Towards *Allegoria Amoris*', in Heelas (ed.), *Religion, Modernity and Postmodernity*, pp. 233–57 (p. 233).

56. Ibid., pp. 233–4. Also: Jean-Luc Marion, *God Without Being* (Chicago: Chicago University Press, 1991), p. 178.

57. Graham Ward, 'Suffering and Incarnation', pp. 194, 197.

58. By contrast, Jasper, in *The Sacred Desert*, prioritizes the Christian atheological form of kenoticism, and his analysis of *Quarantine*, particularly its images of the empty land, draws on the work of Altizer. See, for example, p. 186.

59. Ward, 'Suffering and Incarnation', p. 203.

60. Albert Schweitzer, *Geschichte der Leben-Jesu-Forschung* (1906), translated into English as *The Quest of the Historical Jesus*. Quoted in Alister McGrath, *The Making of Modern German Christology* (Oxford: Blackwell, 1986), p. 2.

61. Owen Chadwick cites this maxim, without giving a specific source, in *The Secularization of the European Mind in the Nineteenth Century* (Cambridge: Canto, 1990), pp. 194–5. Chadwick notes that the idea is 'disprovable by instances'.

62. Jürgen Moltmann, *The Crucified God: the Cross of Christ as the Foundation and Criticism of Christian Theology* (London: SCM, 1974), p. 83.

63. Gunton 1997, p. 53.

64. Charlotte Allen, 'The Search for a No-Frills Jesus', *Atlantic Monthly* (December 1996), pp. 52, 55. Allen also describes the figure who emerges from the Seminar's work as a 'dirt-poor, illiterate peasant sage from Galilee influenced perhaps by Greek Cynic philosophers'. Quoted in Mark Allan Powell, *The Jesus Debate: Modern Historians Investigate the Life of Christ* (Oxford: Lion, 1998), p. 83.

65. Richard Kearney, 'Transfiguring God', in *The Blackwell Companion to Postmodern Theology*, pp. 369–93 (pp. 380–81).

66. Crace, 'Introduction to *Quarantine*'.

67. de Certeau 1971, p. 145.

68. Jean Baudrillard, *Simulacra and Simulation*, trans. Sheila Faria Glaser (Ann Arbor: University of Michigan Press, 1994), p. 6. Ingraffia also uses this passage to explore post-secular fiction in 'Is the Postmodern Post-Secular?', p. 58.

69. Kearney, 'Transfiguring God', in *The Blackwell Companion to Postmodern Theology*, pp. 371, 374.

70. Graham Ward, 'Deconstructive Theology', in *The Cambridge Companion to Postmodern Theology*, p. 91.

71. Jasper 2004, p. 103.

72. Rowan Williams, *Lost Icons: Reflections on Cultural Bereavement* (Edinburgh: T&T Clark, 2000), p. 162.

73. de Certeau 1971, pp. 145, 147.

74. Placher 1996, p. xi.

75. Buechner 1992, p. 61.

3. John Updike's Holy Heresy: Between Grace and 'the Devil's motley'

1. John Updike, 'Remarks upon receiving the Campion Medal' in *John Updike and Religion: The Sense of the Sacred and the Motions of Grace*, James Yerkes (ed.) (Grand Rapids, Michigan: Eerdmans, 1999), pp. 3–6 (p. 4).

2. Marshall Boswell, 'Updike, religion, and the novel of moral debate', in *The Cambridge Companion to John Updike*, Stacey Olster (ed.) (Cambridge: Cambridge University Press, 2006), pp. 43–57 (p. 48).

3. John Updike, *Seek My Face* (London: Penguin, 2004), p. 11. All subsequent references will be given parenthetically to this edition as *SMF*, followed by page number.

4. Michael Edwards, *Towards a Christian Poetics* (London: Macmillan, 1984), pp. 12–13.

5. David Lodge, for example, has argued that 'narrative literature, and especially the novel' has the capacity to create 'fictional models of what it is like to be a human being, moving through time and space. It captures the density of experienced events by its rhetoric, and it shows the connectedness of events through the device of plot'; *Consciousness and the Novel* (London: Secker and Warburg, 2002), p. 14. Patrick Sherry, using Francois Mauriac as his example, suggests that the novel is 'the ideal medium' to explore metaphysical questions 'because it can capture the nature of unseen movements and processes that are worked out only gradually in human lives, and because of its capacity to convey psychological truth';, 'The Novel' in *The Oxford Companion to Christian Thought: Intellectual, Spiritual and Moral Horizons of Christianity*, Adrian Hastings, Alistair Mason and Hugh Pyper (eds) (Oxford: Oxford University Press, 2000), pp. 489–91 (p. 490).

6. David Lyle Jeffrey, 'North American Literature', in Metzger, Bruce M. and Michael D. Coogan (eds) *The Oxford Companion to The Bible* (New York and Oxford: Oxford University Press, 1993), pp. 454–60 (p. 459).

7. Sherry, *op. cit.*, p. 490.

8. John W. Aldridge described this alleged absence of ideas as 'the Private Vice of John Updike'; *Time to Murder and Create: the Contemporary Novel in Crisis* (New York: McKay, 1966). Essay reprinted in Harold Bloom (ed.), *John Updike: Modern Critical Reviews* (New York: Chelsea House, 1987), pp. 9–13 (p. 13).

9. Updike, 'Remarks upon receiving the Campion Medal', p. 3.

10. G. R. Evans, *A Brief History of Heresy* (Oxford: Blackwell, 2003), p. 164.

11. 'Religion and Literature' in *The Religion Factor: an Introduction to How Religion Matters*, William Scott Green and Jacob Neusner (eds) (Louisville: Westminster John Knox Press, 1996), pp. 227–41 (p. 238).

12. Wood's essay, 'John Updike's Complacent God', is the most eloquent, if rather one-sided, attack on the novelist's credentials as a writer of genuine spiritual force; *The Broken Estate: Essays in Literature and Belief* (London: Jonathan Cape, 1999), p. 227.

13. Harold Bloom, 'Introduction', in Bloom 1987, pp. 1–7 (p. 7).

14. *People of the Book: Christian Identity and Literary Culture* (Grand Rapids: Eerdmans, 1996), p. 340. Jeffrey places Updike in a tradition of twentieth-century writers, including Wallace Stevens and John Cheever, who sceptically disavow Puritanism. He argues that the Puritan legacy re-emerges most dynamically in the Southern writing of Flannery O'Connor and Wendell Berry.

15. James Yerkes, '*As Good as it Gets*: the Religious Consciousness in John Updike's Literary Vision', in Yerkes 1999, pp. 9–30 (p. 10).

16. John Updike, *In the Beauty of the Lilies* (London: Hamish Hamilton, 1996), p. 5. All subsequent references will be given to this edition as *ITBOTL*, followed by page number.

17. A. O. Scott, 'God Goes to the Movies', *The Nation*, 12 February 1996, pp. 25–8 (p. 26).

18. Martin Corner, 'Opening the Literal: Spirituality in Updike and Ford', in *Biblical Religion and the Novel, 1700–2000*, Mark Knight and Thomas Woodman (eds) (Aldershot: Ashgate, 2006), pp. 137–51 (p. 146).

19. Valentine Cunningham, 'Introduction: The Necessity of Heresy', in *Figures of Heresy: Radical Theology in English and American Writing*, Andrew Dix and Jonathan Taylor (eds) (Brighton: Sussex Academic Press, 2006), pp. 1–18 (pp. 2, 7).

20. Evans 2003, p. xv.

21. Donald J. Greiner, 'Body and Soul: John Updike and *The Scarlet Letter*', *Journal of Modern Literature*, 15.4 (1989), pp. 475–95 (p. 478).

22. 'Hawthorne's Creed', in *Hugging the Shore: Essays and Criticism by John Updike* (Harmondsworth: Penguin, 1985), pp. 73, 76. See Greiner's commentary on this essay, *op. cit.* pp. 476–7.

23. J. Todd Billings, 'John Updike as Theologian of Culture: *Roger's Version* and the Possibility of Embodied Redemption', *Christianity and Literature*, 52.2 (2003), pp. 203–213 (p. 203).

24. Updike, 'Hawthorne's Creed', p. 77. See also Greiner 1990, p. 477.

25. James Schiff, *Updike's Version: Rewriting the Scarlet Letter* (Columbia and London: University of Missouri Press, 1992), p. 9.

26. Terry Eagleton, *Literary Theory: An Introduction* (Minneapolis: University of Minnesota Press, 1983), p. 12.

27. 'Hawthorne's Creed', p. 78.

28. John Updike, *Roger's Version* (London: Penguin, 1987), p. 19. All subsequent references to the novel will be given to this edition as *RV*, followed by page numbers.

29. Schiff 1992, p. 61.

30. John N. Duvall, 'The Pleasure of Textual/Sexual Wrestling: Pornography and Heresy in *Roger's Version*', *Modern Fiction Studies*, 37.1 (1991), pp. 81–95 (p. 82).

31. The most comprehensive study of Updike's Barthian qualities is Stephen H. Webb's 'Writing as a Reader of Karl Barth: What Kind of Religious Writer is John Updike Not?' in Yerkes 1999, pp. 145–61. Crews's essay, 'Mr. Updike's Planet', offers an illuminating engagement with the influence of Barth on Updike: *The New York Review of Books*, 4 December 1986, 33. 19, pp. 7–14. See also Greiner 1990.

32. Karl Barth, *The Humanity of God* (Atlanta: John Knox Press, 1976).

33. For James Wood (1999) all fiction begins with a belief in the 'as if' (p. xv).

34. Barth 1976, p. 43.

35. Barth 1976, p. 51.

36. Barth 1976, p. 63.

37. Barth 1976, p. 54.

38. Barth 1976, p. 54.

39. Duvall 1991, p. 84.

40. Schiff 1992, p. 10. See also Greiner 1990.

41. Crews, p. 14.

42. Mark A. Buchanan, 'Rabbit Trails to God', *Christianity Today*, www.christianitytoday.com/ct/2003/007/4.42.html (page accessed 26/9/03).

43. Scott, *op. cit.*, p. 27.

44. 'To the Tram Halt Together', review of books on Paul Tillich and Karl Barth, included in *Hugging the Shore*, pp. 825–36.

45. Updike, 'To the Tram Halt Together', p. 828. Updike is quoting from Barth's 'Man and Woman' in *Church Dogmatics* III/4.

46. Updike, 'Hawthorne's Creed', p. 75.

47. Emerson, 'Divinity School Address', *The Norton Anthology of American Literature*, ed. Baym *et al.*, 6th edn, 5 vols (New York: Norton, 2003), pp. 1148–59 (p. 1153). All subsequent references will be given in the text to this edition as *DSA*, followed by page number.

48. Harold Bloom, 'The Sage of Concord', *The Guardian*, 24 May 2003, pp. 4–6 (p. 4).

49. Harold Bloom, *Omens of Millennium: The Gnosis of Angels, Dreams, and Resurrection* (London: Fourth Estate, 1996), p. 18. Also quoted by Michael York, 'New Age

Commodification and Appropriation of Spirituality', *Journal of Contemporary Religion*, 16.3 (2001), pp. 361–72.

50. Zygmunt Bauman, 'Postmodern Religion?', in *Religion, Modernity and Postmodernity*, Paul Heelas (ed.), with David Martin and Paul Morris (Oxford: Blackwell, 1998), pp. 55–78 (p. 57).

51. Zygmunt Bauman, *Intimations of Postmodernity* (London and New York: Routledge, 1992), pp. 1–24.

52. Greiner (1990) argues that in this child 'Updike concludes the essay not with praise of the head but with hope for the soul', p. 481.

53. Updike, 'To the Tram Halt Together', p. 835.

54. Evans 2003, p. 165.

55. Sherry, *op.cit.*, p. 490.

56. Frederick Buechner, *The Sacred Journey: a memoir of early days* (San Francisco: Harper Collins, 1982), p. 46.

4.   Miracles and the Mundane: Signs, Wonders and the Novel

1. Salman Rushdie, *Imaginary Homelands: Essays and Criticism, 1981–1991* (London: Granta, 1992), p. 376.

2. David Hume, *Enquiry Concerning Human Understanding* (1748); Section 10 is anthologized in *Miracles*, edited by Richard Swinburne (New York: Macmillan, 1989), pp. 23–40 (p. 27).

3. J. Houston, *Reported Miracles: A Critique of Hume* (Cambridge: Cambridge University Press, 1994), p. 2.

4. Robert Bruce Mullin, *Miracles and the Modern Religious Imagination* (New Haven: Yale University Press, 1996), p. 2.

5. William C. Placher, *The Domestication of Transcendence: How Modern Thinking about God Went Wrong* (Louisville: Westminster John Knox Press, 1996), p. 135.

6. Howard Clark Kee, 'Miracle in the Biblical World', in Coggins, R. J. and J. L. Houlden (eds), *A Dictionary of Biblical Interpretation* (London: SCM Press, 1990), pp. 461–5 (p. 461).

7. Hume, *op. cit.*, p. 37, p. 40.

8. James Robertson, *The Testament of Gideon Mack* (London: Penguin, 2007), p. 53.

9. Bernd Kollmann, 'Images of Hope: Towards an Understanding of New Testament Miracle Stories' in *Wonders Never Cease: The Purpose of Narrating Miracle Stories in the New Testament and Its Religious Environment*, Michael Labahn and Bert Jan Lietaert Peerbolte (eds) (London: Continuum, 2006), pp. 244–64 (p. 251).

10. M. Cameron Gray (ed.), *Angels and Awakenings: Stories of the Miraculous by Great Modern Writers* (New York: Doubleday, 1994), p. xv.

11. Paul Wilson, *Someone to Watch Over Me* (London: Granta, 2001), p. 7.

12. Rupert Shortt, *God's Advocates: Christian Thinkers in Conversation* (London: Darton, Longman and Todd, 2005), p. 25.

13. Attributed to Petronius, and translated in the novel as follows: 'that by your kindness I may find life after death'. Salley Vickers, *Miss Garnet's Angel* (London: Fourth Estate, 2000), p. 337.

14. 'Angel Levine' is included in *Angels and Awakenings*, pp. 3–16.

15. Don DeLillo, *Underworld* (London: Picador, 1999), p. 806. All subsequent references will be given parenthetically to this edition as *U*, followed by page number.

16. David Mitchell, *Ghostwritten* (London: Sceptre, 1999), p. 337.

17. Tony Tanner, *The Reign of Wonder: Naivety and Reality in American Literature* (Cambridge: Cambridge University Press, 1965), p. 361.

18. Ibid., p. 361.

19. Paul Maltby, *The Visionary Moment: A Postmodern Critique* (Albany: SUNY, 2002), p. 3. Although Maltby includes a detailed reading of DeLillo's *White Noise* (1985), pp. 73–85, he does not explore *Underworld*.

20. Maltby 2002, p. 3.

21. Maltby 2002, p. 3.

22. Hume, *op. cit.*, p. 27.

23. Valentine Cunningham, 'Shaping Modern English Fiction: The Forms of the Content and the Contents of the Form', in *On Modern British Fiction*, Zachary Leader (ed.) (Oxford: Oxford University Press, 2002), pp. 149–80 (p. 167).

24. Cunningham 2002, pp. 177–80.

25. Maltby 2002, p. 3.

26. John L'Heureux, *The Miracle* (New York: Grove, 2002), p. 4. All subsequent references will be given in the main body of the text as *TM*, followed by page number in this edition.

27. Mark Corner, *Signs of God: Miracles and Their Interpretation* (Aldershot: Ashgate, 2005), p. 7.

28. Nick Hornby, *How To Be Good* (London: Viking, 2001), p. 93. All subsequent references will be given in the main body of the text as *HTBG*, followed by page number in this edition.

29. Rhidian Brook, *The Testimony of Taliesin Jones* (London: Flamingo, 1997), p. 191. All subsequent references will be given parenthetically in the main body of the text as *TTJ*, followed by page number in this edition.

30. Terry Eagleton, *The English Novel: An Introduction* (Oxford: Blackwell, 2005), p. 3.

31. Eagleton 2005, p. 3.

32. James Robertson, *The Testament of Gideon Mack* (London: Penguin, 2007), p. 93.

33. Gillian Beer, *The Romance* (London: Methuen, 1970), p. 1.

34. A variety of differing forms of conversion are identified by John Lofland and Norman Skonovd in 'Conversion Motifs', *Journal for the Scientific Study of Religion*, 20 (1981), 373–85.

35. Douglas Coupland, *Generation X: Tales for an Accelerated Culture* (London: Abacus, 1992), p. 174.

36. Alasdair MacIntyre, *After Virtue* (2nd edition; London: Duckworth, 2006), p. 5.

37. Jodi Picoult, *Keeping Faith* (New York: Harper, 2006), p. 50. All subsequent references will be given to this edition as *KF*, followed by page number.

38. David Guterson, *Our Lady of the Forest* (London: Bloomsbury, 2004), p. 125. All subsequent references will be given to this edition as *OLOTF*, followed by page number.

39. Robert Wuthnow, *The Struggle for America's Soul: Evangelicals, Liberals and Secularism* (Grand Rapids: Williams B. Eerdmans, 1989), p. 116. Cited in Linda Woodhead and Paul Heelas (eds), *Religion in Modern Times: an Interpretive Anthology* (Oxford: Blackwell, 2000), p. 365.

40. Hume, *op. cit.*, p. 36.

41. David Johnson, *Hume, Holism and Miracles* (Ithaca: Cornell University Press, 1999), p. 4.
42. Swinburne 1989, p. 6.
43. Maltby 2002, p. 19.

5.   Little Wonder: John Irving's Modern Miracles

1. John Irving, *Trying to Save Piggy Sneed* (London: Black Swan, 1994), p. 24. All subsequent references will be given parenthetically to this edition as *TTSPS*, followed by page number.
2. Henry Jansen, *Laughter Among the Ruins: Postmodern Comic Approaches to Suffering* (Frankfurt: Peter Lang, 2001), pp. 122–3.
3. Frederick Buechner, *The Sacred Journey: a memoir of early days* (San Francisco: Harper Collins, 1982), p. 4.
4. Joan Smith, Interview with John Irving, *Salon*, 3 March 1997 (www.salon.com/march97/interview2970303.html) (accessed 30 April 2007).
5. Richard Bernstein, 'John Irving: Nineteenth-Century Novelist for These Times', *New York Times*, 25 April 1989, p. 13; Joan Smith, *Salon* Interview (see note 4).
6. Douglas Coupland, *Life After God* (London: Simon and Schuster, 1994), p. 273.
7. Frederick Buechner, *A Room Called Remember: Uncollected Pieces* (San Francisco: Harper Collins, 1992), p. x.
8. John A. McClure, 'Postmodern/Post-Secular: Contemporary Fiction and Spirituality', *Modern Fiction Studies*, 41.1 (1995), 141–63 (pp. 142–3).
9. John Irving, *A Prayer for Owen Meany* (London: Black Swan, 1990), p. 33. All future references will be given parenthetically to this edition as *APFOM*, followed by page reference.
10. Graham Ward, *Theology and Contemporary Critical Theory* (2nd edition; Basingstoke: Macmillan, 2000), p. 167.
11. Stephen R. Haynes, 'Footsteps of Anne Hutchinson and Frederick Buechner: A Religious Reading of John Irving's *A Prayer for Owen Meany*', *Religion and Literature*, 27.3 (1995), 73–98. For other readings of the religious characteristics of Irving's fiction see also Jansen 2001, pp. 101–34; John Sykes, 'Christian Apologetic Uses of the Grotesque in John Irving and Flannery O'Connor', *Literature and Theology*, 10 (1996), 58–67.
12. From *The Crown of Wild Olive*, in E. T. Cook and Alexander Wedderburn (eds), *The Works of John Ruskin* (39 vols; London: George Allen, 1903–12), XVIII, p. 497.
13. Sykes 1996, p. 59.
14. David Lyle Jeffrey, *People of the Book: Christian Identity and Literary Culture* (Grand Rapids, Michigan: Eerdmans, 1996), pp. 317–8.
15. *NIV Study Bible* (London: Hodder, 1985), p. 1768.
16. Haynes argues that John Wheelwright 'alternates, in fact, between several Johannine identities: he is the John who prepares the way for his Messiah, relentlessly pointing away from himself toward one who is greater; he is John the author who writes of an extraordinary life originating in another world; and he is the John of Revelation who a generation after the Christ's departure is exiled by an evil empire and can only pray for his return', Haynes 1995, pp. 83–4. See also pp. 80, 82.

17. Frederick Buechner, *Now and Then: a Memoir of Vocation* (San Francisco: Harper Collins, 1991), p. 57.

18. Sacvan Bercovitch, 'Introduction', *The American Puritan Imagination: Essays in Revaluation*, ed. Sacvan Bercovitch (Cambridge: Cambridge University Press, 1974), pp. 1–18 (p. 7).

19. Richard Bernstein, 'John Irving: Nineteenth-Century Novelist for these Times', *New York Times*, 25 April 1989, p. 13.

20. Haynes offers a detailed reading of Irving's use of Puritan culture, what he styles the 'Historical Clue' of seventeenth-century New England. In particular, he explores Anne Hutchinson and John Wheelwright's conflict with the religious authorities in Massachusetts and the narrative parallels between Hawthorne's evocation of Puritan theocracy in *The Scarlet Letter* and *A Prayer for Owen Meany*: Haynes 1995, pp. 84–7.

21. Philip Page, 'Hero Worship and Hermeneutic Dialectics: John Irving's *A Prayer for Owen Meany*', *Mosaic*, 28.3 (1995), 137–56 (p. 151).

22. The implications of these references, together with others to Charles Dickens, for example, have been identified by a number of critics, including Philip Page, Stephen R. Haynes and Henry Jansen. See, for example, Page on Irving's references to Fitzgerald and John's similarity to Nick Carraway (Page 1995, pp. 142–3); Haynes on Hardy's bitter atheism (Haynes 1995, p. 78) and Irving's explicit use of elements of plot and characters from *The Scarlet Letter* (p. 86); and Jansen's brief exploration of the novel's reference to Hardy, disbelief and determinism (Jansen 2001, p. 106).

23. Sykes 1996, p. 59.

24. Robert Lowell, 'Memories of West Street and Lepke' (1959), lines 12, 14.

25. See, in particular, Buechner's autobiography, *Now and Then: a Memoir of Vocation* (New York: Harper Collins, 1991) (originally published in 1983), pp. 8 ff.

26. John Irving, *The Imaginary Girlfriend: a Memoir* (London: Black Swan, 1997), pp. 35–6. All subsequent references will be given parenthetically to this edition as *TIG*, followed by page number.

27. Buechner 1991, p. 20.

28. Haynes 1995, pp. 87–90.

29. Theodore Ziolkowski, *Fictional Transfigurations of Jesus* (Lawrenceville, NJ: Princeton University Press, 1972), pp. 22–3.

30. Sykes 1996, p. 59.

31. John Schad, *Queer Fish: Christian Unreason from Darwin to Derrida* (Brighton: Sussex Academic Press, 2004), pp. 2–3.

32. Ibid., p. 5.

33. Eric Auerbach, *Mimesis: the Representation of Reality in Western Literature*, trans. Willard R. Trask (Princeton: Princeton University Press, 1968), p. 15. For commentaries on this passage and Auerbach's wider impact on twentieth-century biblical criticism and theology see, for example, Hans W. Frei, *The Eclipse of Biblical Narrative: A Study of Eighteenth and Nineteenth-Century* (New Haven: Yale University Press, 1974), p. 14 and Nicholas Wolterstorff, 'Living within a Text', in Keith E. Yandell (ed.), *Faith and Narrative* (Oxford: Oxford University Press, 2001), pp. 202–13.

34. Auerbach 1968, p. 16.

35. Graham Ward, *True Religion* (Oxford: Blackwell, 2003), pp. 132–3.

36. See M. Cameron Grey's discussion of Dostoyevsky and 'the real miracle' in her foreword to *Angels and Awakenings* (New York: Doubleday, 1994), p. xv.

37. John Irving, *A Son of the Circus* (London: Black Swan, 1995), p. 751. All subsequent references will be given parenthetically to this edition as *ASOTC*, followed by page reference.

38. See Haynes's comparison of Pastor Merrill's course with the reading that Buechner assigned students while at Exeter as described in *Now and Then*; Haynes 1995, p. 88.

39. Entry on Léon Bloy in Peter France (ed.), *The New Oxford Companion to Literature in French* (Oxford: Clarendon Press, 1995), p. 98.

40. Léon Bloy, quoted by Irving on the epigraph page of *A Prayer for Owen Meany*.

41. Graham Greene, *The End of the Affair* (London: Viking, 2001), p. 146. All subsequent references will be given parenthetically to this edition as *TEOTA*, followed by page number.

42. T. R. Wright, *Theology and Literature* (Oxford: Blackwell, 1988), p. 123.

43. Ibid., p. 123.

44. Debra Shostak, 'Plot as Repetition: John Irving's Narrative Experiments', *Critique*, 37.1 (1995), 51–70 (p. 52).

45. See epigraph to John Irving, *Until I Find You* (London: Bloomsbury, 2005).

46. Mark Ledbetter, *Virtuous Intentions: The Religious Dimension of Narrative* (Atlanta: Scholars Press, 1989), p. 75.

47. Alasdair MacIntyre, *After Virtue* (2nd edn; London: Duckworth, 2006), p. 216. Also quoted by Roger Lundin, 'Interpreting Orphans: Hermeneutics in the Cartesian Tradition', in Roger Lundin, Clarence Walhout and Anthony C. Thistleton, *The Promise of Hermeneutics* (Grand Rapids: Eerdmans, 1999), pp. 1–64, pp. 3–4.

48. Georg Lukács, *The Theory of the Novel: A Historico-Philosophical Essay on the Forms of Great Epic Literature*, trans. Anna Bostock (London: Merlin, 1971), pp. 88–89.

49. Shostak 1995, p. 61.

50. Page 1995, pp. 138–9.

51. Valentine Cunningham, 'It is No Sin To Limp', *Literature and Theology*, 6 (1992), 303–9.

52. Roland Barthes, *Image-Music-Text*, trans. Stephen Heath (London: Fontana Press, 1977), p. 147.

53. Haynes 1995, p. 79.

54. Jansen 2001, p. 109.

55. Shostak 1995, p. 64.

56. Page 1995, p. 152.

57. Flannery O'Connor, 'On Her Own Work', *Mystery and Manners: Occasional Prose* (London: Faber, 1972), p. 109.

58. Shostak 1995, p. 62.

59. McClure 1995, p. 143.

60. Frei 1974, p. 14. Frei, again, is responding to Auerbach.

61. William C. Placher, *The Domestication of Transcendence: How Modern Thinking About God Went Wrong* (Louisville: Westminster John Knox Press, 1996), p. 202.

62. Jansen 2001, p. 102.

63. Jansen 2001, p. 109.

64. Haynes 1995, p. 76.

65. James Wood, *The Broken Estate: Essays in Literature and Belief* (London: Jonathan Cape, 1999), p. 311.

6. 'How Clear is Your Vision of Heaven?': Douglas Coupland at the End of the World

1. Douglas Coupland, *Girlfriend in a Coma* (London: Flamingo, 1998), p. 4. All subsequent references with be given parenthetically to this edition as *GIAC*, followed by page number.

2. Paul S. Fiddes, *The Promised End: Eschatology in Theology and Literature* (Oxford: Blackwell, 2000), p. 6.

3. Frank Kermode, *The Sense of an Ending: Studies in the Theory of Fiction* (Oxford: Oxford University Press, 1967), p. 6.

4. Fiddes, *op.cit.*, p. 6.

5. Jacques Derrida, *Spectres of Marx: The State of the Debt, the Work of Mourning, and the New International*, trans. Peggy Kamuf (London: Routledge, 1994), p. 14.

6. Ibid., p. 15.

7. James Annesley, *Blank Fictions: Consumerism, Culture and the Contemporary American Novel* (London: Pluto Press, 1998), p. 108.

8. G. P. Lainsbury, 'Generation X and the End of History', *Essays on Canadian Writing*, 58 (1996), 229–40 (p. 233).

9. Lainsbury, *op. cit.*, pp. 233–4.

10. Annesley 1998, p. 108.

11. Derrida 1994, xix, p. 177.

12. Kevin J. Vanhoozer, 'Theology and the condition of postmodernity: a report on knowledge of God', in Kevin J. Vanhoozer (ed.), *The Cambridge Companion to Postmodern Theology* (Cambridge: Cambridge University Press, 2003), pp. 3–25 (p. 18).

13. Vanhoozer, *op. cit.*, p. 18.

14. For a detailed analysis of Coupland's place in the genealogy of Generation X, see John M. Ulrich's first-rate introduction to John M. Ulrich and Andrea L. Harris (eds), *GenXegesis: Essays on Alternative Youth Culture* (Madison: University of Wisconsin Press, 2003), pp. 3–37.

15. Matthew Reynolds, 'Play Again?' (Review of *JPod*), *The London Review of Books*, 28.15 (3 August 2006), 34–5 (p. 34).

16. Ali Smith, 'Amazing Grace', *The Guardian*, 9 October 2004, p. 26; Alan Bilton, *An Introduction to Contemporary American Fiction* (Edinburgh: Edinburgh University Press, 2002), p. 220.

17. Gordon Lynch, *After Religion: 'Generation X' and the Search for Meaning* (London: Darton, Longman and Todd, 2002), p. 90.

18. Ibid., p. 91.

19. Tom Beaudoin, *Virtual Faith: The Irreverent Spiritual Quest of Generation X* (San Francisco: Jossey-Bass, 2000), p. 23.

20. Richard W. Flory, 'Conclusion: Toward a Theory of Generation X Religion', in Richard W. Flory and Donald E. Miller (eds), *GenX Religion* (New York: Routledge, 2000), pp. 231–49 (p. 241). Unlike Lynch and Beaudoin's studies, Flory and Miller's collection does not cite Coupland as a significant influence in the shape of 'Generation X' religion.

21. Douglas Coupland, *Generation X: Tales for an Accelerated Culture* (London: Abacus, 1992), p. 68. All subsequent references will be given parenthetically to this edition as *GX*, followed by page reference.

22. Douglas Coupland, *Eleanor Rigby* (London: Fourth Estate, 2004), p. 12. All subsequent references will be given parenthetically to this edition as *ER*, followed by page reference.

23. Theodor Adorno, *The Culture Industry: Selected Essays on Mass Culture*, J. M. Bernstein (ed.) (London: Routledge, 2001), p. 192.

24. Ibid., p. 187.

25. Roger Lundin, 'Interpreting Orphans: Hermeneutics in the Cartesian Tradition', in Roger Lundin, Clarence Walhout and Anthony C. Thistleton, *The Promise of Hermeneutics* (Grand Rapids: Eerdmans, 1999), pp. 1–64 (p. 2).

26. Kermode 1967, p. 47.

27. Nicholas Blincoe, 'Feeling Frail', *The Daily Telegraph*, 16 October 2004, pp. 1–2 (p. 2).

28. Keith Ward, *Christianity: A Short Introduction* (Oxford: Oneworld, 2000), p. 166.

29. Douglas Coupland, *Polaroids from the Dead* (London: Flamingo, 1997), p. 1. All subsequent references will be given parenthetically to this edition as *PFD*, followed by page reference.

30. Douglas Coupland, *Souvenir of Canada 2* (Vancouver: Douglas & McIntyre, 2004), p. 12.

31. David Lyle Jeffrey, 'North American Literature', in Metzger, Bruce M. and Michael D. Coogan (eds), *The Oxford Companion to The Bible* (New York and Oxford: Oxford University Press, 1993), pp. 454–60 (p. 454).

32. Robert McGill, 'The Sublime Simulation: Vancouver in Douglas Coupland's Geography of Apocalypse', *Essays on Canadian Writing*, 70 (2000), 252–76 (p. 254).

33. Ibid., p. 254.

34. Douglas Coupland, *Hey Nostradamus!* (London: Flamingo, 2003), p. 3. All subsequent references will be given parenthetically to this edition as *HN*, followed by page reference. Pierre Huyghe and Douglas Coupland, *School Spirit* (Paris: Editions Dis Voir, 2003), p. 1. All subsequent references will be given parenthetically to this edition as *SS*, followed by page reference.

35. Walter Benjamin, *Illuminations: Essays and Reflections*, Hannah Arendt (ed.) (London: Jonathan Cape, 1970), p. 265.

36. For a wider discussion of Coupland's religious themes see also my book, *Douglas Coupland* (Manchester: Manchester University Press, 2007), pp. 130–61.

37. Douglas Coupland, *Microserfs* (London: Harper, 2004), p. 15. All subsequent references will be given parenthetically to this edition as *MS*, followed by page reference.

38. Jefferson Faye, 'Canada in a Coma', *The American Review of Canadian Studies*, 31.3 (2001), 501–10 (p. 505–6).

39. Douglas Coupland, *JPod* (London: Bloomsbury, 2006), p. 134. All subsequent references will be given parenthetically to this edition as *JP*, followed by page reference.

40. Andrew Tate, ''Now Here is My Secret': Ritual and Epiphany in Douglas Coupland's Fiction', *Literature and Theology*, 16. 3 (2002), 326–38.

41. Elizabeth Deeds Ermath, *Sequel to History: Postmodernism and the Crisis of Representational Time* (Princeton: Princeton University Press, 1992), p. xi.

42. Gerard Loughlin, *Telling God's Story: Bible, Church and Narrative Theology* (Cambridge: Cambridge University Press, 1999), p. 4.

43. L. Joseph Kreitzer, *The New Testament in Fiction and Film: On Reversing the Hermeneutical Flow* (Sheffield: JSOT Press, 1993).

44. Douglas Coupland, *Miss Wyoming* (London: Flamingo, 2000), p. 9.

45. N. T. Wright, *Simply Christian* (London: SPCK, 2006), p. 81.

46. Brian Draper, 'Novelist Who's Telling Us a Mystery', *The Church Times*, 26 September 2003; http://churchtimes.co.uk/churchtimes/website/pages.nsf/httppublicpages/1401D530D3 (17 November 2005).

47. Douglas Coupland, *Shampoo Planet* (London: Simon & Schuster, 1993), p. 20. All subsequent references will be given parenthetically to this edition as *SP*, followed by page number.

48. Fiddes, *op. cit.*, p. 6.

49. Douglas Coupland, *Life After God* (London: Simon and Schuster, 1994), p. 127.

50. Bilton 2002, p. 234.

51. Reynolds, *op. cit.*, p. 34.

52. McGill, *op. cit.*, p. 270.

53. Jason Cowley, 'Prophet of Doom' (Review of *Hey Nostradamus!*), *The New Statesman*, 8 September 2003, pp. 52–3 (p. 53).

54. Robert Detweiler, 'Theological Trends of Postmodern Fiction', *Journal of the American Academy of Religion*, 44.2 (1976), 225–37 (p. 234).

55. Benjamin 1970, pp. 258–9.

56. Mark Forshaw, 'Douglas Coupland: In and Out of "Ironic Hell"', *Critical Survey*, 12. 3 (2000), 39–58 (p. 40).

57. Fiddes, *op. cit.*, p. 12.

58. Detweiler 1976, p. 235.

59. MacIntyre 2006, pp. 215–6.

7.   Conclusion: Miraculous Realism

1. Peter C. Hodgson, *Theology in the Fiction of George Eliot: The Mystery Beneath the Real* (London: SCM Press, 2001), p. 24.

2. Philip Sheldrake, *A Brief History of Spirituality* (Oxford: Blackwell, 2007), p. 208.

3. Philip Blond, 'The primacy of theology and the question of perception', in Paul Heelas (ed.), with David Martin and Paul Morris, *Religion, Modernity and Postmodernity* (Oxford: Blackwell, 1998), pp. 285–313 (p. 285).

4. David Tracy, 'Fragments: The Spiritual Situation of our Times', in John D. Caputo and Michael J. Scanlon (eds), *God, the Gift and Postmodernism* (Indiana and Bloomington: Indiana University Press, 1999), pp. 170–84 (p. 176).

5. Christopher Deacy, *Screen Christologies: Redemption and the Medium of Film* (Cardiff: University of Wales Press, 2001), p. 2.

6. Paul S. Fiddes, *The Promised End: Eschatology in Theology and Literature* (Oxford: Blackwell, 2000), p. 7.

7. Jon McGregor, *If Nobody Speaks of Remarkable Things* (London: Bloomsbury, 2002), p. 239.

8. Ibid., p. 272.

9. Ibid., p. 273.

10. Michael Cunningham, *The Hours* (London: Fourth Estate, 2003), pp. 34–5. Roy M. Anker quotes the phrase 'animating mysteries of the world' in *Catching Light: Looking for God in the Movies* (Grand Rapids: William B. Eerdmans, 2004), p. 10.

11. Mark Knight and Thomas Woodman, 'The Word in the Word: An Introduction' in Mark Knight and Thomas Woodman (eds), *Biblical Religion and the Novel, 1700–2000* (Aldershot: Ashgate, 2006), pp. 1–12 (p. 2).
12. Ian McEwan, *Atonement* (London: Vintage, 2002), p. 371.
13. Mark Ledbetter, *Virtuous Intentions: The Religious Dimension of Narrative* (Atlanta: Scholars Press, 1989), pp. 17–18.
14. Paul Tillich, *Theology of Culture*, Robert C. Kimball (ed.) (Oxford: Oxford University Press, 1964), p. 9.
15. Paul Fiddes, *Freedom and Limit: A Dialogue between Literature and Christian Doctrine* (Basingstoke: Macmillan, 1991).

Bibliography

Fiction

Amis, Martin, *Heavy Water and Other Stories* (London: Vintage, 1998).

Barker, Pat, *Double Vision* (London: Penguin, 2004).

Brook, Rhidian, *The Testimony of Taliesin Jones* (London: Flamingo, 1997).

Cameron Gray, M. (ed.), *Angels and Awakenings: Stories of the Miraculous by Great Modern Writers* (New York: Doubleday, 1984).

Coe, Jonathan, *The Rotters' Club* (London: Penguin, 2002).

Coupland, Douglas, *Generation X: Tales for an Accelerated Culture* (London: Abacus, 1992).

—— *Shampoo Planet* (London: Simon & Schuster, 1993).

—— *Life After God* (London: Simon and Schuster, 1994).

—— *Polaroids from the Dead* (London: Flamingo, 1997).

—— *Girlfriend in a Coma* (London: Flamingo, 1998).

—— *Miss Wyoming* (London: Flamingo, 2000).

—— *All Families are Psychotic* (London: Flamingo, 2001).

—— *Hey Nostradamus!* (London: Flamingo, 2003).

—— *Eleanor Rigby* (London: Fourth Estate, 2004).

—— *Microserfs* (London: Harper, 2004).

—— *JPod* (London: Bloomsbury, 2006).

Crace, Jim, *Quarantine* (London: Penguin, 1998).

Cunningham, Michael, *The Hours* (London: Fourth Estate, 2003).

DeLillo, Don, *White Noise* (London: Picador, 1985).

—— *Underworld* (London: Picador, 1999).

Doctorow, E. L., *City of God: a Novel* (London: Abacus, 2001).

Greene, Graham, *The End of the Affair* (London: Viking, 2001).

Guterson, David, *Our Lady of the Forest* (London: Bloomsbury, 2004).

Hogg, James, *The Private Memoirs and Confessions of a Justified Sinner* (London: Penguin, 1987).

Hornby, Nick, *How To Be Good* (London: Viking, 2001).

Huyghe, Pierre and Douglas Coupland, *School Spirit* (Paris: Editions Dis Voir, 2003).

Irving, John, *A Prayer for Owen Meany* (London: Black Swan, 1990).

—— *A Son of the Circus* (London: Black Swan, 1995).

—— *Trying to Save Piggy Sneed* (London: Black Swan, 1994).

—— *The Fourth Hand* (London: Bloomsbury, 2001).

—— *Until I Find You* (London: Bloomsbury, 2005).

L'Heureux, John, *The Miracle: a Novel* (New York: Grove, 2002).

Lodge, David, *Paradise News* (London: Penguin, 1992).

McEwan, Ian, *Atonement* (London: Vintage, 2002).

McGregor, Jon, *If Nobody Speaks of Remarkable Things* (London: Bloomsbury, 2002).

Mailer, Norman, *The Gospel According to the Son* (London: Abacus, 2000).

Maine, David, *The Flood* (Edinburgh: Canongate, 2005).

Mantel, Hilary, *Beyond Black* (London: Harper Perennial, 2005).

—— *Fludd* (London: Harper Perennial, 2005).

Martel, Yann, *Life of Pi* (Edinburgh: Canongate, 2002).

Mitchell, David, *Ghostwritten* (London: Sceptre, 1999).

Picoult, Jodi, *Keeping Faith* (New York: Harper, 2006).

Roberts, Michèle, *The Wild Girl* (London: Methuen, 1987).

Robertson, James, *The Testament of Gideon Mack* (London: Penguin, 2007).

Rushdie, Salman, *The Ground Beneath Her Feet* (London: Vintage, 2000).

Updike, John, *Roger's Version* (London: Penguin, 1987).

—— *In the Beauty of the Lilies* (London: Hamish Hamilton, 1996).

—— *Seek My Face* (London: Penguin, 2004).

Vickers, Salley, *Miss Garnet's Angel* (London: Fourth Estate, 2000).

Wilson, Paul, *Someone to Watch Over Me* (London: Granta, 2001).

Winterson, Jeanette, *Oranges Are Not The Only Fruit* (London: Vintage, 1991).

Wood, James, *The Book Against God* (London: Vintage, 2004)

Secondary Texts

Adorno, Theodor, *The Culture Industry: Selected Essays on Mass Culture*, ed. J. M. Bernstein (London: Routledge, 2001).

Anker, Roy M., *Catching Light: Looking for God in the Movies* (Grand Rapids: William B. Eerdmans, 2004).

Annesley, James, *Blank Fictions: Consumerism, Culture and the Contemporary American Novel* (London: Pluto Press, 1998).

Auerbach, Eric, *Mimesis: The Representation of Reality in Western Literature*, translated by Willard R. Trask (Princeton: Princeton University Press, 1968).

Bal, Mieke, 'Postmodern Theology as Cultural Analysis', in Ward (2001), pp. 3–23 .

Barth, Karl, *The Humanity of God* (Atlanta: John Knox Press, 1976).

—— *Dogmatics in Outline* , trans. G. T. Thomson (London: SCM, 2001).

Barthes, Roland, *Image-Music-Text*, trans. Stephen Heath (London: Fontana Press, 1977).

Baudrillard, Jean, *Simulacra and Simulation*, trans. Sheila Faria Glaser (Ann Arbor: University of Michigan Press, 1994).

Bauman, Zygmunt, *Intimations of Postmodernity* (London: Routledge, 1992).

—— 'Postmodern Religion?' in Heelas, Martin and Morris (1998), pp. 55–78.

Beaudoin, Tom, *Virtual Faith: The Irreverent Spiritual Quest of Generation X* (San Francisco: Jossey-Bass, 2000).

Beer, Gillian, *The Romance* (London: Methuen, 1970).

Benjamin, Walter, *Illuminations: Essays and Reflections*, ed. Hannah Arendt (London: Jonathan Cape, 1970).

Bercovitch, Sacvan (ed.), *The American Puritan Imagination: Essays in Revaluation*, (Cambridge: Cambridge University Press, 1974).

Berger, Peter L. 'The Desecularization of the World. A Global Overview', in Peter L. Berger, ed., *The Desecularization of the World: Essays on the Resurgence of Religion in World*

Politics (Washington: Ethics and Public Policy Center; Grand Rapids: William B. Eerdmans, 1999).

Bernstein, Richard, 'John Irving: Nineteenth-Century Novelist for These Times', *New York Times*, 25 April 1989, p. 13.

Billings, J. Todd, 'John Updike as Theologian of Culture: *Roger's Version* and the Possibility of Embodied Redemption', *Christianity and Literature*, 52.2 (2003), pp. 203–13.

Bilton, Alan, *An Introduction to Contemporary American Fiction* (Edinburgh: Edinburgh University Press, 2002).

Blincoe, Nicholas, 'Feeling Frail', *The Daily Telegraph*, 16 October 2004, pp. 1–2.

Blond, Phillip, 'The primacy of theology and the question of perception', in Heelas, Martin and Morris (1998).

Bloom, Harold (ed.), *John Updike: Modern Critical Reviews* (New York: Chelsea House, 1987).

—— *Omens of Millennium: The Gnosis of Angels, Dreams, and Resurrection* (London: Fourth Estate, 1996).

'The Sage of Concord', *The Guardian*, 24 May 2003, pp. 4–6.

Bockmuehl, Marcus (ed.), *The Cambridge Companion to Jesus* (Cambridge: Cambridge University Press, 2001).

Borg, Marcus J. and N. T. Wright, *The Meaning of Jesus: Two Visions* (San Francisco: Harper Collins, 1999).

Bowers, Maggie Ann, *Magic(al) Realism* (London: Routledge, 2004).

Bradley, Arthur, *Negative Theology and Modern French Philosophy* (London: Routledge, 2004).

Brown, Callum, *The Death of Christian Britain: Understanding Secularisation, 18002000* (London: Routledge, 2001).

Bruce, Steve, *Religion in the Modern World: from Cathedrals to Cults* (Oxford: Oxford University Press, 1996).

—— *God is Dead: Secularization in the West* (Oxford: Blackwell, 2002).

Buechner, Frederick, *The Sacred Journey: a memoir of early days* (San Francisco: Harper Collins, 1982).

—— *Now and Then: a Memoir of Vocation* (New York: Harper Collins, 1991).

—— *A Room Called Remember: Uncollected Pieces* (San Francisco: Harper Collins, 1992).

Butler, Judith, John Guillory and Kendall Thomas (eds), *What's Left of Theory: New Work on the Politics of Literary Theory* (New York: Routledge, 2000).

Caputo, John D., *On Religion* (London: Routledge, 2001).

Caputo, John D. and Michael J. Scanlon, *God, the Gift and Postmodernism* (Indiana and Bloomington: Indiana University Press, 1999).

Carruthers, Jo, 'Literature', in Sawyer (2006), pp. 253–67.

Cartwright, Justin, 'After the Plague' (Review of Jim Crace's *The Pesthouse*), *The Guardian*, 17 March 2007, p. 16.

Chadwick, Owen, *The Secularization of the European Mind in the Nineteenth Century* (Cambridge: Canto, 1990).

Coggins, R. J. and J. L. Houlden (eds), *A Dictionary of Biblical Interpretation* (London: SCM Press, 1990).

Connolly, William E., *Why I Am Not a Secularist* (Minneapolis: University of Minnesota Press, 1999).

—— 'Refashioning the Secular', in Butler, Guillory and Thomas (2000), pp. 157–91.

Corner, Mark, *Signs of God: Miracles and Their Interpretation* (Aldershot: Ashgate, 2005).

Coupland, Douglas, *Souvenir of Canada 2* (Vancouver: Douglas & McIntyre, 2004).

Cowley, Jason, 'Prophet of Doom' (Review of *Hey Nostradamus!*), *The New Statesman*, 8 September 2003, pp. 52–3.

Cox, Harvey, 'The Myth of the Twentieth Century: The Rise and Fall of Secularization' in *The Twentieth Century: A Theological Overview*, edited by Gregory Baum (New York: Obis/London: Geoffrey Chapman, 1999), pp. 135–43.

Crews, Frederick, 'Mr. Updike's Planet', *The New York Review of Books*, 4 December 1986, 33. 19, pp. 7–14.

Cunningham, Valentine, 'It is No Sin To Limp', *Literature and Theology*, 6 (1992), 303–9.

—— 'Shaping Modern English Fiction: The Forms of the Content and the Contents of the Form', in Leader (2002), pp. 149–80.

—— 'Introduction: The Necessity of Heresy', in Dix and Taylor (2006), pp. 1–18.

Dauwen Zabel, Morton, (ed.), *The Portable Henry James* (London: Penguin, 1977).

Deacy, Christopher, *Screen Christologies: Redemption and the Medium of Film* (Cardiff: University of Wales Press, 2001).

de Certeau, Michel, 'How is Christianity Thinkable Today?' (1971) in Ward (1997), pp. 145–6.

Derrida, Jacques, *Spectres of Marx: The State of the Debt, the Work of Mourning, and the New International*, trans. Peggy Kamuf (London: Routledge, 1994).

—— *Acts of Religion* (London: Routledge, 2002).

Detweiler, Robert, 'Theological Trends of Postmodern Fiction', *Journal of the American Academy of Religion*, 44.2 (1976), 225–37.

—— *Breaking the Fall: Religious Readings of Contemporary Fiction* (Louisville: Westminster John Knox Press, 1995).

de Vries, Hent, *Philosophy and the Turn to Religion* (Baltimore: Johns Hopkins University Press, 1999).

Dix, Andrew and Jonathan Taylor (eds), *Figures of Heresy: Radical Theology in English and American Writing* (Brighton: Sussex Academic Press, 2006).

Duvall, John N., 'The Pleasure of Textual/Sexual Wrestling: Pornography and Heresy in *Roger's Version*', *Modern Fiction Studies*, 37. 1 (1991), 81–95.

Dyer, Geoff, 'God and Me', *God's Own Countries*, *Granta*, 93 (Spring 2006), 96–100.

Eagleton, Terry, *The English Novel: an Introduction* (Oxford: Blackwell, 2005).

—— *The Meaning of Life* (Oxford: Oxford University Press, 2007).

Edwards, Michael, *Towards a Christian Poetics* (London: Macmillan, 1984).

Ermath, Elizabeth Deeds, *Sequel to History: Postmodernism and the Crisis of Representational Time* (New Jersey: Princeton University Press, 1992).

Evans, G. R., *A Brief History of Heresy* (Oxford: Blackwell, 2003).

Faye, Jefferson, 'Canada in a Coma', *The American Review of Canadian Studies*, 31.3 (2001), 501–10.

Ferreter, Luke, *Towards a Christian Literary Theory* (Houndmills: Palgrave, 2003).

Fiddes, Paul S., *Freedom and Limit: A Dialogue between Literature and Christian Doctrine* (Basingstoke: Macmillan Press, 1991).

The Promised End: Eschatology in Theology and Literature (Oxford: Blackwell, 2000).

Fiddes, Paul S. (ed.), *The Novel, Spirituality and Modern Culture* (Cardiff: University of Wales Press, 2000).

Fisch, Harold, *New Stories for Old: Biblical Patterns in the Novel* (Basingstoke: Macmillan, 1998).

Flory, Richard W. and Donald E. Miller (eds), *GenX Religion* (New York: Routledge, 2000).

Flory, Richard W., 'Conclusion: Toward a Theory of Generation X Religion', in Flory and Miller (2000), pp. 231–49.

Forshaw, Mark, 'Douglas Coupland: In and Out of "Ironic Hell" ', *Critical Survey*, 12.3 (2000), 39–58.

France, Peter (ed.), *The New Oxford Companion to Literature in French* (Oxford: Clarendon Press, 1995).

Frei, Hans W., *The Eclipse of Biblical Narrative: A Study in Eighteenth and Nineteenth Century Hermeneutics* (New Haven: Yale University Press, 1974).

Fuller, Peter, *Images of God: Art and the Consolation of Lost Illusions* (London: Hogarth, 1993).

Greiner, Donald J., 'Body and Soul: John Updike and *The Scarlet Letter*', *Journal of Modern Literature*, 15.4 (1989), 475–95.

Gunton, Colin E., *Yesterday and Today: A Study of Continuities in Christology* (London: SPCK, 1997).

Habgood, John, *Varieties of Unbelief* (London: Darton, Longman and Todd, 2000).

Harries, Richard, *Art and the Beauty of God: A Christian Understanding* (London: Mowbray, 1993).

Hart, Kevin, *The Trespass of the Sign: Deconstruction, Theology and Philosophy* (New York: Cambridge University Press, 1989).

Hastings, Adrian, Alistair Mason and Hugh S. Pyper (eds), *The Oxford Companion to Christian Thought* (Oxford: Oxford University Press, 2000).

Haynes, Stephen R., 'Footsteps of Anne Hutchinson and Frederick Buechner: A Religious Reading of John Irving's *A Prayer for Owen Meany*', *Religion and Literature*, 27.3 (1995), 73–98.

Head, Dominic, *The Cambridge Introduction to Modern British Fiction, 1950–2000* (Cambridge: Cambridge University Press, 2002).

Heelas, Paul (ed.), with David Martin and Paul Morris, *Religion, Modernity and Postmodernity* (Oxford: Blackwell, 1998).

Hodgson, Peter C., *Theology in the Fiction of George Eliot: The Mystery Beneath the Real* (London: SCM Press, 2001).

Houston, Joseph, *Reported Miracles: a Critique of Hume* (Cambridge: Cambridge University Press, 1994).

Hutcheon, Linda, *A Poetics of Postmodernism: History, Theory, Fiction* (New York: Routledge, 1988).

Ingraffia, Brian D., *Postmodern Theory and Biblical Theology: Vanquishing God's Shadow* (Cambridge: Cambridge University Press, 1995).

—— 'Is the Postmodern Post-Secular?', in Westphal (1999), pp. 44–68.

Irving, John, *The Imaginary Girlfriend: a Memoir* (London: Black Swan, 1997).

Jansen, Henry, *Laughter Among the Ruins: Postmodern Comic Approaches to Suffering* (Frankfurt: Peter Lang, 2001).

Jasper, David, *The Study of Literature and Religion: an Introduction* (Basingstoke: Macmillan, 1989).

—— *The Sacred Desert: Religion, Literature, Art and Culture* (Oxford: Blackwell, 2004).

Jeffrey, David Lyle, *People of the Book: Christian Identity and Literary Culture* (Grand Rapids: William B. Eerdmans, 1996).

John, Jeffrey, *The Meaning in the Miracles* (Norwich: Canterbury Press, 2001).

Johnson, David, *Hume, Holism and Miracles* (Ithaca: Cornell University Press, 1999).

Kearney, Richard, 'Transfiguring God' in Ward (2001), pp. 369–93.

Kermode, Frank, *The Sense of an Ending: Studies in the Theory of Fiction* (Oxford: Oxford University Press, 1967).

King, Jeanette, *Women and the Word: Contemporary Women Novelists and the Bible* (Houndmills: Palgrave, 2000).

Knight, Mark and Emma Mason, *Nineteenth-Century Religion and Literature: an Introduction* (Oxford: Oxford University Press, 2006).

Knight, Mark, and Thomas Woodman, 'The Word in the Word: An Introduction', in Mark Knight and Thomas Woodman (eds), *Biblical Religion and the Novel, 1700–2000* (Aldershot: Ashgate, 2006).

Kreitzer, L. Joseph, *The New Testament in Fiction and Film: On Reversing the Hermeneutical Flow* (Sheffield: JSOT Press, 1993).

Labahn, Michael and Bert Jan Lietaert Peerbolte, *Wonders Never Cease: The Purpose of Narrating Miracle Stories in the New Testament and Its Religious Environment* (London: Continuum, 2006).

Lainsbury, G. P. *'Generation X* and the End of History', *Essays on Canadian Writing* 58 (1996), 229–40.

Lane, Richard J., Rod Mengham and Philip Tew (eds), *Contemporary British Fiction* (Cambridge: Polity Press, 2003).

Lane, Richard J., 'The Fiction of Jim Crace: Narrative and Recovery', in Lane, Mengham and Tew (2003), pp. 27–39.

Larmer, Robert A., *Water into Wine? An Investigation of the Concept of Miracle* (Montreal: McGill-Queen's University Press, 1996).

Leader, Zachary (ed.), *On Modern British Fiction* (Oxford: Oxford University Press, 2002).

Ledbetter, Mark, *Virtuous Intentions: The Religious Dimension of Narrative* (Atlanta: Scholars Press, 1989).

Lodge, David, *Consciousness and the Novel* (London: Secker and Warburg, 2002).

Loughlin, Gerard, *Telling God's Story: Bible, Church and Narrative Theology* (Cambridge: Cambridge University Press, 1999).

Lukács, Georg, *The Theory of the Novel: A Historico-Philosophical Essay on the Forms of Great Epic Literature*, trans. Anna Bostock (London: Merlin, 1971).

Lundin, Roger, Clarence Walhout and Anthony C. Thistleton, *The Promise of Hermeneutics* (Grand Rapids: Eerdmans, 1999).

Lynch, Gordon, *After Religion: 'Generation X' and the Search for Meaning* (London: Darton, Longman and Todd, 2002).

Lyon, David, *Postmodernity* (Buckingham: Open University, 1994).

—— *Jesus in Disneyland: Religion in Postmodern Times* (Cambridge: Polity, 2000).

McClure, John A., 'Postmodern/Post-Secular: Contemporary Fiction and Spirituality', *Modern Fiction Studies*, 41.1 (1995), 141–63.

McFague, Sallie, *Metaphorical Theology: Models of God in Religious Language* (London: SCM, 1983).

McGill, Robert, 'The Sublime Simulation: Vancouver in Douglas Coupland's Geography of Apocalypse,' *Essays on Canadian Writing*, 70 (2000), 252–76.

McGrath, Alister E., *The Making of Modern German Christology* (Oxford: Blackwell, 1986).

—— *The Future of Christianity* (Oxford: Blackwell, 2002).

McHale, Brian, *Postmodern Fiction* (London: Routledge, 1989).

MacIntyre, Alasdair, *After Virtue* (2nd edition; London: Duckworth, 2006).

Macquarrie, John, *Jesus Christ in Modern Thought* (London: SCM/Philadelphia: Trinity Press International, 1990).

Maitland, Sara, 'Religious experience and the novel: a problem of genre and culture', in Fiddes (2000), pp. 77–96.

Maltby, Paul, *The Visionary Moment: A Postmodern Critique* (Albany: SUNY, 2002).

Marion, Jean-Luc, *God Without Being* (Chicago: Chicago University Press, 1991).

Mauser, Ulrich, 'Temptation of Christ', in Metzger and Coogan (1993), pp. 735–6.

Mazur, E. M. and K. McCarthy (eds), *God in the Details: American Religion in Popular Culture* (New York and London: Routledge, 2001).

Metzger, Bruce M. and Michael D. Coogan (eds), *The Oxford Companion to The Bible* (New York and Oxford: Oxford University Press, 1993).

Miller, J. Hillis, *The Disappearance of God: Five Nineteenth-Century Writers* (Cambridge: Belknap, 1975).

Moltmann, Jürgen, *The Crucified God: The Cross of Christ as the Foundation and Criticism of Christian Theology* (London: SCM, 1974).

Moore, Stephen D., *Mark and Luke in Poststructuralist Perspective: Jesus Begins to Write* (New Haven: Yale University Press, 1992).

Morrison, Blake, 'God and Me', *God's Own Countries, Granta*, 93 (Spring 2006), 183–4.

Mullin, Robert Bruce, *Miracles and the Modern Religious Imagination* (New Haven: Yale University Press, 1996).

Nicol, Bran, *Postmodernism and the Contemporary Novel* (Edinburgh: Edinburgh University Press, 2002).

O'Connor, Flannery, *Mystery and Manners: Occasional Prose* (London: Faber, 1972).

Olster, Stacey (ed.), *The Cambridge Companion to John Updike* (Cambridge: Cambridge University Press, 2006).

Page, Philip, 'Hero Worship and Hermeneutic Dialectics: John Irving's *A Prayer for Owen Meany*', *Mosaic*, 28.3 (1995), 137–56.

Percy, Martyn, *The Salt of the Earth: Religious Resilience in a Secular Age* (London and New York: Sheffield Academic Press, 2001).

Placher, William C., *The Domestication of Transcendence: How Modern Thinking About God Went Wrong* (Louisville: Westminster John Knox Press, 1996).

Polkinghorne, John, *The Work of Love: Creation as Kenosis* (Grand Rapids: Wm. B. Eerdmans, 2001).

Powell, Mark Allan, *The Jesus Debate: Modern Historians Investigate the Life of Christ* (Oxford: Lion, 1998).

Pyper, Hugh S., 'Desert', in Hastings, Mason and Pyper (2000), p. 161.

Rose, Stuart, 'Is the term "Spirituality" a word that everyone uses, but nobody knows what anyone means by it?', *Journal of Contemporary Religion*, 16.2 (2001), 193–207.

Rushdie, Salman, *Imaginary Homelands: Essays and Criticism, 1981–1991* (London: Granta, 1992).

Ryken, Leland, *The Christian Imagination* (Colorado Springs: WaterBrook, 2002).

Sawyer, John (ed.), *The Blackwell Companion to the Bible and Culture* (Oxford: Blackwell, 2006).

Schad, John (ed.), *Writing the Bodies of Christ: The Church from Carlyle to Derrida* (Aldershot: Ashgate, 2001).

Schad, John, ' "These Are My Bodies": An Introduction', in Schad (2001), pp. 1–7.

—— *Queer Fish: Christian Unreason from Darwin to Derrida* (Brighton: Sussex Academic Press, 2004).

Schiff, James A., *Updike's Version: Rewriting the Scarlet Letter* (Columbia and London: University of Missouri Press, 1992).

Scott Green, William and Jacob Neusner (eds), *The Religion Factor: An Introduction to How Religion Matters* (Louisville: Westminster John Knox Press, 1996).

Shaw, Philip, *The Sublime* (London: Routledge, 2006).

Sheldrake, Philip, *A Brief History of Spirituality* (Oxford: Blackwell, 2007).

Sherry, Patrick, *Images of Redemption: Art, Literature and Salvation* (London: T&T Clark, 2003).

Sherwood, Yvonne and Kevin Hart (eds), *Derrida and Religion: Other Testaments* (New York: Routledge, 2005).

Shortt, Rupert, *God's Advocates: Christian Thinkers in Conversation* (London: Darton, Longman and Todd, 2005).

Shostak, Debra, 'Plot as Repetition: John Irving's Narrative Experiments', *Critique*, 37.1 (1995), 51–70.

Smith, Ali, 'Amazing Grace', *The Guardian*, 9 October 2004, p. 26.

Smith, Joan, Interview with John Irving, www.salon.com, 3 March 1997 (www.salon.com/march97/interview2970303.html) (accessed 30 April 2007).

Steiner, George, 'The Scandal of Revelation', in Yandell (2001), pp. 68–85.

Swinburne, Richard (ed.), *Miracles* (New York: Macmillan, 1989).

Swinburne, Richard, 'Introduction' in Swinburne (1989), pp. 1–17.

Sykes, John, 'Christian Apologetic Uses of the Grotesque in John Irving and Flannery O'Connor', *Literature and Theology*, 10 (1996), 58–67.

Tanner, Tony, *The Reign of Wonder: Naivety and Reality in American Literature* (Cambridge: Cambridge University Press, 1965).

Tate, Andrew, ' "Now – Here is My Secret": Ritual and Epiphany in Douglas Coupland's Fiction', *Literature and Theology*, 16. 3 (2002), 326–38.

—— *Douglas Coupland* (Manchester: Manchester University Press, 2007).

Tartt, Donna, 'The Spirit and Writing in a Secular World', in Fiddes (2000), pp. 25–40.

Tew, Philip, *Jim Crace* (Manchester: Manchester University Press, 2006).

Tillich, Paul, *Theology of Culture*, ed. Robert C. Kimball (Oxford: Oxford University Press, 1959; 1964).

Tracy, David, 'Fragments: The Spiritual Situation of our Times', in Caputo and Scanlon (1999), pp. 170–84.

Ulrich, John M. and Andrea L. Harris, *GenXegesis: Essays on Alternative Youth (Sub)Culture* (Madison: University of Wisconsin Press, 2003).

Updike, John, *Hugging the Shore: Essays and Criticism* (Harmondsworth: Penguin, 1985).

Vanhoozer, Kevin J. (ed.), *The Cambridge Companion to Postmodern Theology* (Cambridge: Cambridge University Press, 2003).

Vanhoozer, Kevin J., 'Theology and the condition of postmodernity: a report on knowledge (of God)', in Vanhoozer (2003), pp. 3–25.

—— 'Scripture and Tradition', in Vanhoozer (2003) pp. 149–69.

Ward, Graham, *Barthes, Derrida and the Language of Theology* (Cambridge: Cambridge University Press, 1995).

—— 'Kenosis and Naming: Beyond Analogy and Towards *Allegoria Amoris*', in Heelas, Martin and Morris (1998), pp. 23357.

—— *Theology and Contemporary Critical Theory* (2nd edition; Basingstoke: Macmillan, 2000).

—— 'Suffering and Incarnation', in Ward (2001), pp. 192–208.

—— *True Religion* (Oxford: Blackwell, 2003).

—— 'Deconstructive Theology', in Vanhoozer (2003), pp. 76–91.

—— *Christ and Culture* (Oxford: Blackwell, 2005).

Ward, Graham (ed.), *The Postmodern God: A Theological Reader* (Oxford: Blackwell, 1997).
—— *The Blackwell Companion to Postmodern Theology* (Oxford: Blackwell, 2001).
Ward, Keith, *Christianity: A Short Introduction* (Oxford: Oneworld, 2000).
—— 'Cosmos and Kenosis', in Polkinghorne (2001), pp. 152–166.
Watson, Francis, 'The quest for the real Jesus', in Bockmuehl (2001), pp. 156–69.
Webb, Stephen H., 'Writing as a Reader of Karl Barth: What kind of Religious Writer is John Updike Not?' in Yerkes (1999), pp. 145–61.
Westphal, Merold (ed.), *Postmodern Philosophy and Christian Thought* (Bloomington: Indiana University Press, 1999).
Williams, Rowan, *Lost Icons: Reflections on Cultural Bereavement* (Edinburgh: T&T Clark, 2000).
Williams, T. C., *The Idea of the Miraculous: The Challenge to Science and Religion* (Houndmills: Macmillan, 1990).
Wolterstorff, Nicholas, 'Living within a Text', in Yandell (2001), pp. 21–36.
Wood, James, *The Broken Estate: Essays in Literature and Belief* (London: Jonathan Cape, 1999).
The Celestial Teapot', *The New Republic*, 18 December 2006, pp. 27–32.
Wood, Ralph C., *The Comedy of Redemption: Christian Faith and Comic Vision in Four American Novelists* (Notre Dame: University of Notre Dame Press, 1988).
Woodhead, Linda and Paul Heelas (eds), *Religion in Modern Times: An Interpretive Anthology* (Oxford: Blackwell, 2000).
Wright, N. T., *The Challenge of Jesus* (London: SPCK, 2000).
—— *Simply Christian* (London: SPCK, 2006).
Wright, T. R., *Theology and Literature* (Oxford: Blackwell, 1988).
—— 'Religion and Literature From the Modern to the Postmodern: Scott, Steiner and Detweiler', *Literature and Theology*, 19.1 (2005), 3–21.
Yandell, Keith E. (ed.), *Faith and Narrative* (Oxford: Oxford University Press, 2001).
Yerkes, James (ed.), *John Updike and Religion: The Sense of the Sacred and the Motions of Grace* (Grand Rapids, Michigan: Eerdmans, 1999).
Yerkes, James, '*As Good as it Gets*: the Religious Consciousness in John Updike's Literary Vision', in Yerkes 1999, pp. 9–30.
York, Michael, 'New Age Commodification and Appropriation of Spirituality', *Journal of Contemporary Religion*, 16.3 (2001), 361–72.
Ziolkowski, Theodore, *Fictional Transfigurations of Jesus* (Lawrenceville, NJ: Princeton University Press, 1972).
Žižek, Slavoj, *The Fragile Absolute or, Why is the Christian Legacy Worth Fighting For?* (London: Verso, 2001).
—— 'Christ's Breaking of the "Great Chain of Being"', in Schad (2001), pp. 105–10.

Index

The Testament of Gideon Mack

Miss Garnet's Angel
Keeping faith - Jodi Picoult
How to be good - Nick Hornby
♫ We are all enlisted ♫
Alma - "we are all conscripted"

Brother Rimmer - last
scene, something about
being brave.

Printed in Great Britain
by Amazon.co.uk, Ltd.,
Marston Gate.

Foreword

Being a lover of steam locomotives is a bit like chasing a setting sun, with the real diehards searching out survivors further and further from their home territory. Many enthusiasts would mark August 1968 as the end of 'proper' steam locomotives in the United Kingdom, the date when British Rail withdrew their final examples. However, for those 'in the know' steam continued to contribute to the British economy in industrial settings for nearly two decades more. In the coal and ironstone mining industry, in power generation, in chemical factories, steelworks and foundries, small rugged locomotives continued to toil away on a daily basis. Some were lovingly cared for, while others were worked into the ground.

I discovered colliery steam by accident – a boring afternoon in the Social Science library at Nottingham University saw me daydreaming out of the window, when I suddenly spotted a column of steam in what was, by then, an area devoid of steam-hauled trains. On examining a map I realised it was from Clifton Colliery and that began a journey of discovery, often accompanied by my younger, equally enthusiastic brother. I discovered the Industrial Railway Society and their invaluable handbooks listing every industrial railway in the UK. This led me to some of the more obscure and less scenic parts of the country, but some industrial settings had a haunting beauty of their own. This collection is by no means exhaustive but it gives a taste of this particular setting for steam workhorses.

For us relative youngsters who were in their teens and early twenties as non-heritage steam died out, there were economic restraints on our activities – cheap cameras with limited performance and cheap film that did not wear the passage of time well. Work and limited incomes also constrained our activities. As a result, my collection is biased towards the North West of England, where I was born and have lived most of my life. Occasional excursions to the Midlands, South Wales and Scotland yielded some variety but, to my regret, the North East and Yorkshire were neglected, and the small Kent coalfield was ignored completely.

Coal has been a crucial, some might say dominating, factor in the development of the United Kingdom as, in earlier years, the world's industrial giant. I was fortunate to have gone down Gresford Mine as a boy – no, I'm not that old, it was part of my grammar school's course in 'Industrial Studies'! My admiration for those who worked in that environment was considerably enhanced. Crawling on one's hands and knees to reach the working coalface, where standing was impossible, and knowing that 266 men and boys died in that mine in 1934 following an explosion and only eleven bodies were recovered made a lasting impression on a fifteen-year-old. I also latterly discovered, while researching my ancestry, that my great-grandmother was a coalminer's daughter, her father being employed in the mines of the North Somerset coalfield.

By the 1960s the writing was on the wall for coal as the driving power behind the British economy. The national rail company had phased out its steam locomotives by 1968 and electric power generation had been diversified, with nuclear and gas plants being built. Domestic use declined with the increased reliance on gas and oil central heating. Coal production was concentrated on newer, larger mines, often with 'merry-go-round' trains of larger hoppers constantly circulating between the mega-power station and rapid loading bunkers at the mine. Then came the 1984 miners' strike, which, ironically, hastened the closure of the very mines it sought to keep open. Closures were inevitable, but reliance on cheaper, imported, coal accelerated the process, and by 2015 all the deep mines had closed, with just open-cast production remaining.

Fortunately many of the locomotives that worked in the last years of the collieries have survived in preservation, where they provide invaluable service on the shorter heritage lines.

Lancashire and Cumbrian Coalfields

Here we have two contrasting coalfields located in the North West of England. The Lancashire coalfield spread from Cronton Colliery on the outskirts of Liverpool through its heartlands in Wigan, St Helens and the western edge of Greater Manchester and up to the foothills of the Pennines around Burnley. Originally fuelling the great Lancashire cotton industry, latterly much of the coal went to power generation.

By contrast the Cumbrian coalfield clung to the western edge of the county along the coastal strip. Here coal had been linked to the other essentials of the iron and steel industry, with haematite iron ore being mined near Barrow and limestone being quarried further east in the Shap area. Large ironworks existed at Millom and Workington. Being coastal there was access to the ports at Whitehaven, Workington, Maryport and Barrow. Whitehaven in particular offered a treasure trove for the industrial railway enthusiast, with rope-worked inclines, steep cliff-top lines and harbour sidelines.

Above: An Austerity 0-6-0ST glimpsed through
the rotting roller shutter doors of the locomotive
shed at Bold Colliery near St Helens.
August 1981.

Right: Bold Colliery saw a late return to steam
traction. Two coal power stations were built
next to the colliery and coal was sent directly
by conveyor belt. What coal left by rail went in
standard 16-ton mineral wagons rope-hauled
up the short incline visible in this photograph,
which then went on to the exchange sidings.
When it was necessary to convert to 21-ton
hopper wagons for merry-go-round services
the incline was unsuitable, and a diversion line
was installed instead. The small diesel locos
then in use proved to have insufficient power
to tackle the new line and so steam locos were
reintroduced. Here, *Joseph* (Hunslet works
No. 3163 of 1944) prepares for the assault on the
new incline.

Joseph climbs away from the screens at Bold Colliery with loaded 21-ton hopper wagons, probably destined for Fiddlers Ferry Power Station. August 1981.

Joseph running back from the exchange sidings parallel to the old Liverpool to Manchester main line with reclaimed spoil tips in the background, August 1981.

Joseph stands on the weighbridge between duties at Bold. *Joseph* changed gender late in his life, having been named *Alison* at his former home at Gresford Colliery! Changing names was not unusual for North West area locos.

In an almost identical position stands another Bold stalwart, *Robert* (Hudswell Clark works No. 1752 of 1943). *Robert* had formerly been No. 7 at Littleton Colliery in Staffordshire. (Photograph C. Pope)

Robert returns from the exchange sidings with a load of empty 21-ton hoppers. The Liverpool to Manchester main line is just behind the loco and wagons. *Robert* is currently preserved on the Great Central Railway. (Photograph C. Pope)

The third Austerity working at Bold in the 1980s was *Whiston* (Hunslet works No. 3694 of 1950). Here, she is seen alongside the loco shed with one of the underpowered North British-built diesels. She had arrived from Cadely Hill in the Midlands. *Whiston* is appropriately preserved on the Foxfield Railway in Staffordshire – a former colliery branch. (Photograph C. Pope)

Robert stands under the water tank, made from an old 'Lancashire' boiler, at the loco shed on a very wet St Helens day in August 1981.

Joseph rests in the shed at Bold Colliery. *Joseph* was named to commemorate a well-known member of staff at Walkden shops, where the North West area's locomotives were overhauled. Like its companions at Bold, *Joseph* survives in preservation. After moving around several preserved railways, *Joseph* returned to his own county, being based at the East Lancashire Railway, and is now named *Sapper*.

Bold Colliery is just a short distance from Rainhill, site of the famous Trials won by Stephenson's *Rocket*. 150 years later, in 1980, a celebration of the Rainhill Trials took place with a run past of famous and historic locomotives. The locomotives were stabled at Bold Colliery. It was quite fitting that, among all the famous locomotives, there should be a representative of the unsung heroes that toiled away in industry on a daily basis. This task fell to *Robert*, and here he is having his big day out. It brought a lump to the throat!

Astley Green Colliery, Tyldesley, and one form of coal transport passes another. A barge on the Bridgewater Canal passes Austerity *Respite* (Hunslet No. 3696 of 1950) on a rake of internal mineral wagons. Part of the colliery now serves as a museum to this local industry, but sadly no steam locomotives are on site.

Harry (Hudswell Clarke No. 1776 of 1944) runs through the yard at Astley Green Colliery in 1969. Astley Green was at the western extremity of the Manchester Collieries system that served many pits in the area and had Walkden shed and workshops at its heart. (January 1970)

Astley Green had a small loco shed of its own. Here, Giesl ejector-fitted Austerity *Respite* (Hunslet No. 3696 of 1950) stands outside the shed. Like many of the North Western area's Austerities, *Respite* was a much-travelled loco. After leaving Astley Green it worked in Cumbria before ending its days at Bickershaw Colliery.

A pair of Austerities shunting internal wagons at Astley Green in 1969.

There were two rail routes out of the colliery – northwards towards the modern Mosley Common Colliery, and the heart of the system at Walkden, and southwards over Chat Moss to join with the old Liverpool & Manchester Railway. Here, an Austerity, probably *Stanley*, brings a rake of wagons over the Bridgewater Canal from the waste tip.

Stanley (Hunslet No. 3302 of 1946) with a load of colliery waste at Astley Green. Like fellow Astley Green engine *Respite*, *Stanley* ended up at Ladysmith Washery in Cumbria and was scrapped there in 1975.

Bickershaw Colliery was located between Wigan and Newton-le-Willows and was designated a 'super pit' when modernisation joined it underground to two other local pits. The pit had its own washery for cleaning the coal. A steeply graded branch connected with the national system near Kenyon Junction. Bickershaw remained open until 1992.

A snowy April finds Austerity *Warrior* (Hunslet No. 3778 of 1952) at work at Bickershaw, shunting a 21-ton hopper.

Warrior with a rake of 16-ton mineral wagons. The snow manages to cover what was normally a very muddy environment!

Above: *Warrior* runs round its rake. Walkden had a liking for themed names – alongside *Warrior* it also maintained *Warspite*, *Wasp*, *Whiston*, *Wizard* and *Witch*, and also named a batch after Royal Navy battleships: *Renown*, *Repulse*, *Respite* and *Revenge*.

Right: Austerities at rest outside the shed at Bickershaw: *Warrior* (Hunslet No. 3823 of 1954) in North West area red livery, complete with Giesl ejector chimney; and, with conventional chimney, *Gwyneth* (Robert Stephenson & Hawthorn No. 7135 of 1944), which had recently transferred from Gresford Colliery, Wrexham.

A general view of Bickershaw, unusually devoid of wagons, with the screens and wash plant in the background and the loco shed with *Gwyneth* in residence in the foreground. The yellow Ford Cortina Mark 2 is typical of the period!

The waste tip at Bickershaw offered a grandstand view of trains heading up the grade from the screens to the exchange sidings. Here, *Gwyneth* heads a rake of six loaded hopper wagons.

A ground-level view of *Gwyneth* charging the gradient to the exchange sidings. Latterly, much of the coal went to Fiddlers Ferry Power Station, near Warrington.

Gwyneth drifts back into the colliery yard having delivered her load to the exchange sidings.

Gwyneth putting up another storming performance on a grey Wigan day.

Gwyneth stands in the yard at Bickershaw with a rake of 16-ton mineral wagons.

A profile of *Gwyneth* in the yard at the colliery. She lost her name for a while when at Gresford, but regained it going through Walkden shops prior to transfer to Bickershaw. At some point Walkden had ceased painting its locomotives in the distinctive lined maroon livery seen on *Warrior*.

Gwyneth leaving a pall of smoke and steam as she heads for the exchange sidings.

An earlier resident at Bickershaw was *Spitfire* (Hunslet No. 3831 of 1955), which survived there until 1976. For a while it shared its home with the appropriately named *Hurricane* (Hunslet No. 3830 of 1955).

A latter-day view inside the shed at Bickershaw with the ominous front end of one of the new replacement diesels on the far right. The Austerities are *Gwyneth* and No. 8 (Hunslet No. 3776 of 1952), a transfer from West Cannock Colliery in Staffordshire. (Photograph C. Pope)

Gwyneth with the screens and washing plant in the background.

Warrior outside Bickershaw's loco shed.

Gwyneth in Bickershaw yard with *Warrior* on shed under the water tank, which is a typical recycled 'Lancashire' stationary boiler conversion.

Warrior with steam leaks enhanced by the cold weather. (Photograph C. Pope)

Being something of a wanderer, *Respite* (Hunslet No. 3696 of 1950) ended her days at Bickershaw, having previously worked at Astley Green and Ladysmith Washery in Cumbria. Along with *Gwyneth* she was given to the National Railway Museum in 1981 with the intention that parts would be used to construct a replica broad gauge Great Western *Iron Duke*. In fact, *Gwyneth* donated most of the required parts, while *Respite*, minus a few parts, went to the Ribble Steam Railway in Preston for restoration.

Respite pulling a load of 16-ton mineral wagons away from the loco shed at Bickershaw.

The hub of the Manchester Collieries system and the main repair depot for North West area locos was Walkden Yard. Here, locos awaiting repair or scrapping could be found stored. The Austerity in steam is *Repulse* (Hunslet No. 3698 of 1950).

Some Austerities are meeting their fate in Walkden Yard. I think the intact loco is probably *W.H.R* (Robert Stephenson & Hawthorn No. 7174 of 1944). The North West area was seemingly blessed with a good stock of these relatively modern and powerful locomotives, unlike some other areas, which had a more mixed collection of locally manufactured designs.

The harbour lines at Whitehaven, Cumbria, are host to unnamed and unnumbered Robert Stephenson & Hawthorn 0-4-0ST works No. 7049 of 1942. The work included moving coal from other pits further up the coast to the Ladysmith Washery incline and for export to the Isle of Man and Northern Ireland by sea. March 1970.

The 0-4-0ST moves some 21-ton hopper wagons from the incline foot.

The harbour lines included some tight curves and so the four-coupled type was most suited for the work.

The loco picks up a new load from the foot of the incline.

Another loco used on the harbour lines was the Peckett-built *Victoria* (works No. 2028 of 1942). Some sources claim *Victoria* as being owned by the Whitehaven Harbour Company, being hired to the NCB when they were short of power. September 1969.

Victoria crosses a harbour road with NCB internal user wagons. September 1969.

Victoria again, with the lifebelt fastened to the telegraph pole indicating the proximity to the harbour.

Locomotives working on the harbour lines were based at the nearby William Pit loco shed. The pit itself had closed many years earlier. Here, *Askham Hall* (Avonside works No. 1772 of 1917), another regular, is under repair, along with a Robert Stephenson & Hawthorn four-coupled loco. September 1969.

William Pit loco shed in September 1969 with *Askham Hall* inside. The locomotive survives in unrestored condition at the Threlkeld Mining Museum near Keswick.

The Howgill incline connecting the Whitehaven harbour lines to Haig Colliery and Ladysmith Washery in 1969. Coal stacked for shipping to Ireland and the Isle of Man can just be seen on the far right.

Running lines along a clifftop, as happened at Ladysmith, could have some disastrous consequences! This landslip in 1972 closed the line to the washery and coal was then transported by a conveyor belt running up the old incline.

Before the landslip, Austerities *Revenge* (Hunslet No. 3699 of 1950) and *Charles* (Hudswell Clarke No. 1778 of 1944) stand on the clifftop at the head of the Howgill incline, waiting to take loads to and from Haig pit and the washery. March 1970.

Above: *Charles* at the incline top, having been given the green light to proceed. An example of the rough life experienced by Ladysmith locos can be seen in the damage to the loco's cab! March 1970.

Right: *Revenge* attacks the gradient, heading towards Ladysmith Washery, with the Irish Sea visible in the background.

A cab view from one of the Austerities – it was a bumpy ride!

Austerity *Stanley* (Hunslet No. 3302 of 1944) came to Ladysmith in January 1971 and survived there until closure in 1975.

An Austerity trundles back down the gradient to the incline. Typical west Cumbrian weather, with a hint of mist from the nearby sea.

This is the 0-4-0ST *King* (Andrew Barclay No. 1448 of 1919), which had led a comparatively leisurely existence at Bank Hall pit near Burnley, Lancs. When that pit closed in 1971 *King* went to Walkden workshop, where a rather incongruous Giesl ejector was fitted in place of a regular chimney, following which the loco was sent to Ladysmith. With only 14-inch cylinders, and having only four coupled wheels, *King* was felt to not be up to the duties at Ladysmith, but a typical motive power shortage forced it into service, where it performed heroically – maybe it was the Giesl!

King trundles back down the grade with a rake of hoppers.

A good view of an old loco with a modern chimney!

Above: *King* running round wagons at the washery.

Right: Cleaning the smokebox of another four-coupled loco at Ladysmith. This is *Carr* (Hudswell Clarke No. 1812 of 1948). *Carr* worked at Astley Green Colliery for most of its life before transfer to William Pit shed and the harbour lines. It then spent its last days on the clifftop before being scrapped in 1972. (September 1969)

Carr in the washery yard at Ladysmith. (September 1969)

The shed at Ladysmith was at almost right angles to the main lines through the complex and was approached via a steep curve. Conditions inside were primitive compared to those at many other collieries, there being no roof or doors.

Ladysmith loco shed could be described as 'light and airy' – because it had no roof! Conditions for maintenance were basic.

Another view of the shed shortly after closure, the site being cleared in 1975.

Another view inside the loco shed with an Andrew Barclay loco under the remaining scrap of roof at the rear.

A low angle view from the inspection pit showing the burned and rusting smokebox – the product of a working life at Ladysmith.

Ladysmith usually had a scrapline of locos that had been worked into the ground or transferred from elsewhere, more in hope than in confidence that they would prove useful! *Risehow No. 1* (Yorkshire Engine Company No. 2430 of 1948) was an example of the latter, having been transferred from Risehow Colliery, Flimby, just along the coast to the north.

The family resemblance to *Risehow No. 1* is unmistakeable. This is her sister engine, formerly *Risehow No. 2* (Yorkshire Engine Company No. 2432 of 1948), which was previously employed at Lakeland Disposal site at Risehow Colliery, Flimby. It has, quite literally, reached the end of the line.

This unnamed Andrew Barclay (No. 2271 of 1949) six-coupled loco was formerly active at Ladysmith, but by this time, in 1973, had been relegated to the scrap-line.

Spider (Hawthorn Leslie No. 2623 of 1905) had come a long way for nothing. *Spider* had been one of four locos that worked at Ifton Colliery in Shropshire. On closure two had been sent to Cumbria and two to the Wrexham area. *Spider*, allegedly in working order on arrival, lacked a steam brake, which would probably be a recipe for disaster on this line. As a result, it did no work at its new home.

After closure the locos on the scrap-line were shuffled around to await the scrap man's torch.

This Peckett-built four-coupled engine (Peckett No. 2158 of 1955) was owned by Albright & Wilson and, along with the Sentinel diesel in the background, worked at their chemical works, which adjoined Ladysmith Washery. When they were pressed for motive power this loco was sometimes loaned to the NCB.

Harrington Coal Preparation Plant at Lowca, a little to the north of Whitehaven, had originally served a colliery at the same location and was also connected to Workington steelworks by the former Lowca Light Railway. When Harrington Colliery closed the plant remained in operation to wash coal from other local pits. The loco shed at Harrington was luxurious compared to the one at Ladysmith! April 1970.

The two locos present at Harrington shed in this picture are the Austerity *Amazon* (Vulcan Foundry No. 5297 of 1945) and the former *Solway No. 2* (Hudswell Clarke No. 1814 of 1948), a transfer from the nearby Solway Colliery. April 1970.

Another view of *Amazon* at Harrington.

A view from inside Harrington shed.

The driver oils round *Amazon*, having cleared out the ashes.

Unity (Hudswell Clarke No. 1587 of 1927) was, like *Spider* at Ladysmith, a transfer from Ifton Colliery in Shropshire. In theory she should have been a useful loco for this system but I don't think, even after some tinkering in the shed, that she ever worked at her new home.

Unnamed Hudswell Clarke No. 1814 crosses the road in Lowca village with a flagman holding up the traffic. (April 1970)

Approaching the loading point at Harrington. April 1970.

Amazon on the clifftop at Harrington. Behind the loco the line heads on towards Workington. September 1969.

Amazon has drawn a rake of hopper wagons out of the washery. September 1969.

Above: A view to the south, with Whitehaven Harbour breakwater visible in the distance. September 1969.

Right: A final look at *Amazon* at Harrington.

North and South Wales Coalfields

Both extremes of the principality had thriving iron and steel industries and so coal was an important factor in the development of those industries. South Wales had traditionally also been the source of much exported coal and the nature of the product varied across the coalfield, east to west, from softer to harder anthracite type coals. In terms of the National Coal Board in the 1960s and early 1970s, the southern coalfield was divided into two administrative areas: East and West Wales. The landscape in the south is aptly described by the well-known term 'The Valleys' as the pits tended to be located in these confines and disgorged their products southwards towards the coast. The North Wales coalfield was much smaller and was centred on Wrexham. By the mid-1960s only three pits remained, with two of these being near to the English border, and these operated steam locomotives. These pits were the responsibility of the English North West.

This Austerity is named *Llewellyn* (Hunslet No. 3817 of 1954) and, on a crisp spring morning, was working at Hafodyrynys Colliery in the Glyn Valley near Pontypool. This was another 'modernised' pit, combining the output from other smaller concerns.

Llewellyn again, with a rake of 16-ton mineral wagons. I feel an attachment to *Llewellyn* – it was my mother's family name and they came from this part of the country!

The other locos present on this visit were stored by the screens. The first, No. 31, was a 'Frankenstein' loco rebuilt from parts of two Peckett locomotives, the main bits being allegedly from No. 1465 of 1917. The Austerity at the rear is *Glendower* (Hunslet No. 3810 of 1954), now preserved un-restored at the South Devon Railway, Buckfastleigh.

This is the loco shed at Mountain Ash in the Cynon Valley, Glamorgan. This was another example of a coal-centred industrial system as it served Deep Duffryn Colliery, Aberaman Phurnacite Plant, a landsale yard and a loading point. Its main line had once been part of the national network. Mountain Ash also had workshops maintaining wagons and other equipment.

This is *Sir Gomer* (Peckett No. 1859 of 1932), a loco associated with the latter days at Mountain Ash. The loco is parked next to the coaling facilities – a 16-ton mineral wagon with its door open!

Coaling in action – replenishing *Sir Gomer's* bunker! The locomotive in the right of the picture is the ex-British Railways pannier tank No. 7754. It is now preserved on the Llangollen Railway but sadly it was never in steam when I visited Mountain Ash. *Sir Gomer* is preserved at the Battlefield Line in Leicestershire.

At Mountain Ash one usually found locos that were discarded or awaiting repair. Here, on the end of the coaling siding, is *The Earl* (Peckett No. 1203 of 1910), which was never to work again.

Another popular member of Mountain Ash's varied family was *Llantanam Abbey* (Andrew Barclay No. 2074 of 1949). It is now preserved on the Pontypool & Blaenavon Railway.

Completing the list of active locomotives on my last visit to Mountain Ash was No. 1 (Hudswell Clarke No. 1885 of 1955), a powerful-looking machine that was working to the loading point and landsale yard.

Here, No. 1 is shunting the landsale yard, which was located south of the loco shed.

No. 1 blasts up the valley from the landsale yard with hoppers from Penrikyber Colliery or the stocking site.

No. 1 in the Mountain Ash complex near the wagon repair shop, with *Sir Gomer*, an Andrew Barclay diesel and a rail-mounted crane in the background.

No. 1 has passed the loco shed and is heading north towards Aberaman.

This rake of wagons is for internal use only, as signified by the large 'X'.

On an earlier date this little gem was working across the river. This is *Sir John* (Avonside No. 1680 of 1914) in nicely lined out but slightly grubby green livery.

Here, *Sir John* sits behind Hudswell Clarke No. 1 in the shed yard, both awaiting their next duties. *Sir John* is preserved at the Pontypool & Blaenavon Railway.

Above: *Sir Gomer* again on a cool, damp morning that enhances the slight steam leaks.

Left: This is Merthyr Vale Colliery, where the active locomotive on this day was No. 6 (Peckett No. 2061 of 1945). Not long before this the colliery, like Mountain Ash, was operating an ex-Great Western pannier tank.

The Peckett seemed in good condition and bore a full set of works and Railway Executive plates.

The spare loco at Merthyr Vale at this time was No. 1, a typical Andrew Barclay six-coupled side tank (No. 2340 of 1953). She looked in need of a new coat of paint and the remains of her blue livery suggest she must have looked smart when it was new; however, I don't think she worked for very much longer.

Here is *Illtyd* (Andrew Barclay No. 2331 of 1952) near Talywain landsale yard in a complex of colliery lines in the Eastern Valleys near Pontypool – a long way from her Scottish birthplace. A sister loco, *Islwyn*, was also delivered new here in 1952. So extensive and remote were the mines in the area that the NCB operated passenger trains to get the workforce to them. March 1973.

For years this system included the remote branch to Blaenserchan Colliery high in the hills and it was a former workplace for ex-GWR pannier tank No. 7754, which went to Mountain Ash. A local rationalisation scheme saw the coal from that mine go underground to Hafodyrynys for washing. The system closed in the mid-1970s. March 1973.

Blaenavon was another of those locations where the iron manufacturing industry had developed due to the presence of the essentials – iron ore, coal and limestone. Here, *Toto* (Andrew Barclay No. 1680 of 1920) is shunting mineral wagons under the screen at Big Pit. This pit closed in 1980 but a few years later volunteers took over the site and it now operates as a heritage museum. *Toto* was preserved and is currently at the Mangapps Railway Museum in East Anglia. March 1973.

Dereliction at Maerdy. This is No. 9792, one of several ex-British Railways pannier tanks bought by the Coal Board. Unlike its sisters it did not survive in preservation and was already missing many parts when seen in 1973.

Above: Dereliction at Maerdy. Peckett is not known for constructing big locomotives, but this loco, No. 2150 of 1954, is the most powerful steam locomotive built for British industry, and was known latterly to enthusiasts as the 'Maerdy Monster'. One sister locomotive worked at the same location but by this date a hired diesel was doing the work. The 'Monster' is preserved at the Elsecar Heritage Railway.

Left: Maesteg was another popular location for industrial enthusiasts. Here, one of its fleet of Austerities heads up the valley to one of the three pits it served. Sadly, time limited my visit, and I never had the opportunity to return.

Above: A sad sight at the Wern Tarw pit prop yard, Pencoed, Glamorgan, is this rusty Peckett (No. 2030 of 1942), formerly belonging to the Royal Ordnance Factory in Sellafield, Cumbria, where it was their No 3. This was not an NCB loco, but one owned by a local timber merchant.

Right: Fitted with a rather ineffective spark arrestor, this is *Norma* (Hunslet No. 3770 of 1952), seen in the exchange sidings at Pontarddulais at the end of the line from Graig Merthy Colliery in Glamorgan.

Two locomotive sheds served Graig Merthyr Colliery, a remote pit high in the local hills. One, used mainly for maintenance, was at the pit itself, while the other, at Pontarddulais, contained exchange sidings for the national network. When this photograph was taken the Andrew Barclay locomotives, one of which can be seen just inside the lower shed, were just ending their careers at the location and the work was being taken over by Austerities.

Graig Merthyr pit was set high in the hills and the line serving it had some steep gradients. As well as transporting workers to the mine, the line also, unofficially, delivered items and produce to isolated homes en route. The conveyor climbing the hill on the left took colliery waste to a tip.

Here is Austerity *Norma* (Hunslet No. 3770 of 1952), seen shunting in the exchange sidings at Pontarddulais.

In the village of Pontarddulais the line to the colliery crossed the main A48 road, which was protected by gates.

Above: Another Austerity working at Graig Merthyr was an unnamed William Bagnall-built loco (No. 2758 of 1944), seen here pausing at one of the low 'platforms' where miners could mount or dismount. This locomotive is preserved at the Cefn Coed Colliery Museum, Crynant.

Left: Departing from the yard at Pontarddulais, one of *Norma*'s footplate men adopts an unconventional method of getting from the bunker to the cab!

Descending from the colliery, a loaded train passes the mangled remains of a recent load that ran away on the steep gradient and derailed.

Brynlliw Colliery in West Glamorgan produced a hard coal known as anthracite. A short branch from the pit passed under a road bridge (which was a convenient place for photography), through a landsale yard and on to the exchange sidings with the national network. At the time of this visit the mine operated three Peckett-built locomotives.

The two active Pecketts –
No. 1426 of 1916 (rebuilt with
parts from No. 1187) and her
unnamed and unnumbered sister
(Peckett No. 2114 of 1951) – drop
hot ash as they pass under the
road bridge. Both locomotives
have been preserved.

A view in the opposite direction
shows the landsale yard,
where coal was offloaded to
local coal deliverers, and the
exchange sidings, with No. 1426
in residence.

No. 1426 again, returning to the
screens for another load. This
locomotive is preserved in the
Swansea Museum collection.

Peckett No. 2114 at rest outside the shed at Brynlliw. It is currently preserved in Kidwelly.

The North Wales coalfield was much smaller than that in the south. By the mid-1960s only three pits remained active. This is Gresford, just north of Wrexham. Here, in 1919, an underground explosion killed many miners. The colliery closed in 1973, but the distinctive waste tip survives, if somewhat lowered.

Although more modern locomotives worked at Gresford – the last being the Austerity *Alison*, which moved on to Bold and became *Joseph* – a latter-day stalwart was, appropriately, *The Welshman* (Manning Wardle No. 1207 of 1890). Looking somewhat down on the rear springs, this old-timer could still manage the short run down to the exchange sidings. *The Welshman* is rare in being fitted with a long boiler, which reflects its antiquity. It is preserved by the National Coal Board.

Here, *The Welshman*, with a friendly driver, is at the points where the lines from the colliery and the link to the main line meet at the exchange sidings. The main line here is the former Great Western main line from Birkenhead to Paddington, and Gresford is located at the top of the bank, where the line rises from the Cheshire Plain.

While the elderly Manning Wardle was doing the work at Gresford, this unnamed Austerity (Hunslet No. 3206 of 1945) was stored out of use beside the loco shed.

As closure at Gresford drew closer, the scrap-line grew longer. The Austerity has lost its cab and behind *The Welshman* is *Richboro* (Hudswell Clarke No. 1243 of 1917), an exile from Ifton Colliery in Shropshire. *Richboro* never worked at Gresford and went to Llangollen, where it acted as a gate guard at the Dapol model railway factory before going to the Aln Valley Railway in Northumbria, where it has been restored to working order.

The other colliery in the Wrexham area operating steam locomotives was Bersham, a compact system located right beside the Wrexham to Shrewsbury main line to the south of the town. Here, a pair of British Railways Class 25 diesels pause next to *Hornet* (Peckett No. 1935 of 1937), shunting wagons in the exchange sidings.

Left: With the winding gear visible in the background, *Hornet* pulls a rake of wagons from under the screen and prepares to place them in the exchange siding.

Below: The chimney on *Hornet* cannot pass without mention, nor can her low profile. *Hornet* was built for Black Park Colliery in Shropshire, where there were limited clearances. The chimney was fabricated by one of the fitters at Ifton Colliery, who was impressed by American smokestacks. At one time it had apparently been larger but he was ordered to cut it down! *Hornet* is under restoration at the Ribble Steam Railway in Preston.

The other working locomotive at Bersham was this attractive little four-coupled loco, *Shakespeare* (Hawthorn Leslie No. 3072 of 1914), seen here in the colliery yard. The short wheelbase was useful as there was a tight curve from the screens to the exchange siding.

Shakespeare has its ash pan emptied and the hot ash shovelled off the wooden sleepers. Sadly, this attractive locomotive went for scrap in 1980. Bersham closed in 1986, by which time diesel locomotives worked modern merry-go-round hopper traffic. (Photograph C. Pope)

Somerset, East Midlands and North East Coalfields

Yorkshire, the East Midlands and the North East all sat on huge coal reserves that served iron and steel industries in those locations as well as, in the past, providing domestic coal and fuel for other industries. Being a poor student, and later on a beginner's wage, these were areas that I regrettably only visited briefly. The East Midlands disposed of its steam power quite early and many of its locomotives were stored as nominal 'spares' in the 1960s. Yorkshire on the other hand had several locations that hung on to steam power.

For administrative purposes the small Somerset coalfield around the town of Radstock was actually part of the East Wales area. By the 1970s only two pits survived – Kilmersdon and Lower Writhlington – and these had been linked underground. Lower Writhlington was connected to the Somerset & Dorset line at Radstock and Kilmersdon to the ex-Great Western Bristol to Frome branch by means of a rope-worked incline. Only Kilmersdon had locomotives and the picture above is of the 1929-built Peckett No. 1788, which did virtually all the work. March 1973.

Above: Here, the immaculate Kilmersdon Peckett appears to have steamed into a woodland thicket, where no rails are visible. The reason for that is based on a tragic incident. In 1966 a colliery tip at Aberfan in South Wales collapsed, burying a primary school and killing many local children and adults. After this the National Coal Board wisely decided to survey other spoil heaps to check their safety. Kilmersdon were asked to prepare access to their old spoil heap and the Peckett and the regular driver, Herbert Loader, were instructed to clear a path using an old overgrown siding.

Right: Here, Bert Loader is working with his bow saw to clear the bushes. The Peckett, one of the company's R3 design, was, unsurprisingly, saved for preservation and is based at the West Somerset Railway.

Mr Loader always made visiting enthusiasts very welcome. Here he is cleaning the ash pan of his locomotive. A small diesel was tried at the colliery but unfortunately on one occasion it ran away down the incline and was damaged. There was also a small Hunslet loco transferred from another colliery but it was rarely, if ever, used.

This loco does not belong to the National Coal Board, but can justifiably be counted as involved in the coal industry. It belongs to the Birchenwood Gas & Coke Company at Kidsgrove, Staffordshire, and is a 1953-built Peckett, works No. 2154. The company had originally mined its own coal but in later years was concerned with coke production from other local mines.

Holditch Colliery was located near Newcastle-under-Lyme in Staffordshire. *Cornist* (Hudswell Clarke No. 1503 of 1923), with interesting smokebox decoration, was one of three locomotives operating there in the early 1970s. The pit, which closed in 1990, was allegedly the gassiest one in the country in terms of methane, and the gas was used to power a local brickworks.

West Cannock Colliery, near Hednesford, Staffordshire, was the last remaining pit in a group bordering Cannock Chase, and was an amalgam of several smaller pits. This locomotive is *Topham* (William Bagnall No. 2193 of 1922), seen standing outside its shed on a cold winter's morning with an improvised brazier keeping the water hydrant from freezing. The colliery closed in 1982 and *Topham* is preserved on the Spa Valley Railway.

No. 8 (Hunslet No. 3777 of 1952) has appeared elsewhere in this book, having latterly been transferred to Bickershaw Colliery in Lancashire. Here she is seen at Cannock Wood Colliery, Rawnsley, in Staffordshire.

This big beast is *Littleton No. 5* – Manning Wardle No. 2018 of 1922, one of the larger locomotives built by this firm. This is Littleton Colliery in Staffordshire to the west of Cannock Chase. Motorists on the M6 motorway would have sometimes seen its locomotives heading under them on the way to the exchange sidings on the West Coast Main Line, near Penkridge.

This is the locomotive shed at Littleton. Taking on water on the left is No. 5, while just visible inside is *Robert Nelson No. 4* (Hunslet No. 1800 of 1936) and outside on the right is Austerity No. 7. Littleton was very welcoming to enthusiasts and even had open days, when travel behind the locomotives was possible.

Sentinel four-wheeled, vertical-boilered, geared locomotives were quite rare in colliery work. They were not really suited to use on longer industrial branches. This is an unnamed example (Sentinel No. 9535 of 1951), which is seen out of use at Silverdale Colliery in Staffordshire.

Cadley Hill Colliery in October 1980. Standing outside the shed are blue 0-6-0ST *Empress* (W. G. Bagnall No. 3061 of 1954) and the virulent yellow Hunslet Austerity 0-6-0ST No. 65 (No. 3889 of 1964). The latter was one of the last steam locomotives built for the National Coal Board but was found to be in poor condition after transfer from Manvers Main Colliery near Rotherham. It was used only as a source of spares. *Empress* is preserved at the Mangapps Railway in Essex. (Photograph C. Pope)

Ashington, north of Newcastle, was the hub of an extensive system running to 15 miles in length, and which ran passenger trains for miners, as well as coal traffic. The town of Ashington was built to serve the industry. The shed and associated repair shop served a number of collieries. This is the coal plant, where No. 44 (Robert Stephenson & Hawthorn No. 7760 of 1953) is seen with a wagonload of coal. It is currently preserved but unrestored at the Tanfield Railway in Durham.

Here is No. 41 (RSH No. 7759 of 1953), a loco from the same builder and to the same design as No. 44. It is coupled to another wagon, whose purpose is neatly identified.

Miner's passenger trains, or 'paddy trains' as they were known in some areas, operated on the Ashington system and No. 29 (Robert Stephenson & Hawthorn No. 7607 of 1950), a big inside cylinder side tank, was often used on these trains. Sadly, it was scrapped in 1972.

Another Ashington loco used on passenger services was No. 40 (Robert Stephenson & Hawthorn No. 7765 of 1954). Like most Ashington locos, the livery is the preferred 'house style' of medium blue. This loco was fitted with an electric headlight, which is just visible in front of the chimney. The local manufacturer, Robert Stephenson & Hawthorn, was naturally well represented among the locomotives here and at other collieries in the area.

Backworth Colliery was the home base for locomotives also serving Fenwick Colliery and Whitehill Point Staithes. No. 48 (Hunslet No. 2843 of 1943) was one of several Austerity locomotives based there.

Burradon was another location with a large locomotive depot serving several collieries and a washery. Locos with side tanks were less well represented among the host of Robert Stephenson & Hawthorn saddle tanks. However, No. 38 (Hudswell Clarke No. 1823 of 1949) is an example of the former, seen at Burradon shed. The Northumberland area seemed to have a liking for colourful wagons! No. 38 is currently at the Tanfield Railway in Durham.

Scottish Coalfields

Similar to the South Wales coalfield, Scotland's collieries could be in diverse landscapes ranging from wild moorland to grubby industrial areas. The coal measures stretched broadly north-east to south-west from coastal Fife across the central belt between Glasgow and Edinburgh and into Ayrshire and the Southern Uplands. After the deep mines had closed some coal continued to be taken from open-cast quarries. The motive power at most Scottish mines was the product of the Kilmarnock-based company of Andrew Barclay, and few English-made locos made it across the Border!

One of the more scenic Scottish locations was the Waterside system, based near Dalmellington in Ayrshire. Formerly serving a long-established ironworks, the mines remained active after this closed. The locomotives were based at Dunaskin near Dalmellington and worked traffic to the exchange sidings from the Minnivey and Pennyvenie mines higher up on the moors, and also to a waste tip partway down the line. Here, a four-coupled No. 10 (Andrew Barclay No. 2244 of 1947) descends from the mine to Dunaskin. The shed at Dunaskin remains in use as a base for the Scottish Industrial Railway Centre heritage group and No. 10 is part of their collection.

An interesting feature of the locomotives at Waterside was the wooden-bodied wagons adapted, by removal of one end, as 'tenders' to carry extended coal supplies for the long trip to the mine. No. 10 is seen again, on some well-laid track by most colliery standards. The line boasted three Andrew Barclay tanks at this time.

Above: The other locomotive type to be found on the Waterside system was the six-coupled Andrew Barclay side tank. This is No. 17 (Andrew Barclay No. 1338 of 1913) with a conventional chimney. Its sister engine, No. 24, was fitted with a Geisl ejector chimney. All locos here were kept in clean external condition.

Right: No. 24 is also distinguished from its sister by the sloping side tanks. Here, a rake of typical wooden-bodied wagons are arriving at Dunaskin Washery.

No. 17 is seen near the washing plant with the weighbridge in the foreground. No. 17 is preserved and awaiting restoration at the Llangollen Railway.

This is the Cutler Tip, situated between the mines and the exchange sidings, where colliery waste was dumped. No. 17 is pushing a rake of chaldron-type tipping wagons onto the tip siding.

No. 17 makes the trip to Cutler Tip with a rake of tipping wagons.

Another of the Andrew Barclay four-coupled locomotives, No. 19 (Andrew Barclay No. 1614 of 1918), stands in the tidy, modern shed at Dunaskin. She remains at Dunaskin, having been bought for preservation.

It's Scotland and it's another Andrew Barclay product from Kilmarnock! This is Mauchline Coal Preparation Plant, with No. 16 (Andrew Barclay No. 1116 of 1910) in view. I was looking for this location when I saw wisps of steam emanating from a cutting just by the roadside. On investigation I found this locomotive quietly resting with no crew in sight – it must have been break time! This is another locomotive now preserved by the Scottish Industrial Railway Centre at Dunaskin. August 1970.

Polkemmet Colliery, Whitburn, in West Lothian. Working locomotives Andrew Barclay 0-6-0ST No. 2358 of 1954 and Andrew Barclay 0-6-0T No. 1296 of 1912, both in filthy condition, work double-headed to lift a line of loaded wagons up the steep grade out of the colliery yard towards the BR exchange sidings. August 1979. (Photograph C.Pope)

Although loaded trains went up the bank double-headed, the two locomotives habitually returned to the colliery yard separately in follow-my-leader fashion. At this time 21-ton double-door wagons were being used to ship out coal from Polkemmet and rakes of empties can be seen behind the loco. August 1979. (Photograph C. Pope)

Polkemmet Colliery and Andrew Barclay 0-6-0T (No. 1296 of 1912) drifts back down the gradient light engine from the BR exchange sidings. In the background stands a line of empty wagons waiting to be dropped down by gravity under the coal preparation plant. It should be noted that this is another locomotive sporting a Geisl ejector in place of a normal chimney. August 1979. (Photograph C. Pope)

The two Andrew Barclay locomotives at rest outside the locomotive shed at Polkemmet. Both locomotives survived to be preserved at the Ayrshire RPS at Dalmellington. August 1979. (Photograph C. Pope)

The most modern steam locomotive at Polkemmet was No. 25, a 1954-built Andrew Barclay. Here, she stands beside an abandoned relic of the steam age in the form of an ancient steam crane, resting off the rails in the yard. (Photograph C. Pope)

Another view of a double-headed Polkemmet train with a panorama of the colliery buildings and waste tips in the background. The side tank seems to be making the lesser effort, judging by the exhaust, but this might just be a result of the modified chimney. August 1979. (Photograph C. Pope)

Photographs taken at Polkemmet often appeared to be in monochrome as everything assumed a mantle of grey! On an earlier occasion the locos under the water tank were another Andrew Barclay six-coupled tank, unidentified but probably No. 8 (Andrew Barclay No. 1175 of 1909), and a Hunslet-built Austerity, No. 17 (Hunslet No. 2880 of 1943). Both locomotives have been preserved: the Barclay is plinthed in a local country park and the Austerity is at the Scottish Railway Preservation Society at Bo'ness. August 1970.

The coastal area around the port of Methil in Fife contained many pits and most were served by the Wemyss Private Railway, a company that had survived nationalisation of both the mines and the railways. Sadly, pit closures led to its demise in 1970 and my only photographs are of its derelict locomotives. Some pits, Wellesley being an example, had their own locomotive and one usually shunted round the dock at Methil for a little longer. This is No. 10 (Andrew Barclay No. 1245 of 1911). It looks as if another wooden-bodied NCB wagon is being used as an improvised 'tender' for replenishing the bunker. August 1970.

Bedlay Colliery, Glenboig, Lanarkshire. Working loco Andrew Barclay 0-4-0ST No. 17 (No. 2296 of 1952) runs light engine down the rural connection from the BR exchange sidings to the colliery. The pit head is visible in the background, along with the spoil heap or 'bing'. The rake of empty wagons in the siding on the extreme right wait to be propelled by the loco around to the far side of the screens prior to loading. 25 May 1981. (Photograph C. Pope)

In these sylvan surroundings it is hard to believe that this mine was within sight of the outskirts of Glasgow. No. 17 (Andrew Barclay No. 2296 of 1952) propels empty wagons towards the colliery yard. The pit closed later in 1981 and had latterly supplied coking coal for the steel industry, mainly the Ravenscraig plant near Glasgow. 25 May 1981. (Photograph C. Pope)

Bedlay Colliery. Four-coupled No. 17 (Andrew Barclay No. 2296 of 1952) waits patiently while the crew takes a lunch break. The diesel fuel tank was for the use of road vehicles. 25 May 1981. (Photograph C. Pope)

Bedlay Colliery and No. 6 stands in the siding that served as a loco depot here. A pit is visible under the engine, and there was also a sand furnace and tin 'bothy' for the crew, but if a shed building ever existed it had long since disappeared. The pit had a massive refurbishment completed in 1958, as confirmed by the modern buildings in the background. They clearly forgot about the needs of the locomotives! 7 August 1979. (Photograph C. Pope)

On another occasion at the same location, the primitive conditions in which some locomotives were maintained are apparent. The locomotive is jacked up on wooden blocks and one assumes that the bearings may be the part under scrutiny. 26 May 1981. (Photograph C. Pope)

Andrew Barclay No. 6 is hard at work after its transfer from Kinneil Colliery. Here, it backs down towards to screens in order to pick up a rake of loaded wagons. These will then be taken up to be weighed on the weighbridge visible in the centre background. The connection to the BR exchange sidings runs in the direction of the electricity pylon. The open area to the right was once occupied by a brickworks. 7 August 1979. (Photograph C. Pope)

No. 9 (Hudswell Clarke 0-6-0T No. 895 of 1909) stands out of use at Bedlay Colliery. 25 May 1981. (Photograph C. Pope)

On the fringes of the Firth of Forth stood Frances Colliery, near Dysart. Here, No. 21 (Andrew Barclay 0-4-0ST No. 2292 of 1951) is in action, shunting in the colliery yard. Unusually, BR locomotives worked rakes of empty wagons right through the colliery to a set of sidings beyond the screens, and the colliery engine basically just shunted in the vicinity. Occasionally, though, the Barclay was called upon to bank BR trains up the connecting branch towards the main line. 8 August 1979. (Photograph C. Pope)

Another view of No. 21, standing near the weighbridge at Frances Colliery. The pit was temporarily closed by the miner's strike in 1984, and then permanently in 1988, fires due to spontaneous combustion having caused damage. 8 August 1979. (Photograph C. Pope)

Faint wisps of steam are coming from No. 20 (Andrew Barclay No. 1833 of 1924) as she cools down at Newbattle Coal Stocking Plant near Edinburgh, the day's work having ended. Currently, No. 20 is under restoration at the Ribble Steam Railway.

The spare loco at Newbattle Coal Stocking Plant was No. 17 (Andrew Barclay No. 2219 of 1946). The site, closed in 1971, was close to Lady Victoria Colliery, which became a museum of Scottish coal mining.

Bibliography and Acknowledgements

Locomotive details have mostly come from *Industrial Locomotives*, the excellent handbooks published over the years by the Industrial Railway Society.

Further information was provided by the Warwickshire Railway Society's *Industrial Steam Locomotives of North East and North West England* (1968), as well as Alan Davies' *Locomotives of the Lancashire Central Coalfield* and Gordon Edgar's *Industrial Locomotives and Railways of Cumbria*, both from Amberley Publishing.

Detail on individual collieries owes much to the excellent articles published in Irwell Press's *Railway Bylines* magazine.

Finally, I would like to thank my brother Chris, who has contributed his own photographs to this project and accompanied me on several trips.